Class Action
DESEGREGATION AND DIVERSITY IN SAN FRANCISCO SCHOOLS

Rand Quinn

University of Minnesota Press

Minneapolis | London

Published by the University of Minnesota Press
111 Third Avenue South, Suite 290
Minneapolis, MN 55401-2520
http://www.upress.umn.edu

Printed in the United States of America on acid-free paper

The University of Minnesota is an equal-opportunity educator and employer.

Library of Congress Cataloging-in-Publication Data
Names: Quinn, Rand, author.
Title: Class action : desegregation and diversity in San Francisco schools / Rand Quinn.
Description: Minneapolis : University of Minnesota Press, [2020] | Includes
    bibliographical references and index.
Identifiers: LCCN 2019014733 (print) | ISBN 978-1-5179-0475-3 (hc) |
    ISBN 978-1-5179-0476-0 (pb)
Subjects: LCSH: School integration—California—San Francisco—History. | Segregation
    in education—California—San Francisco—History. | Public schools—California—San
    Francisco—History. | African Americans—Education—California—San Francisco—
    History. | School choice—California—San Francisco—History.
Classification: LCC LC214.23.S23 Q56 2020 (print) | DDC 379.2/630973—dc23
LC record available at https://lccn.loc.gov/2019014733

UMP BmB 2020

For Amy Yuen

Contents

Introduction

It was February 1969 and the San Francisco Citizens Advisory Committee had just finished drafting its proposed desegregation plan, Educational Equality/Quality. The plan was to be submitted without comment to the school board at its next meeting. Public deliberation would happen later once parents and other residents had enough time to review the details. Equality/Quality was modest. Once fully implemented, it would cover just one-fifth of the city's elementary population.[1] The plan stitched together adjacent elementary school attendance zones in two predominantly White neighborhoods. Students from these neighborhoods would be bused such that the racial distribution at each individual school would approximate that of the neighborhood as a whole. In addition, curriculum resource centers would be established and staff would receive specialized training.[2] "This is much more than just a plan for desegregating schools," remarked Laurel Glass, the school board chair. "It is an exciting plan for improving the quality of education in the district."[3]

In the days leading up to the school board meeting, superintendent of schools Robert Jenkins saw flyers with such extreme antibusing sentiments that he requested a police presence. The night of the meeting, over one thousand people filled the Nourse, a grand auditorium in the Beaux-Arts style built in 1927 for the High School of Commerce. The first hour was spent on routine business. Then Marjorie Lemlow, president of Mothers Support Neighborhood Schools, approached the podium. "Madame chairman, I want to speak about busing," she began. Lemlow was resolutely against Equality/Quality, sight unseen, and as she made her case to the school board, some in the audience shouted out their support and others their opposition.[4] At one point during Lemlow's testimony, several people rushed the dais and attempted to disable her microphone. The meeting soon fell into disarray. The *San Francisco Chronicle* reported on an organized group of thirty or more "burly White men" that moved intimidatingly through the aisles in search of busing proponents. Several fights broke out. The few police on hand were unable to take control of the situation. All told, the ensuing frenzy left four people seriously injured.[5]

When pressed on the issue the following day, Mayor Joseph Alioto remarked, "I am opposed to expanded busing in the city at this time. I don't think the White community wants it and I don't think the Black community wants it. It's too emotional an issue."[6] The mayor was correct in noting that opposition to busing was not limited to White parents. But opposition was not universal, and there was more popular support for desegregation than suggested by the mayor. Local advocacy groups representing various constituencies had long fought for school desegregation, and many San Franciscans were in favor of busing. In the months that followed, Equality/Quality would continue to be a contentious plan that divided neighborhoods and communities into those in support and those opposed. It would be nearly a year—not until January 1970—before the school board would give its final approval.[7] But even with the approval of Equality/Quality, most of the city was left unaffected.

The incremental and slow-moving pace toward desegregation angered its proponents. To force a resolution, the local chapter of the NAACP filed a lawsuit on behalf of San Francisco's Black elementary schoolchildren. The suit, *Johnson v. San Francisco Unified School District*, charged the district with maintaining a segregated school system in violation of the Equal Protection Clause of the Fourteenth Amendment (no state shall "deny to any person within its jurisdiction the equal protection of the laws") and the 1964 Civil Rights Act.[8] David Johnson, the first of six named plaintiffs, sought relief for his daughter Patricia who attended Dudley Stone School, which was 75 percent Black. Patricia's experience was characteristic of Black elementary students across the city. The lawsuit maintained that 80 percent of San Francisco's Black elementary students attended twenty-nine segregated schools that ranged from 62 percent to 97 percent Black. San Francisco is "behind such places as Mississippi and Texas in offering equal educational opportunity to Black students," stated chapter president Charles Belle to the *Chronicle* in June 1970. "We intend to change that and to insure that San Francisco again becomes a progressive city."[9]

The court would rule in favor of the NAACP the following year, setting aside Equality/Quality, which was limited to just two neighborhoods, and ordering citywide elementary school desegregation to commence September 1971. But systemic change remained elusive. Court supervision would last decades, all the way to December 2005. Over this thirty-four-year period, San Francisco witnessed additional desegregation lawsuits, protracted episodes of community contention, and a succession of different busing schemes and student assignment plans. By the time the district was released from court oversight, a generation of students had spent their entire educational career under a desegregation regime. Only briefly during this period, from the mid-1980s to the early 1990s, was the school district considered desegregated. In fact, in 2005 when court supervision ended, the school district was more segregated than it ever had been since 1971.

In the pages that follow, I will tell the story of San Francisco's highly contested school desegregation policies over the last half century.[10] San Francisco is an important chapter in the history of American school discrimination. It was the first large city outside of the South to face court-ordered school desegregation following *Brown v. Board of Education*,[11] and it experienced the same demographic shifts that transformed other cities throughout the urban West. As such, San Francisco provides an ideal vantage point from which to understand school desegregation and the complicated racial politics that emerged from it. In this book, I explain why desegregation was relatively short lived and why the school district gradually resegregated despite the court's mandate. I argue that the district's assignment of students to particular schools—through busing and other desegregative mechanisms—began as a remedy for state discrimination but transformed into a tool intended to create diversity. I describe how this transformation was facilitated by the rise of school choice, evolving social and legal landscapes, and local community advocacy and activism.

Beyond providing a political history of school desegregation in San Francisco, I have three objectives. First, I seek to illuminate the interrelated and evolving relationship between "court" and "community" in education—how jurisprudence and community-based advocacy and activism have shaped the trajectory of equal educational opportunity in the decades since *Brown*. Second, I seek to bring a deeper understanding to the multiracial and multiethnic politics of urban education reform. Third, I offer the case in response to recent calls by scholars to better specify the ideational mechanisms that lead to policy change.

Court and Community

The process of desegregating formerly segregated school systems was complicated. Early on, jurisprudence was rapidly evolving as a string of court rulings that trailed *Brown* served to clarify, strengthen, and, in time, diminish school desegregation. In 1974, the Supreme Court placed severe limits on city–suburban desegregation, making it nearly impossible to desegregate metropolitan areas where Black families were concentrated in central cities.[12] From this point in time forward, desegregation jurisprudence has typically been described as increasingly conservative: On balance, courts held that racially segregated schools are acceptable so long as they are not the result of overt discrimination but rather the result of demographic or housing patterns. In 2007, the Supreme Court determined that the use of racial classifications in student assignment when part of a voluntary effort by a district to integrate its schools violated the Equal Protection Clause.[13] So while the proscription on statutory dual (i.e., segregated) school systems remains, permissible remedies for de facto segregation are limited.

Additional complicating factors to desegregation include federal-level administrative retrenchment, diminished resources and capacity of civil rights groups to pursue desegregation, and an absence of political will among elected officials.[14] Desegregation has also been foiled by an array of local factors including an absence of support from community leaders, resistant school boards and superintendents, unwelcoming political climates, and poorly designed student assignment plans. We know relatively little about the process under which court expectations to desegregate schools are frustrated or enhanced by community mobilization and advocacy efforts. In addition, we lack theory on the dynamics of community collaboration and contention that shape school desegregation policy.

The weight of desegregation literature resides in the 1970s and early 1980s, when desegregation efforts were embedded in the larger Civil Rights movement, when the federal courts were more significantly engaged in the desegregation process, and when desegregation was seen as a viable way to improve the academic achievement of African American students. Without longer periods of examination, we are left with an incomplete understanding of the political thrusts and parries between proponents and opponents that resulted in the decline of desegregation in recent decades. Although several recently published books have considered the long trajectory of school desegregation from multiple stakeholder perspectives, we still have an impoverished view of how the courts and communities—some in favor and some opposed to desegregation— evolved and played off of one another.[15] *Class Action* articulates the interplay and evolution of desegregation jurisprudence and community advocacy and activism over a three-decade-plus period in a large urban city. By doing so, it provides a model of desegregation outside of the South, as the courts determined the parameters of our nation's equal educational opportunity ideal and dynamic community action shaped local school desegregation plans.

Multiracial and Multiethnic Politics of Urban Education Reform

Desegregation was also complicated by changes in student populations. Nowhere was this more the case than in the urban West. In the decades following *Brown*, cities from San Diego to Seattle experienced dramatic racial and ethnic demographic changes with the arrival and subsequent departure of African American families, the arrival of families from Mexico and countries throughout Central America and Asia, and the departure of White families. Amid an ever-changing social and legal context, local efforts were continuously challenged as communities wrestled over the terms and conditions of court-mandated desegregation plans.

San Francisco was a focal point for these struggles. Similar to other urban centers in the West, San Francisco received an influx of Black families migrating from the South in the years during and following World War II.[16] The city's Black population, which stood at 4,846 in 1940, swelled to 96,078 by 1970 (Table 1). In addition, Chinese, Mexican, Filipino, and other communities with long, multigenerational histories in the city grew larger with the arrival of new immigrants following the 1965 passage of the Immigration and Nationality Act. At the same time, the city's White population declined beginning in the 1960s. San Francisco's school district mirrored the citywide demographic trends. The district expanded rapidly in the postwar years, adding more than twenty-five thousand students in two decades, and exceeding ninety thousand students by the end of the 1960s, making it one of the largest districts in the nation and one of the most racially and ethnically diverse. By 1967, San Francisco had the highest percentage of Black (26 percent) and Chinese (14 percent) public school students and the second lowest percentage of White (44 percent) public school students among the fifty-eight counties of California.[17]

However, the district lost over thirty-five thousand students in the twelve years that followed. After the 1971 implementation of the city's elementary school desegregation plan, Black students overtook White students as the largest of the nine racial and ethnic subgroups the district tracked, a trend that lasted throughout the 1970s. By the 1980s, Chinese students became the largest subgroup, followed by Latino students. Today, White students are one of the smaller subgroups in the district (Figure 1).

Table 1. San Francisco's Postwar Demographic Changes, 1940–2000

Year	White	(%)	Black	(%)	Chinese	(%)	Latino	(%)	Total
1940	602,701	95.0	4,846	0.8	17,782	2.8	n/a		634,536
1950	693,888	89.5	43,502	5.6	24,813	3.2	31,433	4.1	775,357
1960	604,403	81.6	74,383	10.0	36,445	4.9	51,602	7.0	740,316
1970	511,186	71.4	96,078	13.4	58,696	8.2	69,633	9.7	715,674
1980	402,131	59.2	86,190	12.7	82,244	12.1	84,194	12.4	678,974
1990	388,341	53.6	78,931	10.9	130,753	18.1	96,640	13.3	723,959
2000	385,728	49.7	60,515	7.8	152,620	19.6	109,504	14.1	776,733

Sources: United States Census. Data compilation by Metropolitan Transportation Commission and Association of Bay Area Government, Bay Area Census website; Chinese population in 1940 reported in Rose Hum Lee, "The Recent Immigrant Chinese Families of the San Francisco-Oakland Area," *Marriage and Family Living* 18, no. 1 (1956): 14–24.

Note: Census questions and categories have changed over time. The indicator for Latino residents in 1950 and 1960 is "White, Spanish Surname." From 1970 on, respondents who identified as Latino could also identify as White, Black, or some other race. In 2000, respondents could report multiple races. Total includes other subgroup populations.

Despite the changes in the racial and ethnic makeup of the city, desegregation had been primarily cast in Black–White terms until the 1990s. Chinese and Latino families, as well as their advocates and community leaders, were largely left out of formal desegregation negotiations.

Class Action resides among recent scholarship untangling and clarifying the history and politics of school desegregation as it moved out of the South.[18] This work assesses Black activism, White resistance, legal mobilization, and the rise and eventual fall of desegregated school systems. Despite extensive scholarship, there are areas where contributions can be made. We know less about the response to desegregation from racial and ethnic communities beyond Black and White. This is an understandable bias since the primary dynamic of desegregation has always been Black–White, particularly early on in its history. However, the increasing diversity of urban districts from the 1970s to the present day necessitates an understanding of the multiracial and multiethnic politics of desegregation. This book seeks to address that shortfall.

Michael Omi and Howard Winant's racial formation perspective provides a framework for understanding the multiracial and multiethnic politics of education reform.[19] Omi and Winant understand race as a concept that is socially constructed and culturally defined. Race permeates the

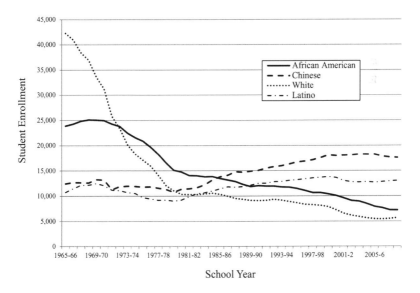

Figure 1. San Francisco's student enrollment by the four largest subgroups, 1965–2009.

economic and political realms of our society. Racial *formation* refers to the "sociohistorical process by which racial categories are created, inhabited, transformed, and destroyed."[20] This process occurs through historically situated projects that serve to connect broadly held meanings of race to the structures and routines that guide and constrain everyday life. In the words of Omi and Winant, a racial project is "simultaneously an interpretation, representation, or explanation of racial dynamics, and an effort to reorganize and redistribute resources along particular racial lines."[21]

Desegregation operates as a racial project. Efforts to desegregate schools encompass policies and programs to implement busing, redraw catchment boundaries, redistribute school resources, create magnet programs, and, in more recent years, institute systems of choice designed to create diverse school communities. Racial projects of desegregation are context-specific. The interpretive and redistributive components of desegregation racial projects differ across school systems and over time. In San Francisco, the racial project of desegregation was marked by an ever-shifting demographic terrain that led to waves of contention as new and politically emergent constituencies sought to intervene in school district policy and in the courts. The racial categorization of students and the most appropriate distribution of those students across schools were constantly contested. New solutions emerged as existing solutions were abandoned.

The racial formation perspective of Omi and Winant views each racial group on a distinct and independent racial trajectory. Claire Jean Kim complicates this approach by examining changing power dynamics between Asian Americans and African Americans.[22] According to Kim, understanding multiracial and multiethnic politics requires an understanding of both racial power—the "systemic tendency of the racial status quo to reproduce itself"—and racial ordering—the process of reproducing racial categories and meanings in a distinct racial order. Kim maintains that Asian Americans have been racially triangulated in relation to White and Black people through two simultaneous, interrelated mechanisms of "relative valorization" and "civic ostracism." In the former, Asian Americans are valorized as model minorities, placing them above African Americans on a superior/inferior axis. In the latter, Asian Americans are understood to be perpetual foreigners and are ostracized from politics, placing them below African Americans on an insider/foreigner axis. The ways these communities are stereotyped bear on the interracial tensions they endure. In San Francisco, while the legal effort to force school desegregation was principally about correcting government racial discrimination of Black students, desegregation could not occur without affecting the city's other racial and ethnic communities. Local advocacy and activism relied on and exploited discursive frames and arguments that ordered racial and ethnic communities in relation to each other—not just Black and White students but also Chinese and Latino students, as well as five other student subgroups "recognized" by the district.

Institutional Logics: A Framework for Understanding

My third objective is to respond to recent calls by scholars to better specify the ideational mechanisms that lead to policy change.[23] In education—as in other sectors of society—policy change does not emerge simply from economic-based assessments that seek to maximize efficiency or efficacy. Policy change is also determined by political processes that cluster around conflicting sets of ideas held and deployed by stakeholders. An institutional logics perspective, which incorporates the role of ideas as mechanisms for policy change, serves as an organizing framework for this book.[24]

Scholars use the term *institutional logics* to refer to sets of ideas, assumptions, practices, values, and rules that constitute patterns of organization and dictate appropriate behavior.[25] In contentious domains, such as school desegregation, individuals and organizations vie for adherents and defend the practices and symbols of one logic from others. Institutional logics perspectives originated from sociological theories of new institutionalism. Institutions are social constructions that provide meaning and stability to our lives—the institution of marriage, for example, with its socially and culturally determined rituals, deeply engrained beliefs and traditions, and enforceable rules set by governments and religious bodies that lay out associated processes and rights. The scholarship first establishing new institutionalism focused on the constraints institutions place on individuals and organizations—how, for instance, the institutional aspects of education led to ritual conformity and ceremonial adoption.[26] This early emphasis led to critiques that the theory suffered from overdeterminism and a lack of attention to how institutions change.[27]

In one such critique, sociologists Roger Friedland and Robert Alford formulate an argument locating individual and organizational behavior within social contexts. They view society as constitutive of institutional orders—corporations, families, markets, professions, religions, and states— each with a fundamental logic.[28] For Friedland and Alford, logics are sets of "material practices and symbolic constructions" available for elaboration.[29] For example, they describe the institutional logic of market capitalism in contemporary Western society as "accumulation and commodification of human activity" and that of the state as "rationalization and the regulation of human activity by legal and bureaucratic hierarchies."[30] Friedland and Alford recognize that one way institutional change occurs is through political contest over contradictory, competing, or overlapping logics governing activity within an organizational field.[31]

In this book, I argue that the politics of desegregation is structured by material practices and symbolic constructions clustered around proximity, choice, and opportunity. Policy alternatives are shaped, framed, and understood by stakeholders through commonly held ideas on the legitimacy and appropriateness of (1) neighborhood schools systems, whereby families live close to their schools and student assignment is based on school catchments of contiguous area (the logic of proximity), (2) assignment systems that allow parents to choose in which schools to enroll their children, independent of home or school address (the logic of choice), and (3) systems of student assignment designed to (or that purport to) address educational inequality (the logic of opportunity). In San Francisco—and in school districts throughout the nation—conceptualizations of student assignment and its beneficiaries developed within the boundaries of these three logics, for different individual and organizational stakeholders, at different points in time. It was these different and overlapping conceptualizations by stakeholders that led to political contention and ultimately induced changes in student assignment policy.

The Backstory: A Century of Legal School Segregation in San Francisco, 1851–1947

California's public education system formally began with the enactment of an 1851 law to apportion state funds for the establishment of public schools.[32] Within a year, a rapidly growing San Francisco had opened six grammar schools throughout the city. Its seventh school was notable. On May 22, 1854, a full century before the Supreme Court would issue its ruling in *Brown*, Reverend John Jamison Moore, a former slave, was called upon to lead California's first public school for Black children. The "Colored School," as it was referred to, was established in the basement of St. Cyprian African Methodist Episcopal Church in what is now Chinatown and provided instruction to several dozen students.[33] In the decades that followed, a string of state laws mandating school segregation were placed on the books. New laws were met with lawsuits challenging their basis. However, legal segregation of one form or another persisted in California until June 14, 1947, when Governor Earl Warren repealed all remaining school segregation laws in the state.[34]

Ward v. Flood

Sometime between 1857 and 1859, following a petition to the school board from members of the local Chinese community, a "Chinese School" was established in a Presbyterian chapel just a few blocks away from the Colored School. It was soon reconstituted into an evening school to accommodate the growing number of Chinese laborers seeking instruction.[35] By 1865, California had legislated that children of "African or Mongolian descent, and Indian children not living under the care of White persons" were to attend separate schools under most circumstances. Only upon approval by the school board and a majority of White parents could non-White students be admitted into a White school. The law coincided with the ratification of the Fourteenth Amendment and the passage of the Civil Rights Act of 1866. In 1870, the California legislature struck the reference to "Mongolians" but retained provisions specifying that only White students qualified for general admission into public schools. The move led San Francisco to shutter its Chinese school in 1871 and, at least on paper, open its public schools to students of Chinese origin.[36]

Around this time, African Americans throughout the state mobilized to challenge school segregation. A legal strategy was devised, and in 1872 a complaint was made to the California Supreme Court on behalf of Mary Frances Ward, a San Francisco student who had been turned away from Broadway Primary School because she was Black. Ward argued that school segregation amounted to a violation of equal protection and other constitutional guarantees. "'Common schools' . . . means public, common to all, in a political sense," argued Ward. With the recent ratification of the Thirteenth and Fourteenth Amendments, "no child who is a citizen of California can be excluded by reason of color or race from any common or public school of the State." The court agreed that the state could not deny public education to a child on the basis of race. However, it noted that while Ward had been denied the right to attend a White school, she was free to enroll in the Colored School.[37]

The ruling notwithstanding, on August 3, 1875, the San Francisco Board of Education voted to create a unitary school system after deciding to allow "colored" students to attend any public school in the district. The *Pacific Appeal* proclaimed, "Thus, with one fell swoop, the caste barrier which has excluded colored children from attending the public schools among White children was broken down with a sudden avalanche. . . . Both White and colored citizens should rejoice that this last relic of slavery has at last disappeared." By 1883, legislators in Sacramento followed suit, amending the law by requiring districts to open all schools to all children. While African Americans in the state would never again be victims of school segregation by law, legal discrimination of other communities would return. It would take several more decades, replete with incremental advances and retreats, before California's school segregation policies would be permanently overturned.[38]

Tape v. Hurley

Despite state and local proclamations suggesting otherwise, Chinese students had little practical access to general admission schools following the 1871 closing of the Chinese School. Instead, many Chinese families enrolled their children in missionary and community-run schools.[39] In 1884, Principal Jennie Hurley barred Mamie Tape, a Chinese American child, from enrolling in Spring Valley Elementary School. Tape sued. The municipal court determined, and the California Supreme Court affirmed, that children of Chinese descent had a right to public education.[40] But the courts also reiterated its earlier position in *Ward*—school segregation by law was constitutional. As the case proceeded, with the tremendous growth of the Chinese community and anti-Chinese racism running rampant, California school law was amended (with near-unanimous support by lawmakers) to permit districts to mandate separate schools for students of Chinese descent. In short order, San Francisco opened a new Chinese School that Tape and all other Chinese students seeking a public education would have to attend.[41]

San Francisco did not have the requisite funds to establish separate schools for its much smaller Japanese and Korean communities, so these students were integrated into their neighborhood schools. But following the massive 1906 earthquake and an ensuing drop in enrollment in the Chinese School, the school board directed all Chinese, Japanese, and Korean students to attend a newly established "Oriental Public School."[42] This act of exclusion strained the relationship between the national governments of Japan and the United States. Under pressure from President Theodore Roosevelt, San Francisco finally agreed to rescind the policy in 1907.[43] However, the state legislature voted to expand its list of subgroups for which separate schools could legally be established in 1921, after several failed attempts. Districts were subsequently permitted to establish separate schools for students of Japanese, Chinese, and "Mongolian" ancestry.[44] By 1929, all exclusionary language had once more been removed from state code. However, in 1943 the legislature reinstated provisions in the Education Code permitting the segregation of Chinese, Japanese, "Mongolian," and, under certain conditions, "Indian" (i.e., American Indian) students.[45]

Mendez v. Westminster

By the mid-1940s, a reported one-fifth of nonmetropolitan schools across California segregated students of Mexican descent.[46] Intent on eliminating the practice, five Orange County fathers, with support from other parents, the League of United Latin American Citizens (LULAC), and the locally based Latin American Organization sued four county elementary school districts in 1945.[47] The class action suit was filed on behalf of five thousand students of "Mexican or Latin descent" on the basis that the districts had violated the Fourteenth Amendment guarantee of equal protection. The policy in place at three of the districts, Westminster, Garden Grove, and El Modeno, was to assign non-English-speaking elementary students to separate schools, apart from English-speaking students.[48] But as implemented, English-speaking Mexican students were grouped together with English learners. The fourth district, Santa Ana, was without a formal policy of segregation but had informal practices in place that made it analogous to the other three. The districts argued that resources were equal across schools and that the segregation was merely a by-product of their pedagogical decisions toward English learners.

The plaintiffs prevailed. Foreshadowing the monumental events to occur at the Supreme Court eight years later, District Court Judge Paul McCormick took issue with *Plessy v. Ferguson*'s separate but equal doctrine: "A paramount requisite in the American system of public education is social equality. It must be open to all children by unified school association regardless of lineage."[49] McCormick's ruling was affirmed by the Ninth Circuit Court of Appeals the following year, albeit on narrower legal grounds.[50] The California Education Code only allowed for the segregation of certain Asian and American Indian subgroups.[51] Provisions allowing for the segregation of Latino subgroups did not exist. Thus, the appeals court determined that the segregation practiced in Orange County was in violation of state law. Although the appeals court did not consider the legality of segregating Asian and American Indian students, months after the ruling, Governor Earl Warren repealed the offending sections, the last remnants of de jure school segregation in California.

The case was truly a precursor to *Brown*. In addition to the similarity in content, the case connected three individuals important to the dismantlement of legal school segregation in America. Governor Warren would later be appointed chief justice of the United States Supreme Court and would deliver the landmark *Brown* opinions. And in the appeal of *Westminster*, utilizing arguments that would remain largely intact for *Brown*, NAACP counsel Thurgood Marshall and Robert L. Carter served as amicus curiae.

Brown v. Board of Education

Brown v. Board of Education resulted in the largest and most contentious public school reform effort in postwar America. The story here is well known. The NAACP employed a decades-long, carefully crafted strategy designed to dismantle racial segregation.[52] By 1950, it had succeeded in challenging the constitutionality of racial segregation in higher education.[53] Two years later, the Supreme Court agreed to consider the issue of segregation at the primary and secondary levels. Linda Brown had been denied admission to her neighborhood elementary school in Topeka, Kansas, because she was Black. Her lawsuit was combined with similar NAACP-initiated cases from South Carolina, Virginia, and Delaware. Respondent school districts operated dual systems (one for Black students and one for White students) but had equalized or were in the process of equalizing various elements of education. Petitioners argued that despite these efforts, the "separate but equal" doctrine established nearly six decades earlier under *Plessy* violated the Fourteenth Amendment by depriving Black students equal educational opportunities.[54] Justices were thus required to consider the question of racial segregation rather than questions of unequal benefits or resources, as they had in prior cases.[55]

On May 17, 1954, the Supreme Court issued its ruling on *Brown*, unanimously declaring the de jure dual systems prevalent in the South unconstitutional. In overturning the "separate but equal" doctrine, the Supreme Court stated for the first time that legalized segregation in public schools violated equal protection under the Fourteenth Amendment to the Constitution. "Today, education is perhaps the most important function of state and local governments," observed the court. As an institution necessary to democracy, educational opportunity "is a right which must be made available to all on equal terms."[56] The following year, the court laid out a process for relief to be accorded.[57] Rather than ordering desegregation to commence immediately across the nation, the court allowed for locally developed solutions and timelines. Dual school systems were directed to desegregate "with all deliberate speed"—an imprecise and undefined standard.[58]

Brown was just one of many components of school desegregation. Numerous rulings in the immediate wake of *Brown* adjusted the court's interpretation of what constituted unlawful school segregation and the parameters within which school districts could appropriately desegregate. In addition, with the enactment of the Civil Rights Act of 1964, the Department of Justice took an active role in school desegregation. While many districts had already been under court mandate to desegregate at the point of its passage, Title IV of the act authorized the attorney general to file a civil action on behalf of parents and their children against school boards to achieve desegregation. In time this became a widely employed strategy.

The creation of unitary (i.e., desegregated) systems in place of these dual systems was a slow, and at times violent, process. Massive resistance to desegregation meant decades of political and legal struggles before progress of real significance was made. But by the 1980s, Southern school districts had been transformed into some of the most integrated systems in the country.[59] Of course, desegregation extended beyond the South, and beyond school districts in which institutionalized discrimination was the principal explanation for racial segregation. Many ostensibly unitary districts were in fact segregated because of attendance boundaries, neighborhood preferences, housing discrimination, and other factors, both deliberate and unintended. For the district that was de facto segregated, proving a constitutional violation—even after *Brown*—was a difficult proposition that required accounting for these various local contextual factors. Consequently, outside of the South, the NAACP employed a district-by-district political and legal strategy. Local chapters of the NAACP, along with local chapters of other civil rights organizations, pressured some districts to voluntarily adopt desegregation programs. But often, desegregation plans were mandated and overseen by a federal district court following legal action by a local chapter of the NAACP.

San Francisco after *Brown*: "We Must Study Our School System"

Soon after the *Brown* rulings, San Francisco's Black community leaders called on the school district to voluntarily desegregate. While laws permitting segregation had been relegated to history, segregation itself remained. "There is discrimination in the drawing of school district lines for new schools," stated a 1959 editorial of the *Sun-Reporter*, a newspaper serving San Francisco's African American community. This "leads to the creation of predominantly Negro schools on one hand, and predominantly White schools on the other, resulting in the development of a 'de facto' segregated school system." Community leaders organized families to formally tackle the issue. They held discussions with school administrators and board members but left these meetings without any resolution. The extent of the problem was difficult to gauge accurately as there was no official racial census of the schools. "We do not have the facts to support or disprove these rather serious charges against our system of education," observed the *Sun-Reporter.* "Invariably these charges against the San Francisco Public Schools have been denied and the school officials have demanded evidence and proof of the charges made."[60]

A campaign led by *Sun-Reporter* publisher Carlton B. Goodlett was launched ahead of the 1959 school year. It began with a "Study Our Schools" conference at the Booker T. Washington Community Center that drew over a hundred participants from "churches, political organizations, civic clubs, labor leaders, PTA members, the NAACP, and the Urban League." School segregation is a "dangerous disease" that must be confronted, community members were warned. The plan crafted by the Study Our Schools committee was to hire an independent authority to lead an investigation of the school system and to commit mayoral candidates to appoint a school board member who represented the Black community. But the district was adamant that school discrimination was not a problem, and in 1960 Superintendent Harold Spears testified before the United States Commission on Civil Rights that student assignment policies in San Francisco were completely colorblind.[61]

The San Francisco branch of the NAACP (SFNAACP) was not alone in its formulation of a plan to address de facto segregation. A number of NAACP branches throughout the North and West were also developing and executing homegrown political action campaigns and litigation strategies. The national office supported this work, creating a community action program to provide technical assistance to local branches. "You *must* and *should* attack school segregation in your communities," wrote Robert Carter, general counsel of the NAACP. But Carter cautioned that campaigns needed to be carefully planned: "The law is not at all settled, and a bad precedent resulting from a decision against you will hurt not only your efforts but countless other districts with similar problems."[62]

In San Francisco, efforts to push the district forward plodded along before intensifying in 1962. Proponents of desegregation from the Congress of Racial Equality (CORE) and the Bay Area Human Relations Clearinghouse came before the board of education in January to persuade it to "officially recognize the existence of de facto school segregation in San Francisco [and] to declare that such a pattern in the schools is educationally undesirable."[63] In April, the SFNAACP formally announced a campaign demanding that San Francisco voluntarily desegregate its

Figure 2. CORE (Congress of Racial Equality) members picketing the school district office demanding desegregation, August 10, 1962. *San Francisco Examiner* (Sacco). Fang family *San Francisco Examiner* photograph archive negative files, BANC PIC 2006.029:137869.05.02--NEG, box 1391. Copyright Regents of the University of California, Bancroft Library, University of California, Berkeley.

schools.[64] Robert Carter traveled to San Francisco to hold a press conference in which he broached the idea of busing as a desegregation mechanism.[65] The district resisted. "I have no educationally sound program to suggest to eliminate the schools in which the children are predominantly of one race," stated Superintendent Spears. "If we were preparing to ship these children to various schools, in predetermined racial allotments, then such brands would serve the same purpose they have been put to in handling livestock."[66]

The district was preparing for the opening of the new Central Junior High School serving the Haight-Ashbury and Western Addition neighborhoods.[67] Its proposed catchment area would create a predominantly African American student population. The SFNAACP was joined by CORE, the Council for Civic Unity, the San Francisco Labor Council, and neighborhood parents in opposing a segregated Central Junior High. Terry Francois, chair of the SFNAACP, demanded that Central's lines be redrawn. "We haven't decided what we will do," he told the *New York Times*. "We've talked about boycotting the school and picketing. Of course, we also probably will go to court."[68] The *San Francisco Chronicle* editorialized:

> Well, the time has come for us to forget Dixieland . . . and to worry about our own backyard. . . . The San Francisco Board of Education should put a reasonable proportion of Whites and Negroes in every public school, even if this means carrying Negro or White children across neighborhood lines.[69]

The district estimated that at least 50 percent of Central's enrollment would be Black. Parents from Grattan Elementary and other proposed feeder schools feared that such a racially imbalanced Central would prompt White families to leave what was considered to be an integrated neighborhood. "People just don't want the city to open another racially segregated school," declared Mara McMurtry, president of the Grattan parents' group. Despite intense lobbying efforts over the summer, at a raucous meeting on August 7, 1962, the school board refused to budge from their support of the original boundaries. Central's catchment would not be redrawn. In response, parents from Grattan filed a lawsuit contending that the anticipated racial demographics of Central would constitute a violation of equal protection.

This was countered by the formation of the Citizens Committee for Neighborhood Schools (CCNS), based in the predominantly White Sunset District. "The committee feels that race has never been a consideration to affect the sound educational policies by the superintendent and the Board of Education, and that the race issue should not now be injected into school administration," argued CCNS in a letter to the superintendent. "For this reason we strongly urge you and the Board of

Figure 3. NAACP representatives Tarea Hall Pittman and June Shagaloff discussing de facto school segregation, August 17, 1962, *San Francisco Examiner* (Sacco). Fang family *San Francisco Examiner* photograph archive negative files, BANC PIC 2006.029:137883.01.12-- NEG, box 1392. Copyright Regents of the University of California, Bancroft Library, University of California, Berkeley.

Education to refuse to change the district lines for Central Junior High School for the purpose of changing the racial composition of that school." With the controversy escalating, the school board, upon the recommendation of Spears, decided to abandon Central altogether. Central was a "symbol of racial strife," declared Judge Alfonso Zirpoli, who commended the board's action before dismissing the lawsuit.[70]

But school segregation remained an issue. In early October 1962, the SFNAACP filed a lawsuit challenging racial imbalance throughout the entire school system.[71] Several weeks later, the California State Board of Education issued a call for the prevention and elimination of school segregation.[72] The following spring, a San Francisco Board of Education committee studying "ethnic factors" determined that school attendance zones were delineated "without intent to manipulate school populations in such a way as to produce racial homogeneity."[73] The committee also determined that the district was in accordance with California's requirement that "boundaries be reasonably drawn on the basis of proximity and equity" for students.[74] However, in an effort to alleviate existing racial imbalance, the committee recommended that "wherever practicable and reasonable and consistent with the neighborhood school plan," race be used as a factor in establishing or redrawing attendance boundaries. Parenthetically, the committee took exception with how the issue had been framed by community activists:

> The term "segregation" whether de jure or de facto is a misnomer as applied to San Francisco schools. Segregation is an overt act that has not occurred in San Francisco. It is a disservice to the City and its schools to fail to distinguish between local racial concentration and the kind of school conditions elsewhere that might merit the term "segregation."[75]

As with the Grattan lawsuit, the SFNAACP's case was eventually dismissed in December 1964.[76] Earlier that year, the district finally succumbed to pressure and agreed to conduct a racial census of its schools.[77] Yet, the school board refused to release the results until August 1965, over six years after demands for a count first surfaced.[78] When the results were finally made public, the data revealed a pattern of widespread racial imbalance, particularly in the lower grades. Districtwide, elementary schools enrolled approximately 57 percent White, 28 percent Black, and 15 percent Asian students.[79] The census revealed that seventeen of the district's ninety-five elementary schools had student enrollments greater than 90 percent White. Twenty-four schools were at least 57 percent Black, and nine were more than 90 percent Black. Fourteen schools had Asian enrollments greater than 30 percent.[80] Proponents of desegregation finally had the hard facts to support what was widely known to be true. The district came under renewed pressure to identify an appropriate method for creating racially balanced schools. "But whatever method is employed," editorialized the *San Francisco Chronicle*, "the discrepancies shown in the newly released school census must be redressed so that the city's children of all races and cultural surroundings may have equal school facilities and equal school environments. Otherwise, serious trouble lies ahead."[81]

School segregation continued to be a deeply polarizing issue. By the mid-1960s, the number of community organizations mobilized to fight for or against school desegregation had grown to thirty.[82] Local government began to shift. The San Francisco Human Rights Commission stepped in to urge the school district to adopt a program of integration.[83] The district hired the Stanford Research Institute to create a set of possible desegregation plans.[84] As terms expired on the school board, the mayor appointed new commissioners supportive of racial balance.[85] A retiring Superintendent Spears was replaced in 1967 by Robert Jenkins, the former leader of Pasadena City School District who had guided that system's desegregation efforts. The new superintendent's first task was to improve racial balance across schools. He promptly rejected all of the plans that had been developed by the Stanford Research Institute for failing to consider instructional quality.[86] In their place, he proposed pairing desegregation with increased resources—his Equality/Quality plan. A task force of teachers and administrators was formed to push the plan forward. To provide constituents a role in the planning process, Jenkins appointed representatives from labor, business, and local community groups to a citizens advisory committee. Equality/Quality would be in place for just one school year before it was replaced by the citywide elementary school desegregation ordered by the federal district court in *Johnson*. *Class Action* begins here, with the start of court supervision in July 1971, and continues to December 2005, when the district was finally released from court supervision.

Scope and Plan

A core element of school desegregation is the district's student assignment policy. The introduction of a desegregation plan challenges accepted principles and practices regarding the assignment of students to schools. Desegregation requires communities to ask: *How are we to de-*

termine which students attend which schools? What is the role of the school district in making this determination? What role do parents have in the process? and *What are the roles of the legal system and other societal institutions?* Over time, demands to desegregate schools disrupted many widely accepted answers to these questions and, with it, many commonly used methods of student assignment. Examining the trajectory of desegregation in relation to competing notions of student assignment shared across stakeholders provides insight into the struggle over principles, practices, and policies in urban education reform.

This book is divided into two main parts that track successive episodes of court action and community mobilization. San Francisco instituted court-mandated desegregation on September 13, 1971. Over the ensuing years, new assignment plans would be proposed and adopted as old plans fell out of favor. The district's student assignment system would be under court supervision of one kind or another until December 31, 2005. Each part of the book centers on a class action lawsuit against the school district and the multiracial and multiethnic politics that structured a transition from one student assignment system to another. In each case, the new system embodied a fundamentally different understanding of student assignment and was a source of political contention as different community stakeholders sought to protect or dismantle the status quo system. During the nearly three and a half decades this book covers, the courts, community stakeholders, and the school district contended with multiple competing and evolving conceptualizations of student assignment. Understanding the course, content, and impact of these conceptualizations lies at the heart of this book.

Part I, "On a Long Road to Desegregation, 1971–1983," explains how and why Horseshoe, a 1971 student assignment plan designed to eliminate "racially imbalanced" schools was replaced by Educational Redesign, a 1978 plan designed to eliminate "racially identifiable" schools. The distinction was nuanced, but the move completely redefined school desegregation, altering the educational experience of a generation of students. In explaining this move, the chapters of Part I chronicle opposition to busing, which was driven by deeply held preferences for neighborhood schools, and school choice, which over the course of the 1970s became an increasingly legitimate means of student assignment.

Two desegregation lawsuits serve as bookends to chapter 1. The lawsuits—*Johnson v. SFUSD* and *SFNAACP v. SFUSD*—shaped student assignment policy through the 1970s and into the 1980s and led to community mobilization and advocacy in support of and against various student assignment policies. Following *Johnson v. SFUSD*, a lawsuit filed by the San Francisco chapter of the NAACP on behalf of African American elementary schoolchildren, the city created a plan that was fundamentally about balancing the ratio of White to Black students at every school so that it was similar to the districtwide White-to-Black ratio. This racial balancing scheme was a common method districts across the nation employed to conform to desegregation orders of the time. The White–Black conceptualization instantiated in student assignment policy was reinforced in the political rhetoric of desegregation's proponents.

In 1978, the student assignment plan was replaced. Rather than racial balance, the new plan sought what came to be known as racial unidentifiability—that "no racial or ethnic subgroup constitutes a majority" at any school. This new multiracial conceptualization met resistance from the NAACP. Members decried the attempt by the school district to redefine racial balance because of its consequences for desegregation. By doing away with fixed ratios, schools without any Black or White students could still comply with the court's desegregation mandate. After the Board of Education gave its final approval of a new student assignment plan in 1978, the NAACP filed a class action lawsuit against the District *(SFNAACP v. SFUSD)*—its fifth in sixteen years—calling for the preservation of the plan established under *Johnson.*

Prior to desegregation, the taken-for-granted process for assigning students to schools was to draw neighborhood-based catchment boundaries. When school desegregation plans were crafted, they typically necessitated busing across neighborhood boundaries because housing discrimination and related factors produced high rates of residential segregation. However, busing faced broad opposition from local elected officials and the general public. Chapter 2 continues the story of the transformation from racial balance to racial unidentifiability by examining the role of the neighborhood school. Throughout the 1970s and early 1980s, student assignment was often understood and debated as a choice between two alternatives: walking to a neighborhood school or being bused to a school outside of one's neighborhood for the purpose of desegregation. When framed in this way, most parents favored a neighborhood system, even if (or because) it meant a continuation of school segregation. Even during the early days of the assignment plan prompted by *Johnson*, when deleterious effects of segregated schools on Black children were widely discussed and commonly accepted, busing as a policy solution faced vigorous opposition. As the years wore on, an inability to reconcile the district's student assignment policy with the popular community preference for neighborhood schools generated tension that ran across and along racial lines, leading to future community mobilization and advocacy.

Chapter 3 assesses the gradual legitimation of school choice in student assignment policies. In the years following *Johnson*, after an initial period of success desegregating schools, the number of racially balanced elementary schools steadily decreased. Resegregation was, in large part, due to the district's transfer policy, an aspect of the student assignment system that allowed families to choose a school other than their assigned school. The policy was widely understood and exploited as a loophole by families unhappy with their assignments. Despite some valid aspects of the program, it soon grew into a mechanism for segregation.

Following the implementation of the 1978 student assignment plan, transfers were allowed only if they maintained the racial unidentifiability of both sending and receiving school. The district promoted the revised transfer policy as its "primary voluntary desegregation" effort. However, the SFNAACP attacked it as segregative and unconstitutional, hearkening to the "freedom of choice" plans in the South that subverted the intent of *Brown* by allowing families to choose between what essentially were either all-White or all-Black schools. Choice, whether as a loophole under the 1971 student assignment plan or as a voluntary desegregation effort under the 1978 plan, was understood and framed by the SFNAACP to be segregatory. Even with controls in place, the chance to undermine or bypass the district's racial balancing mandate was seen as a genuine threat.

Part II, "Desegregation and Diversity, 1983–2005," traces the replacement of a race-conscious integration framework with a race-neutral diversity framework. The chapters of Part II address how a race-conscious assignment system could no longer be justified as providing equal educational opportunity. Diversity, broadly defined, took the place of desegregation, and while racial integration remained the goal of district leaders and other stakeholders, achieving that goal required race-neutral means.

Chapter 4 addresses multiple conceptualizations of equal educational opportunity from the 1980s to the 2000s. The class action lawsuit filed by the SFNAACP against the school district in 1978 led to a 1983 federal consent decree that governed the district's student assignment policy until 2005. During this period, the SFNAACP and the San Francisco school district were, by and large, working together as partners. But as the years wore on, the conditions specified by the consent decree became increasingly untenable for many parents and advocates. The Chinese American Democratic Club mobilized on behalf of Chinese American students—understood by many to be the subgroup most adversely affected by the 1983 settlement. The club's efforts led to a 1994 lawsuit, *Ho v. SFUSD*, challenging the constitutionality of the district's student assignment system. However, rifts formed among advocates representing the city's sizeable and diverse Chinese American community. Chinese for Affirmative Action, a longtime civil rights organization, opposed efforts aimed at ending the race-conscious elements of the consent decree.

In the courtroom, the SFNAACP, now aligned with the SFUSD, sought to preserve the consent decree in its original (1983) form. On the street, a collection of community organizations and ad hoc groupings of parents and students fought to amend student assignment—whether to dismantle, maintain, or strengthen the desegregative mechanisms in place— by employing opposing equal educational opportunity arguments. The consent decree was revised in 1999 to eliminate the use of racial classifications in student assignment. Thereafter, the district introduced a new system that used a set of nonrace factors to determine student assignments.

Chapter 5 describes the gradual rise of school choice as the preferred student assignment mechanism to achieve diversity. Over time, school choice became a central component to student assignment in San Francisco. In the early 1970s school choice policies functioned as loopholes exploited by parents seeking to bypass the district's desegregation efforts. By the end of the decade, choice was framed as the voluntary desegregation complement to the city's designated schools system. In the first decade of the consent decree, during the 1980s, school choice policies were tightly constrained so that racial identifiability was not affected. But by the 1990s, constraints loosened. With the second phase of the consent decree in the 2000s, following the class action lawsuit on behalf of Chinese American students, choice became the centerpiece of student assignment. The district no longer made initial assignments, and all students were expected to choose the schools they wished to attend.

Part II closes with chapter 6, which describes renewed efforts for neighborhood schools during the 1990s and 2000s. Although choice became the central means of assignment and racial diversity remained the central goal (albeit through race-neutral means following the 1999 modification of the consent decree), strong support for neighborhood schools from both community stakeholders and the school district remained an important aspect of the local political landscape throughout the course of the consent decree. The most organized and vocal community proponents of a neighborhood-based system were parents—primarily middle class, primarily Chinese American—residing in the western neighborhoods that were home to the district's most desirable schools. Support for neighborhood schools also emerged among the families that disproportionately bore the burden of busing—African Americans living in the southeastern neighborhoods. And while the use of racial classifications in student assignment was eliminated in 1999, the agreed-upon student assignment plan during the 2000s left some parents as unsatisfied as they were under the prior system.

The conclusion places San Francisco within a broader context of post-*Brown* student assignment policies. Fundamentally, *Brown* addressed school district student assignment policy. Accepted notions of the means by which students were to be assigned to schools were disrupted by the Supreme Court's recognition that in public education "the doctrine of 'separate but equal' has no place."[87] While *Brown* dealt directly with the de jure segregation prevalent throughout the South, its impact (and that of the string of school discrimination lawsuits that followed) was felt in the de facto segregated districts of the North and West. In the decades following the decision, policymakers, parents, advocates, activists, and other stakeholders in urban districts across the country struggled over the terms and conditions of student assignment. Examining the contours of these struggles sheds light on the complicated community politics that emerge when one set of stakeholders challenges policy arrangements in public education that another set of stakeholders seeks to protect.

PART I

On a Long Road to Desegregation, 1971–1983

CHAPTER 1

How Educational Opportunity for San Francisco's African American Students Evolved

Now, changing times and changing conditions have placed a nearly unbearable burden on San Francisco's schools. In spite of past efforts on the part of those charged with responsibility for the schools, problems have remained unsolved—indeed, some have grown worse.

—WILSON RILES, STATE SUPERINTENDENT
OF PUBLIC INSTRUCTION, FEBRUARY 5, 1975.

A Proposal to Redesign the Schools

On December 29, 1977, after months of preparation, San Francisco Superintendent Robert Alioto announced the final and most significant phase of Educational Redesign, a comprehensive new plan for desegregation. The plan proposed a fundamental change to the way students would be assigned to schools and offered a new definition for school segregation. It called for the creation of several new magnet and alternative programs, the closing of underenrolled schools, and an adjustment to elementary, middle, and high school grade levels. It would considerably reduce the level of busing and provide an expanded role for school choice. Under Educational Redesign, one out of every six students would be assigned to a different school at the start of the new term.[1]

As it was in cities across the nation, student assignment in San Francisco was burdened by the complex politics of race and school segregation. Contention over desegregation had been part of the local political landscape for decades. The introduction of Educational Redesign generated a new round of conflict between opponents and proponents of desegregation that would work its way from the district central office to the school board chambers, the federal district court, and the city's many neighborhoods and communities. The conflict over Redesign crossed racial lines and involved policymakers, community organizations and their leaders, and everyday constituents. The compromise that was eventually reached satisfied some but angered many, and, just like the desegregation plan before it, Redesign would eventually be replaced. But contention would remain a part of the local landscape for several decades more as broader changes in the way society regarded school desegregation occurred. Entirely new desegregation programs would be developed, implemented, and, just as with Redesign, eventually dismantled.

Superintendent Alioto understood very well that widespread support would be important to Redesign's ultimate success. Prior to its introduction, school district staff spent several months collecting and incorporating recommendations from the San Francisco Public Schools Commission, the Citizens' Planning Committee, the local grand jury tasked with assessing city schools, and various community organizations and parent groups.[2] A series of public hearings held prior to an authorizing vote from the school board attracted more than three thousand parents, students, teachers, and community advocates. In the days leading up to the first hearing, Assistant Superintendent Isadore Pivnick explained what lay ahead: "You're going to find some people who are very excited and happy, and some who are very upset—to the point where they will be emotional and cry. Some will be relieved because their children can now walk to school. Others will be angry with us because busing meant better education for their kids, so they want buses back." Pivnick's assessment was prescient. At every hearing, amid frequent jeers and outbursts, district officials and school board members attempted to sell Redesign to a largely (though not entirely) skeptical public.[3]

This chapter addresses the political contention surrounding the SFNAACP's struggle to secure equal educational opportunity for African American students throughout the 1970s and early 1980s. Anchoring the SFNAACP's efforts were two lawsuits, *Johnson v. SFUSD* and *SFNAACP v. SFUSD*. The central argument of the chapter is how changes in the broader environment allowed the school district to move from a bimodal desegregation framework to a multimodal integration framework. That is, from a framework that was chiefly about racially "balancing" the proportion of Black and White students across all schools to one that was about creating racially "unidentifiable" schools by drawing from the nine recognized racial and ethnic subgroups to create diverse school communities. For proponents and opponents of desegregation—the SFNAACP, the school district, and others—student assignment policy proposals were framed and constructed in ways that resonated with post-*Brown* mandates to eliminate educational inequality.

Horseshoe and Operation Integrate

The desegregation program Alioto sought to replace with Redesign grew out of *Johnson v. SFUSD*, the federal district court case filed by the San Francisco chapter of the NAACP on behalf of African American elementary schoolchildren.[4] Ruling on *Johnson* in 1971, Judge Stanley Weigel noted that the district maintained a system of de jure segregated elementary schools:

> The law is settled that school authorities violate the constitutional rights of children by establishing school attendance boundary lines knowing that the result is to continue or increase substantial racial imbalance. The law is settled that school authorities violate the Constitution by providing for the construction of new schools or enlargement of existing ones in a manner which continues or increases substantial racial imbalance. The law is settled that school authorities violate the Constitution by assigning Black teachers and teachers of limited experience to "Black" schools while assigning few, if any, such teachers to "White" schools.[5]

The SFUSD did all of this "persistently and over a period of years" for its elementary schools, argued the SFNAACP, whose members had been frustrated with the district's anemic voluntary desegregation efforts throughout the 1960s. The school district followed the court order to immediately desegregate by devising and adopting an assignment system referred to as the Horseshoe plan, so named because when viewed on a map, the zones approximated an inverted "U." Horseshoe divided San Francisco into seven contiguous zones and assigned students within their zones in a way that maintained "racial balance"—a term used to describe the assignment of students such that the racial demographics at each school approximated the racial demographics of the district as a whole. Under Horseshoe, achieving racial balance meant that students were assigned such that in every school the percentage of students from each of four major racial subgroups differed by no more than 15 points from that subgroup's districtwide percentage. Because *Johnson* only addressed the elementary grades, students were assigned to junior high school (grades seven to nine) and senior high school (grades ten to twelve) without regard to this "racial balance."

In the weeks leading up to the new school term, Mayor Joseph Alioto (no relation to Superintendent Robert Alioto) publicly attacked Horseshoe as he had done with its predecessor, Educational Equality/Quality. Before ultimately backing down, he attempted to convince San Franciscans they could disobey the court order. "There is an element of governmental coercion in moving kids against their and their parents' wishes," argued the mayor. "When the people who don't want this are Blacks and Asians and Chicanos, maybe papa isn't always right. Nothing in the Constitution says that you must be integrated by a certain percentage."[6] The mayor's statement was not left unchallenged. Nathaniel Jones, general counsel of the NAACP, charged the mayor and other politicians with attempting to do what others had done in the South: "They confuse the issue, deceive the people and whip up community resentment against the court. They stood in the school house doors and engaged in demagogic appeals to the worst instincts of people."[7]

In 1974, the district—still under court supervision in the desegregation of its elementary schools—voluntarily moved to desegregate its secondary schools in order to circumvent additional legal action by the SFNAACP. The new system, dubbed Operation Integrate, extended the district's desegregation efforts through grade ten, with plans to add grades eleven and twelve in subsequent years, so that the entire district would be racially balanced across all grades by September 1976.[8] The basic contours established under Horseshoe were left essentially unchanged with Operation Integrate, but student assignment would now be based on balancing the percentage of students across nine racial and ethnic subgroups instead of four.[9] (During this period of time, some residents described the district's entire desegregation program, both elementary and secondary, as Operation Integrate, while others continued to refer to desegregation as the Horseshoe plan, especially when referring to the elementary grades.)

While San Francisco now had in place a plan to desegregate all schools, the perennial issue of academic quality remained. The San Francisco Public Schools Commission, which had been originally convened by State Superintendent Wilson Riles to address finance and management issues, released a report in 1976 that called attention to the lack of an academic focus in the city's desegregation efforts: "Although it was not within the original mandate of [this] Commission to address the question of integration, we soon found that it was closely related to many of the problems we addressed. We became especially aware of the lack of a strong educational component in [San Francisco's desegregation program]." By the following year, the board of education agreed to the first phase of Educational Redesign—committing the district to improving reading and math skills of elementary students, reconfiguring grade spans for some elementary schools, and launching an open enrollment academic program. These preliminary measures laid the groundwork for the final phase of reforms under Educational Redesign introduced in late 1977.[10]

Educational Redesign

Although requiring an estimated $2.9 million outlay, Educational Redesign was projected to save the district $9.6 million over five years from its annual budget of approximately $167 million, primarily through a combination of school closures and reduced busing. The district emphasized the plan's expanded "walk enrollment" (in other words, an increase in the number of students within walking distance of their assigned school) and significant fiscal savings. But this did not mean that Redesign would be an easy sell to the board of education and the general public. The board held a public meeting on February 14, 1978, to review the plan. Reminiscent of the audience Superintendent Jenkins faced announcing Equality/Quality nearly a decade prior, close to one thousand San Franciscans squeezed into Nourse Auditorium to listen, criticize, and, in some instances, applaud the board debate. At 3:30 a.m. the following morning the proposal finally passed with ninety amendments, each requiring its own roll call vote. Pending court approval, Redesign was set to take effect in time for the 1978–1979 school year.[11]

The public had been influential. Numerous elements designed to facilitate integration were curtailed. Several schools originally slated for closure were ultimately saved; portions of the busing plan were over-turned; and a handful of proposals to convert neighborhood schools into magnet programs were abandoned. All of these adjustments resulted from public pressure. Still, most of what Educational Redesign originally laid out received board approval. Reflecting on the difficulty of the pro-cess, Superintendent Alioto remarked, "The important thing about this change is what's going to happen in the long run. If nothing else, I think we've cracked the barrier of apathy about education. We've generated enthusiasm—or in some cases concern—but at least the people of San Francisco care. We're going to see a major educational reform."[12]

From Racial Balance to Racial Unidentifiability

While the school district worked to implement Educational Redesign, several community organizations and parent groups—on both sides of the desegregation issue—remained partially or wholly opposed to the plan. Redesign's principal opponent was the SFNAACP, which promptly sued the district and the state of California to preserve the existing de-segregation policy—Horseshoe/Operation Integrate. At issue was the new remedy Educational Redesign proposed for school segregation. Rather than seeking racial balance by setting the schoolwide percentage of stu-dents from each recognized racial subgroup such that it approximated each subgroup's districtwide percentage, Redesign sought what was de-scribed as racial unidentifiability by assigning students so that every school had an enrollment from at least four of the nine recognized racial and ethnic subgroups and that no subgroup enrollment exceeded 45 per-cent of the total school population.

Three shifting conditions facilitated the district's ability to set aside racial balance and institute the new desegregation standard. First, federal and state desegregation jurisprudence evolved in ways that disfavored how student assignment was understood, framed, and constituted under Horseshoe and Operation Integrate. Second, these changes in jurispru-dence altered the California regulatory environment for school desegre-gation. And third, the changing racial demographics of San Francisco's student population made maintenance of the former desegregation pro-gram increasingly burdensome.

Desegregation Jurisprudence

While the injunction issued by the federal district court in *Johnson v. SFUSD* remained in place, desegregation jurisprudence evolved. In 1973, the Supreme Court heard *Keyes v. School District No. 1,* its first desegregation case originating from outside of the South. The court was asked to consider the Denver School Board's neighborhood school policy and its manipulation of school catchment areas and school site selection in ways that maintained racial and ethnic segregation. Up to this point in time, the characteristic situation of unlawful school segregation had been the school district operating a dual system. With *Keyes,* the court clarified the definition of school segregation to allow for petitioners to bring claims against districts that were not dual, thus extending the court's reach in the North and West. The court determined that even in situations where a statutory dual system never existed, a school board's segregative intent may be cause for legal action. In delivering the opinion of the court, Justice Brennan wrote, "We emphasize that the differentiating factor between *de jure* segregation and so-called *de facto* segregation . . . is *purpose* or *intent* to segregate." In a later case originating from Oxnard School District in California, the Ninth Circuit Court of Appeals determined that *Keyes* required a "determination that the school authorities had intentionally discriminated against minority students by practicing a deliberate policy of racial segregation."[13]

Ruling on *Johnson* two years earlier, Judge Weigel noted that it was "well settled law" that any school district policy or regulation that creates or maintains racial imbalance constituted de jure segregation. The distinction between *de facto* and *de jure* was given as such by Weigel in 1971:

> If a school board has drawn attendance lines so that there is a reasonable racial balance among the children attending a given school and if, thereafter, solely due to movement of the neighborhood population, the school attendance becomes racially imbalanced, the segregation thus arising is then *de facto.* On the other hand, if the school board, as in this case, has drawn school attendance lines, year after year, knowing that the lines maintain or heighten racial imbalance, the resulting segregation is *de jure.*[14]

In other words, the question of intent was not relevant. Weigel's ruling in *Johnson* preceded the *Keyes* ruling, so this was not an unreasonable legal standard at the time. Indeed, *Johnson* comported with numerous prior cases won by the Justice Department and other petitioners.[15] However, several months after Weigel's decision, the SFUSD, parents of public schoolchildren of Chinese ancestry, and other opponents filed appeals to *Johnson* in the Ninth Circuit that presented, in part, the question of whether the correct standard of de jure segregation had been applied.[16]

The Ninth Circuit waited until after *Keyes* was decided to issue its ruling since the appellants' claim similarly dealt with a district that employed various techniques resulting in the maintenance of racial segregation. Following *Keyes*, in 1974, Weigel's order was vacated and returned so that the SFUSD's segregative intent could be determined. In the meantime, the school district was ordered by the appellate court to maintain its desegregation program.[17] While much of *Keyes* was viewed favorably by proponents of desegregation, the clarification the Supreme Court provided in determining de jure and de facto segregation proved to be a problem for the SFNAACP. Although Horseshoe remained intact, the decision did not bode well for its ultimate fate. "*[Keyes]* threw us out of court," recalled SFNAACP counsel Arthur Brunwasser. "For the first time the Supreme Court drew the line between school districts that were *de jure* segregated by law and the *de facto* [districts segregated] by practice."[18]

State Regulatory Environment

Throughout much of the 1960s, a majority of members on the California State Board of Education (SBE) proactively supported desegregation efforts undertaken by local education authorities. In 1962, the SBE declared that racial and ethnic segregation in schools stood against equality of educational opportunity and that "all effort to avoid and eliminate segregation" should be put forth by districts. The following year, the SBE required districts to consider the potential impact of school boundaries and attendance practices on racial integration. These policies would soon become a legal obligation imposed by the state supreme court in response to a school desegregation lawsuit originating from Pasadena.[19]

In 1966, the SBE required districts to conduct an annual racial and ethnic census as a means of tracking desegregation efforts across the state.

And in 1969, after months of discussion, the SBE affirmed and elaborated its earlier position on the elimination of segregation by defining a racially imbalanced school as one in which "the percentage of pupils of one or more racial or ethnic groups differs by more than 15 percentage points from that in all the schools of the district." The definition was unanimously approved and, at the time, was considered "one of the most precise definitions of racial imbalance in the nation."[20] This became the standard adopted by the SFUSD for its Horseshoe plan.

As California's regulatory environment evolved to both define and induce desegregation, school districts were compelled to begin busing programs. Instantly, busing became among the more contentious issues up and down the state. Proponents saw busing as a practical solution to racial imbalance. But many parents opposed busing—even parents who generally supported the idea of racially integrated schools. Antibusing sentiment spread rapidly, and in response, the SBE repealed its racial imbalance definition in 1970.[21] Following a failed attempt by the California legislature to add a section to the Education Code preventing school districts from assigning students to nonneighborhood schools (which would have thus hobbled busing efforts), Republican assembly member Floyd Wakefield proposed a ballot initiative to bar districts from using race as a factor in student assignment and to repeal state guidelines for school integration. The initiative—Proposition 21—qualified for the November 1972 ballot, and Californians overwhelmingly supported it.[22] While the California Supreme Court ultimately declared the student assignment section of Proposition 21 unconstitutional, the provisions that eliminated state integration guidelines were allowed to remain.

During this same period, several school desegregation cases were working their way through the state court system. On June 28, 1976, the California Supreme Court handed down sweeping guidelines after considering cases from Los Angeles and San Bernardino. The court held that districts were bound by the state constitution to take steps to "alleviate the racial and ethnic isolation" of students, whether the origin of isolation was de jure or de facto in nature. SFUSD interpreted the decision to mean that litigating the issue of segregative intent was no longer necessary. Whether there was intent to segregate or not, the district was responsible for reducing segregation. In this case, the California Supreme

Court broke from the trial court's original approach by noting that neither segregation nor desegregation could be determined strictly on the basis of a school's racial combination: "Other factors, such as the racial composition of faculty and administration, and community and school board attitudes toward the school, have a place in such a determination."[23] In other words, there could be no definition of racial segregation that would, for example, declare a school segregated solely if it was more than 50 percent White.

Mirroring the language of the court's opinion, the SBE promulgated new regulations in 1977 directing school districts to take "reasonable and feasible steps to alleviate" racial and ethnic segregation. The revised definition of segregated schools put forth by the state board was: "those schools in which the minority student enrollment is so disproportionate as realistically to isolate minority students from other students and thus deprive minority students of an integrated educational experience." Districts with segregated schools were required to work with community representatives to develop and adopt a plan of action by January 1, 1979, and every four years thereafter.[24] The new SBE regulation compelling districts to alleviate segregation was a vague and weak version of its earlier regulation requiring districts to eliminate racial and ethnic imbalance. Horseshoe, with its 15 percentage–point standard for determining racial imbalance, appropriately conformed to the legal and regulatory environment of the early 1970s. But it no longer did so by the late 1970s. Educational Redesign, however, was attuned to the state's new and comparatively imprecise and weak guidance on school segregation and its disfavor of a numerical definition of racial imbalance.

Racial and Ethnic Demographics

During the summer of 1975, the sociologist James Coleman, who nearly a decade earlier rose to prominence by authoring a report documenting the impact of school segregation, once again gained national attention, this time for several comments he made at a research conference on the relationship between school desegregation and demographic change. Coleman expressed concern that busing, rezoning, and other "induced integration" strategies led White families to remove their children from urban public school systems, resulting in resegregation. He concluded, provocatively, that the courts were "probably the worst instrument of social policy" for consequential issues such as school desegregation where individuals may act in ways that ultimately defeat intended policy goals. Because of Coleman's professional stature as a social scientist, his statements were taken as an authoritative explanation for White flight, a phenomenon widely observed once busing became the common remedy to school segregation that resulted from housing discrimination and residential segregation, a pattern endemic in cities throughout the country.[25]

This national debate played out locally in San Francisco. Addressing those who predicted the departure of White students following the 1971 desegregation mandate, Judge Weigel wrote, "By feeding unwarranted fears about busing, those opposing desegregation invite a White flight even before children and parents have had a reasonable opportunity to see for themselves how busing works in actual practice. The testimony in this case makes it clear that in those communities in which busing has been employed, it has worked well. There was no evidence to the contrary."[26]

Despite Weigel's attempt to allay concern, SFUSD was no different than any of the other large urban school districts across the nation experiencing significant enrollment declines among White students. While the number of White public school students in the city had fallen steadily for several years, the steepest drop occurred immediately following the implementation of the Horseshoe plan. Between 1968 and 1976, San Francisco's public schools lost a total 21,040 White students, representing a 57 percent drop in enrollment. In the 1970–1971 school year, just prior to the implementation of Horseshoe, the district enrolled 29,048 White students; in the following school year, White enrollment in the district dropped to 25,808. It was not just White students leaving the public schools of San Francisco. Chinese students also opted out in significant numbers. In the school year prior to Horseshoe, San Francisco enrolled 12,248 Chinese students. The following term, Chinese enrollment dropped by 1,003.[27] Students were encouraged to enroll in "Freedom Schools" established by the San Francisco Chinese Committee for Quality Education, an ad hoc organization of Chinatown parents and leaders.[28]

In the years leading up to Educational Redesign, the district reported a 9 percent drop in student enrollment, mostly due to the loss of White and Chinese students. But at the same time some students were leaving the school district, San Francisco was welcoming new immigrant families. The 1965 Immigration and Nationality Act (INA), principally among several factors, led to an increase in students from Mexico, the Philippines, China, and elsewhere. Schools were overwhelmingly White as late as the 1940s. By the 1960s, the district was composed of primarily White and Black students. And although San Francisco had been home to several Asian and Latino communities for generations, the demographic changes the district witnessed following the INA were considerable (Table 2).[29]

The rapid demographic change and the declining student enrollment taking place in San Francisco served as indicators Superintendent Alioto used to justify the implementation of a new student assignment plan. "In reviewing the shifting racial/ethnic balance, I found that the pupil population had shifted from a two-thirds White and Black mix in 1969 to one which was nearly one half Asian and Latino," stated Alioto. "Demographic

Table 2. SFUSD Student Population by Subgroup (Percent), 1965–1978

School Year	TOTAL	L	OW	AA	C	J	K	AI	F	ONW
1965–1966	93,269	11.5	45.3	25.6	13.3	1.8	-	-	2.5	-
1966–1967	93,045	12.3	44.0	26.1	13.6	1.8	-	-	2.3	-
1967–1968	93,710	12.9	41.0	26.5	13.5	1.8	0.1	0.2	2.3	1.6
1968–1969	92,653	13.1	39.9	27.1	13.6	1.8	0.1	0.2	2.6	1.6
1969–1970	90,790	13.7	37.0	27.6	14.6	1.7	0.2	0.3	3.2	1.7
1970–1971	82,757	13.6	35.1	28.1	14.8	1.8	0.3	0.3	4.1	1.9
1971–1972	80,902	13.8	31.9	30.0	13.9	1.8	0.3	0.3	5.9	2.2
1972–1973	79,042	14.0	29.6	30.1	15.0	1.8	0.4	0.3	6.4	2.5
1973–1974	74,723	14.3	27.0	30.1	16.0	1.7	0.5	0.3	7.4	2.7
1974–1975	72,443	14.5	25.3	29.8	16.4	1.8	0.6	0.4	8.2	3.0
1975–1976	70,045	13.8	24.4	29.8	16.8	1.3	0.8	0.4	8.3	4.1
1976–1977	67,778	13.9	23.5	29.0	17.4	1.5	0.9	0.4	8.7	4.6
1977–1978	63,872	14.3	22.1	28.6	18.1	1.5	1.0	0.6	8.8	5.0

Source: Research, Planning, and Accountability Department, San Francisco Unified School District.

Note: The nine subgroups recognized by the district during this period: Latino (L), Other White (i.e., White) (OW), African American (AA), Chinese (C), Japanese (J), Korean (K), American Indian (AI), Filipino (F), Other Non White (ONW). Note the decline in total enrollment, the decline in the percentage of White (OW) students, and the increase in the percentage of Latino (L) and Chinese (C) students.

projections for the near future show a further decline in White and Black public school populations."[30] These legal regulatory and demographic changes made a revision to the framework of student assignment—from Horseshoe/Operation Integrate's focus on racial balance to Educational Redesign's new emphasis on racial unidentifiability—seem sensible to district leaders and the general public.

Trouble on the Horizon

On April 17, 1978, a few months after the board of education approved Educational Redesign, the district sought authorization from the federal district court to implement it. Court authorization was necessary because the desegregation mandate established in *Johnson v. SFUSD* remained in effect. Superintendent Alioto declared, "Contrary to the Horseshoe [and Operation Integrate] plan, which has failed to achieve its goal of a desegregated quality education for all San Francisco students, I am convinced that implementation of the Educational Redesign will achieve that desegregated quality education to which I and the Board are committed."[31]

The district's request that the court allow the dismantlement of Horseshoe/Operation Integrate in favor of Educational Redesign immediately became a matter of grave concern to the SFNAACP. Several years earlier, soon after the 1974 appeals court remand of *Johnson,* attorneys from both sides discussed resolving the case through a consent decree whereby the recitals would indicate that the board of education "did not acknowledge violating the law and did not admit any wrong doing." A consent decree was compelling to all involved since it would allow for a judgment (which the SFNAACP deemed necessary in order to hold the district accountable) without the political contention that a full-scale evidentiary hearing would bring. By November 1975, the SFNAACP had authorized its attorney, Arthur Brunwasser, to proceed with the settlement plan. But the following March, its membership reversed course, voting to rescind all prior settlement agreements with the district and to instead prepare for a trial.[32]

This was a risky strategy. Because of *Keyes,* unlike the original trial, the SFNAACP would now need to prove segregatory intent on the part of the school district. "In my view, there is insufficient evidence, either in the record or outside of it, to establish acts of *de jure* segregation on the part of the School District, and there does not appear to be any legal means available to prevent the implementation of the Superintendent's proposal [i.e., Educational Redesign]," wrote Brunwasser in a letter to SFNAACP branch president Joseph Hall. "When the School District formally requests Judge Weigel to approve the new proposal, I feel certain that one of the defendants will make a motion to dismiss the case, and such a motion will very likely be successful."[33]

Because no formal action had been taken by either party following the 1974 remand, and because the facts and law had changed since the original 1971 decision, Weigel dismissed *Johnson* on June 22, 1978, without prejudice, for failure to prosecute and mootness. Following the dismissal, the SFNAACP substituted Brunwasser, who continued to favor a settlement, for Thomas Atkins, a well-known desegregation attorney who was special counsel to the NAACP Special Contribution Fund. Reflecting on the strategy differences he had with the SFNAACP, Brunwasser stated, "With the standards of *Keyes* . . . we weren't going to win [at trial]. In fact, after *Keyes* was decided, I knew that we were going to get a reversal in the Ninth Circuit, and I tried to settle that case."[34]

Thomas Atkins was of a different opinion. Sensing that it was premature to discuss a settlement and fearing that Educational Redesign would lead to resegregation, he counseled the SFNAACP to move forward with a trial and validate the court's original 1971 decision. "[The decision] must be defended against any efforts to dilute its vitality or the integrity of the desegregation order which it effected in the fall of 1971," argued Atkins. "As a practical matter, this means the Plaintiffs must be willing and prepared to go back into court in a remand trial and produce such supplemental evidence as is necessary to indicate to the Ninth District Court of Appeals that the original finding of *de jure* segregation was required by the facts."[35]

On June 30, 1978, with Atkins as lead counsel, the SFNAACP filed a new lawsuit on behalf of all Black children attending public schools in San Francisco, *SFNAACP v. SFUSD*.[36] The new lawsuit, as filed, differed from *Johnson* in two important ways. Unlike *Johnson,* which focused on elementary students, *SFNAACP* sought relief for both elementary and secondary students. In addition, the new lawsuit was filed against both local defendants (the school board, the superintendent, and the school district) and state defendants (the State Board of Education, Superintendent of Public Instruction, and California Department of Education), whereas *Johnson* involved only local defendants. A third important distinction would emerge in early 1979 when the SFNAACP's class certification would be modified. Demanding that Black students not be "subjected to any of the badges or indicia of slavery," the SFNAACP requested a temporary restraining order and preliminary injunction requiring the district to maintain the Horseshoe/Operation Integrate plan. "Our immediate concern is the headlong rush of this district to dismantle [desegregation] and to resegregate schools," remarked Benjamin Hooks, national director of the NAACP. "We want the schools to do their job, which is to educate children so that when they graduate they can go to college if they want to, or so they can get a good job if they want to go to work."[37]

Racial Unidentifiability

Under Horseshoe, the SFUSD required parents to declare on behalf of their children the most appropriate of six racial subgroups. Each subgroup belonged to one of two main racial categories tracked by the district, *White* or *Non-White*. Falling under the district's *White* category were the subgroups *Spanish Surname* and *Other White* (as in, White students without a "Spanish Surname"). The subgroups *Negro/Black, Asian/Oriental, American Indian,* and *Other Non-White* belonged to the district's *Non-White* category. The *Asian/Oriental* subgroup brought together Chinese, Japanese, and Korean students, and the *Other Non-White* subgroup was mostly composed of Filipino students and students from other less populous Asian and Pacific Islander communities.[38]

Despite the existence of six subgroups, the specific relief sought and provided for in *Johnson* was narrow. Even in a city as racially diverse as San Francisco, desegregation was principally about balancing the racial percentage of White and Black students in schools. The court defined school segregation as situations in which "the ratio of Whites to Blacks . . . is substantially at variance with the ratio of White children to Black children in the total population of the schools." In line with this definition, the stated objective of the district's Horseshoe plan was the "full integration of all public elementary schools so that the ratio of Black children to White children will then be and thereafter continue to be substantially the same in each school." To accomplish Horseshoe's objective, the district adopted the standard provided by the State Board of Education whereby the segregation threshold for a school's subgroup enrollment was plus or minus 15 percentage points of that subgroup's districtwide population. Consequently, Horseshoe's seven attendance zones were drawn by district officials in such a way that would allow the district to "maintain an excess of Whites to Blacks" within the 15 percentage–point standard.[39]

Despite the court's narrow focus, the district needed the involvement of all students. So, in addition to applying the SBE guidelines to White and Black children, the district "committed itself . . . to extending these guidelines to the third and fourth major groups in the enrollment," Latino and Asian students. "Our case was brought for Black children, a class action. So, it was their rights that were primarily involved," observed SFNAACP attorney Arthur Brunwasser. "However, as a matter of educational policy, it came about that because of the unique racial makeup of San Francisco, that all racial groups would be involved in the program." On this point, the court wrote, "While plaintiffs complain only of segregation of Black students, the plan they have filed, as well as that filed by defendants, provides for a balancing of all races. The fact that the court did not require more than desegregation of Black students does not make the plans invalid. And there are solid reasons supporting the parties in their plans for desegregation of all races."[40]

Nevertheless, while Horseshoe attempted to desegregate the four largest racial subgroups, its principal concern was Black and White students. In its initial year, the *Other White* and *Negro/Black* subgroups had districtwide percentages of elementary students substantially greater than 15 percent. But only 14.4 percent of elementary students were identified as *Asian/Oriental* and only 13.4 percent of elementary students were identified as *Spanish Surname*. Thus, while Horseshoe imposed a maximum 15 percentage point variance on schools for the third and fourth largest subgroups (capping enrollments at 29.4 percent for Asian students and 28.4 percent for Latino students), there was no lower limit for these two subgroups. A school could have no Latino or Asian students and still be considered racially balanced. In contrast, each and every school in the district had to both enroll significant numbers of Black and White students and ensure that neither group constituted a majority; specifically, in order to be considered racially balanced and in compliance with the court's mandate, every school in the district would need to enroll at least 19.8 percent but no more than 49.8 percent White students and at least 13.9 percent but no more than 43.9 percent Black students (Table 3).

Table 3. Elementary School Level Racial Balance with ±15 Percent Standard, 1971

	Districtwide Percent	Minimum	Maximum
Spanish Surname	13.4	-	28.4
Other White	34.8	19.8	49.8
Negro/Black	28.9	13.9	43.9
Asian	14.4	-	29.4
Other Non White	8.5	-	23.5
American Indian	-	-	-

Source: Current Statistics and Evaluation—Horseshoe, July 1, 1971, *Johnson v. SFUSD*, RG 21, NARA. Figures do not include students in special education programs. Racial and ethnic subgroup labels c1971.

Note: *Asian* category included Chinese (12.3), Japanese (1.8), and Korean (0.3) subgroups; *Other Non White* category included Filipino (6.0), American Indian (0.4), Other Non White (1.8), and an Unknown category (0.3). The racial and ethnic subgroup categories established by the State Board of Education: Spanish Surname, Other White, Negro, Oriental, American Indian, and Other Non White (Procedures to Correct Racial and Ethnic Imbalance in School Districts. California State Department of Education, 1969).

To facilitate the district's school-level racial balancing efforts, Horseshoe's attendance zones were drawn so that each contained roughly one-seventh of the districtwide population of Black and White students: zones had between a 10.6 percent and a 25.9 percent share of the districtwide total. This was a relatively narrow band considering that for Latino students, zones ranged from a low of 2.1 percent to a high of 38.0 percent of the subgroup's districtwide total, and for Asian students, zones ranged from 5.0 percent to 35.9 percent of the districtwide total (Table 4). The demographic makeup of Horseshoe's attendance zones similarly suggests attention to White and Black students. Within each zone, White students comprised between 23.0 percent and 44.8 percent of the student population. Likewise, for each zone, Black students comprised between 18.0 percent and 38.5 percent of the student population. But because of the racial demographics and housing patterns of the district, as well as the need to make attendance zones of contiguous areas, three zones contained fewer than 4.0 percent Latino students and two zones had less than 5.0 percent Asian students (Table 5).

Table 4. Share of Districtwide Subgroup Elementary Population (Percent), c1971

Horseshoe Zone	Latino	White	Black	Asian
1. Richmond Complex (5,741 students)	2.4	13.7	11.3	22.9
2. Marina, Chinatown, Western Addition (4,836 students)	2.1	11.7	10.6	17.0
3. Mission, Chinatown, Potrero Hill (9,456 students)	38.0	13.4	12.7	35.9
4. Glen Park, Hunters Point (7,092 students)	24.8	15.2	15.7	5.1
5. West of Twin Peaks, Visitacion Valley, Bayview (10,010 students)	23.6	22.6	25.9	7.1
6. Sunset, Oceanview (4,443 students)	2.7	12.3	12.8	5.0
7. Park South Complex (4,590 students)	6.3	11.0	11.0	6.9

Source: Current Statistics and Evaluation—Horseshoe, July 1, 1971, *Johnson v. SFUSD*, RG 21, NARA.
Note: Population totals includes "Other Non White" students.

Table 5. Racial Percentages by Horseshoe Zone, c1971

Horseshoe Zone	Latino	White	Black	Asian
1. Richmond Complex (5,741 students)	2.6	38.5	26.4	26.4
2. Marina, Chinatown, Western Addition (4,836 students)	2.7	39.3	29.2	23.3
3. Mission, Chinatown, Potrero Hill (9,456 students)	24.9	23.0	18.0	25.1
4. Glen Park, Hunters Point (7,092 students)	21.7	34.7	29.6	4.8
5. West of Twin Peaks, Visitacion Valley, Bayview (10,010 students)	14.6	36.6	34.5	4.7
6. Sunset, Oceanview (4,443 students)	3.8	44.8	38.5	7.4
7. Park South Complex (4,590 students)	8.5	38.6	31.9	10.0
Districtwide (46,168 students)	13.4	34.8	28.9	14.4

Source: Current Statistics and Evaluation—Horseshoe, July 1, 1971, *Johnson v. SFUSD*, RG 21, NARA.
Note: Population totals include "Other Non White" students. Note the distribution of Latino and Asian students in comparison with the distribution of White and Black students.

With the 1974 implementation of Operation Integrate, SFUSD, in addition to extending desegregation to secondary schools, expanded the 15 percent criterion to nine subgroups by disaggregating the Asian category and adding a category for indigenous students. Thereafter, the recognized racial and ethnic subgroups were: *Spanish Surname, Other White, Negro/Black, Chinese, Japanese, Korean, American Indian, Filipino,* and *Other Non White.* During this period, the proportion of public school students who were Chinese gradually increased such that by 1977, schools would need a student enrollment of at least 3.1 percent Chinese to be in compliance with Operation Integrate (Table 6).

Table 6. School Level Racial Balance with ±15 Percent Standard, 1977

	Districtwide Percent	Minimum	Maximum
Spanish Surname	14.3	-	29.3
Other White	22.1	7.1	37.1
Negro/Black	28.6	13.6	43.6
Chinese	18.1	3.1	33.1
Japanese	1.5	-	16.5
Korean	1.0	-	16.0
American Indian	0.6	-	15.6
Filipino	8.8	-	23.8
Other Non White	5.0	-	20.0

Source: Research, Planning, and Accountability Department, San Francisco Unified School District.
Note: Racial and ethnic subgroup labels c1977.

Eventually, the demographic changes in the city, particularly the growth of the Chinese community, would be an important factor challenging the bimodal (Black/White) conceptualization of school desegregation. But at the time, even with the expansion to nine subgroups, the Black/White framework was durable. A 1976 evaluation report by the SFUSD Integration Department found that district officials "tacitly admitted" the difficulty of integrating the comparatively small and geographically concentrated Chinese and Latino populations by drawing the boundaries it did for Zone Three. The zone combined the Mission District (where many Latino students lived) and Chinatown. Schools in Zone Three were out of balance almost from the very start of Horseshoe, and with the growth of language programs for Spanish- and Chinese-speaking students, approximately one-half of the out-of-balance schools across the district were located in the zone within just a few years. "Thus, the desegregation plan may be said to have been aimed at equalizing the proportions of Black and White students in the schools," continued the 1976 evaluation report. "This was very largely achieved in the early years of the plan, both according to the state guidelines and when measured by the number of highly segregated Black or White schools, which was reduced to zero."[41]

The core policy function of Horseshoe/Operation Integrate was narrow. These student assignment systems were designed to ensure that a roughly equivalent ratio of White to Black students existed in every zone and every school. Latino and Asian students were only incidentally assigned. This bimodal conceptualization for desegregation was instantiated in the district's student assignment policies and became the way desegregation was framed and understood. By contrast, Educational Redesign was an early foray into a multimodal conceptualization of integration, one that favored flexibility over fixed ratios. Educational Redesign redefined a racially balanced school as one in which "no ethnic or racial group . . . constitute[s] a majority" in student enrollment. To comply with the new definition, Educational Redesign imposed a new standard requiring schools to enroll at least four of the nine recognized racial and ethnic subgroups and to prevent any subgroup from exceeding 45 percent of the total student population (Figure 4).[42] This was a subtle but

Student Assignment	Definition of Racial Balance	Standard Applied
Horseshoe (1971); Operation Integrate (1974)	In every school, ratio of White to Black students not substantially at variance with districtwide ratio.	In every school, each recognized subgroup must fall within 15 percentage points of their districtwide total.
Educational Redesign (1978)	In every school, no racial or ethnic subgroup constitutes a majority.	In every school, at least four subgroups must be represented with no subgroup constituting more than 45 percent of student population.

Figure 4. From racial balance to racial unidentifiability.

significant break from the status quo. With the implementation of Educational Redesign, San Francisco's student assignment system no longer set minimum subgroup percentages, and it created a standard maximum subgroup percentage, regardless of district demographics. Unlike prior assignment programs, schools could be in compliance with very few or even no Black or White students, and students from less populous subgroups—Filipinos, for example—could be amassed in a school up to the 45 percent limit.

"The Sad History of Educational Neglect"

The SFUSD argued that changes proposed by Educational Redesign conformed to current state regulations and contemporary desegregation jurisprudence. However, critics believed that Educational Redesign was not true desegregation. The SFNAACP argued that the consequence of changing the definition of racial balance would be the immediate re-segregation of schools for reasons unrelated to any possible "educational needs of a racially-neutral nature." Educational Redesign "denied Black children their constitutional right to a desegregated and equal educational opportunity," complained Joseph Hall, the SFNAACP branch president. "It was merely a part of the sad history of the educational neglect of Black children within the SFUSD." The SFNAACP favored the original standard of racial balance put in place by the State Board of Education: when, for a school, the "student racial population for any one group is ±15 percent of that group's percentage of the system wide total student population." Although these provisions had since been repealed in California, similar standards were sanctioned elsewhere, and to bolster its case, the SFNAACP pointed to a recent appellate court affirming opinion allowing a desegregation plan for Columbus, Ohio, in which the percentage of Black students in any given school was to fall within a minimum-maximum range based on the districtwide percentage of Black students, just as in Horseshoe.[43]

The SFNAACP lawsuit came on the heels of the landslide victory of Proposition 13, a ballot initiative limiting property tax receipts. Since property taxes were a core source of school funding, "Prop 13" had the effect of eliminating more than half of local school revenue statewide, obliging the California legislature to provide a backfill to school districts through the state general fund. Prop 13's impact was considerable. In San

Francisco, the share of state and local revenue for the district flipped following its passage.[44] And even with increased support from the state, Prop 13 left the district with a budget shortfall. During the spring of 1978, the SFUSD's projected expenses for the upcoming school year were $186 million.[45] Following the passage of Prop 13, the district was forced to reduce its budget to $167.4 million, necessitating the closure of thirteen elementary schools and twenty-one children's centers and the laying off of 859 employees (Table 7). Amid talk that school funding in the city would be slashed, NAACP national director Benjamin Hooks forcefully stated that the court must "enjoin state school officials from taking away money from children who have already been denied educational opportunities."[46] Accordingly, a motion was included in the SFNAACP lawsuit seeking to prevent the implementation of Prop 13 in San Francisco.

Table 7. SFSUD School Budget before and after Prop. 13 (In Millions)

Category	1977–1978	1978–1979
Basic Instruction	$55.1	$51.5
Education for Handicapped Students	8.3	9.1
Summer School	2.2	0.3
Bilingual Ed	6.2	8.0
After-School Recreation	0.7	-
Children's Centers	15.2	12.8
Administrative Payroll	7.8	5.6
Teachers Payroll	89.6	83.8
Books, Supplies, Equipment	9.9	8.7
Free Community Use of School Buildings	2.8	-

Source: "Slimmer Schools Budget," *San Francisco Chronicle,* August 12, 1978.
Note: Student enrollment was estimated at 65,347 for 1977–1978 and 61,112 for 1978–1979.

Over the summer, Judge Weigel ruled against a request by the SFNAACP to continue Horseshoe while parties prepared for trial. So, in the fall of 1978, amid austere budget cuts, the district implemented Educational Redesign. The following year new presiding judge William H. Orrick, in a ruling that would later be criticized by many community groups and leaders, expanded the plaintiff class. Orrick certified the SFNAACP as class representative of not just all Black public schoolchildren—as the lawsuit originally asserted—but of "all the school children, heretofore, now or hereafter eligible to attend the public elementary and secondary schools of the SFUSD."[47]

Over the next several years, amid various minor legal machinations, three pretrial motions were submitted that became significant to the eventual outcome of the case.[48] First, the state defendants filed a motion for dismissal or abstention, arguing that their presence was unnecessary to resolve the case since the primary responsibility for the establishment and implementation of education policy lay with the state legislature and local school districts. The court denied the motion. Keeping the state defendants on for the entirety of the case facilitated the acquisition of postsettlement funding from the state supporting the city's desegregation activities.

Second, the local defendants (the school district, board of education members, and superintendent) filed a motion for a separate trial to resolve the question of whether the district was in fact operating a dual school system in violation of plaintiffs' constitutional rights. The defendants argued that there would be no basis for additional relief if Educational Redesign succeeded in eliminating all vestiges of segregation. The court denied this motion as well but asked that the issue of current conditions of segregation be the very first issue addressed at a trial.[49]

Third, while the local defendants' motion for a separate trial was pending, the SFNAACP requested a partial summary judgment on the issue of whether the school district was racially segregated as of 1954 or at any point thereafter. Plaintiffs described a long history of de jure school segregation in San Francisco, from the establishment of "Colored" and Chinese schools during the 1850s to discriminatory hiring and segregative assignment of teachers a century later. The motion was denied, as the SFNAACP "failed to assert a sufficient number of undisputed facts to create an inference of segregative intent."[50] The motion did, however, set the stage for a settlement.

Judge Orrick's comments on the motion addressing the strengths and factual deficiencies of the SFNAACP's case provided parameters for the parties to negotiate within, and on December 30, 1982, hours before the court's trial deadline, the SFNAACP and the school district preliminarily entered into a consent decree settlement over the appropriate means to desegregate the schools (see appendix B). The consent decree adopted the basic elements of Educational Redesign and introduced the term *racial identifiability* in place of *racial imbalance.* Its goal was "to eliminate racial/ethnic segregation or identifiability in any SFUSD school, program, or classroom and to achieve the broadest practicable distribution throughout the system of students from the racial and ethnic groups which comprise the student enrollment of the SFUSD."[51]

While the decree called for the elimination of segregation in every "school, program, or classroom," the focus was always placed at the school level. "Too frequently, classrooms are segregated within a school site," argued Lulann McGriff, a parent and active member of the NAACP education issues committee. "I visited schools where the majority of Black students are put in separate classrooms. I have also observed all the Black students seated in the back of the classroom or in a separate grouping within the room. This type of segregation within a class is most harmful to the self concept of all the students." McGriff would become SFNAACP president a few years later.[52]

The consent decree provided for a student assignment system similar to Redesign. Schools were required to enroll students from at least four of the nine recognized racial and ethnic subgroups. For most schools, no subgroup could exceed 45 percent of the student body. For a number of alternative schools, particular subgroups could not have an enrollment comprising more than 40 percent of the student body. The consent decree also included provisions for programs that would enhance school quality, particularly in the predominantly African American Bayview-Hunters Point District.

In the fall of 1971, the SFUSD introduced its Horseshoe plan in order to comply with the elementary school desegregation mandate established in *Johnson.* Several years later, desegregation efforts in the city extended to secondary schools with Operation Integrate. Both plans rested on racial balance, a common desegregation framework of the day. Racial balance, both in concept and in practice, focused on Black/White desegregation by fixing the ratio of Black to White students at every school. But a sizeable portion of San Francisco students were neither. Horseshoe and Operation Integrate were relatively short lived. An evolving institutional environment meant that what was deemed feasible and appropriate at the start of the decade was no longer by its close. This inconsistency between local desegregation policy and institutional environment created an opportunity for a new framework—racial unidentifiability—to take root. Educational Redesign embodied racial unidentifiability by drawing from nine recognized racial and ethnic subgroups to create integrated schools. The transition to the new desegregation program was contentious and soon led to a new lawsuit, *SFNAACP v. SFUSD*. The dominant logic during the period was of opportunity. During the 1970s and early 1980s, the SFNAACP worked primarily through the legal system to provide equal educational opportunity to African American students. At the same time, other stakeholders sought to preserve or amend elements of the district's student assignment policy in ways that ran counter to the desegregative goals mandated by the court. In the next two chapters, I consider these efforts by examining how powerful notions of neighborhood schools (logic of proximity) and school choice (logic of choice) impeded the work of the SFNAACP.

CHAPTER 2
Neighborhood Tensions and Crosstown Busing

Throughout the 1970s, opponents of desegregation often understood and framed it as a choice between two alternatives: walking to a neighborhood school or being bused to a school outside of the neighborhood. When the issue was presented in this way, most parents favored a neighborhood system, even if (or, for some, because) it meant a continuation of school segregation. But busing itself was not new. To alleviate overcrowded conditions during the postwar population surge, the school district had a busing policy that primarily transported Black students to predominantly White schools.[1] It was the busing of children out of their neighborhoods—particularly busing into predominantly Black schools—that troubled many White, Asian, and Latino parents. And for many Black parents, especially those residing in Bayview-Hunters Point, the concern was that their children would be forced to bear the brunt of desegregation by being disproportionately bused out of the neighborhood. In this chapter, I show how the deeply held, taken-for-granted idea of neighborhood schools disrupts desegregation efforts. Throughout the contentious transitions from one court-mandated desegregation policy to the next, a fundamental logic—what I label a logic of proximity—enables particular structures, practices, ideas, and arguments that reinforce the legitimacy of the neighborhood school system.

Like many urban districts throughout the country, San Francisco was residentially segregated. Housing discrimination and residential patterns created neighborhood boundaries that ran along race and class lines. However, the city stood apart from others in that it had sizeable student populations of four racial and ethnic subgroups. Many Black families called the neighborhoods of Bayview-Hunters Point, Western Addition, and Oceanview home; the Mission District was where many Latino families resided; Chinatown was home to many Chinese families; and White families were concentrated in neighborhood pockets across the city, including in the western neighborhoods. Residential segregation coupled with the unease many families had with integrated schools meant that the "stick" of busing was the only method of desegregation that was feasible. The "carrot" of magnet schools, enhanced programs, and additional resources would not draw sufficient numbers of White parents to Black schools. Because a system of neighborhood catchments was understood to be the most appropriate means of assigning students to schools, antibusing advocates and opponents of school desegregation could frame their demands successfully by appealing to the rationale of neighborhood schools. Furthermore, desegregation proponents, forced to operate within the confines of a logic of proximity, acquiesced to busing plans crafted such that they contained elements of a neighborhood school system, to the detriment of full districtwide desegregation.

Even during the earliest days of Horseshoe, when deleterious effects of segregated schools on Black children were widely discussed and commonly accepted, busing as a policy solution faced opposition. Proposition H, a local nonbinding policy declaration measure on the June 1970 ballot, asked if the school district shall "compel elementary school children (kindergarten through sixth grade) to be bused or reassigned to schools out of their immediate neighborhoods without parental consent." The results were definitive. The proposition received just over 132,000 "No" answers and fewer than 39,500 "Yes" answers.[2] Referencing a precinct analysis of Proposition H results the following year, Mayor Alioto said, "If 99 percent of the Chinese, 78 percent of the Black community and 75 percent of the Chicano community is against busing, I don't know why it has to be thrust on the people in a compact city like San Francisco."[3]

Weeks before the 1971 start of the Horseshoe plan, the *San Francisco Examiner* commissioned a poll on public attitudes on busing. Although a majority of African American and Latino adults in San Francisco believed, in a general sense, that children benefit from racially balanced schools, a majority of White and Chinese American adults felt the opposite (Table 8, Questions 1 and 2).[4] And when it came to the specific busing

Table 8. What San Francisco Thinks about Busing (Percent)

	White	Black	Latino	Chinese
1. Our children will benefit from the experiences of racially balanced schools.	38	64	59	28
2. Our children will not benefit from the experiences of racially balanced schools.	51	24	21	54
3. Approve of the plan for busing children to school in order to achieve racial balance in San Francisco.	14	39	38	6
4. Disapprove of the plan for busing children to school in order to achieve racial balance in San Francisco.	83	56	59	92
5. I feel the school my child attends should reflect the racial characteristics of our neighborhood.	60	37	50	58
6. I do not feel the school my child attends should reflect the racial characteristics of our neighborhood.	33	50	36	27

Source: "What San Francisco Thinks about Busing," *San Francisco Examiner,* August 29, 1971. The poll was carried out for the *Examiner* by Multi-Media Research Company.

Note: Actual racial categories were White, Negro, Latin American, and Chinese.

plans prescribed by Horseshoe, most San Franciscans—across all four major racial subgroups—were opposed; fewer than 40 percent of Black and Latino adults, less than 15 percent of White adults, and only 6 percent of Chinese adults expressed approval of the desegregation plan (Table 8, Questions 3 and 4).

Desegregation opponents capitalized on the unpopularity of busing by working to change the composition of the school board. In advance of Horseshoe, a nonbinding policy declaration measure was placed on the ballot asking if the mayor-appointed board of education should be made into a board elected by voters.[5] It was believed that a board determined by the electorate would much more vigorously oppose the desegregation of San Francisco schools.[6] The effort became more important with the retirement of Superintendent Robert Jenkins. His successor, Thomas Shaheen, began his term as the new superintendent in the fall of 1970 and was seen as someone who would vigorously support efforts to desegregate the school system.[7] The policy declaration passed, and in response, the Board of Supervisors placed Proposition S on the 1971 ballot. Proposition S sought to amend the city charter to provide for the election of at-large members of the board of education.[8] Proposition S also passed, and as current board members' terms expired, they were replaced by new members chosen by the electorate.

Shaheen's tenure in San Francisco was contentious and brief. He accused the board of education of impeding the district's integration efforts—a practice "no self-respecting superintendent can accept nor be party to"—and of essentially attempting to "run a private school system for the White community."[9] Although Shaheen had a base of supporters among African American residents, the school board voted to dismiss him in 1972.[10] He was followed by Steven Morena, who served as superintendent for three years. When Robert Alioto was appointed in 1975, he had to contend with the first school board fully composed of elected members, a majority of whom were elected on antibusing platforms.[11]

However, like many other cities across the nation, the dilemma San Francisco faced was that desegregation could only work through busing. This was because of residential segregation. In his 1971 desegregation decree, Judge Weigel wrote, "The evidence demonstrates that there simply cannot be desegregation without some busing of some students because there are districts in the city in which there are great preponderances of members of one particular race." Weigel continued, "This is not to say that busing is a desirable end in itself. It is not."[12] The apprehension among San Franciscans and the sharp decline in White and Chinese student enrollment following Weigel's decree suggested as much. What was actually desirable to most San Franciscans was the traditional neighborhood method of school assignment. The district's neighborhood-based assignment policy, codified in the 1930s, created school catchment zones of contiguous area:

> Pupils in elementary schools shall be enrolled in the schools which are nearest or most convenient to their homes. Pupils shall be permitted to enroll in any secondary school in the city if accommodations permit. If the number enrolled in any secondary school exceeds the number that can be accommodated, preference must be given to those pupils who reside nearest the school.[13]

Decades later, this policy was used to thwart desegregation. The 1962 school board committee formed to study segregation determined that the "neighborhood school plan is generally accepted by the community as the most desirable method of assigning pupils to schools, especially elementary and junior high schools."[14] That year, the district successfully stalled desegregation demands by arguing that its neighborhood system complied with state guidance requiring only that boundaries be drawn such that all students had equal convenience of attendance, facilities, and opportunities.[15] The neighborhood-based assignment policy remained in place until the Horseshoe plan, but the rationale underlying the policy continued on.

In settling the *Johnson* lawsuit, all of the prospective plans, including Horseshoe, incorporated a zone system in order to "retain a feeling of a neighborhood."[16] The Citizens Advisory Committee, charged with developing the district's desegregation plan, wrote to the public: "It would be an easy job to desegregate all the schools with a computer and thus have cross-town busing, children going to several elementary schools and the pairing of schools without regard to the needs of those children."[17] Such a system could more comprehensively integrate the district. Instead, under Horseshoe, children in the same grade and living on the same square block attended the same school—just as in a neighborhood system.

This feature of Horseshoe troubled the SFNAACP. In proposing an alternative plan in 1971, chapter president Charles Belle dismissed Horseshoe as "just an extension of the neighborhood school concept."[18] Several years later, in its efforts to block Educational Redesign's implementation, the SFNAACP argued once again that the school district's intent "is made clear by the repeated references in public statements of the Superintendent and Board Members that a principal purpose of the 'Redesign' was to restore the neighborhood school."[19] The implication of this for Belle and the SFNAACP was that restoring the neighborhood school would critically undermine desegregation efforts.

A Return to Neighborhood Schools

In Horseshoe, elementary schools were designated as either primary level or intermediate level. Primary elementary schools enrolled kindergarten to third-grade students, and intermediate elementary schools enrolled fourth- to sixth-grade students. Under the plan, each student would walk to a nearby school for one level—either primary or intermediate—and ride a bus to school farther away (but within their zone) for the other level, requiring students to enroll in a new school after third grade. When Educational Redesign was introduced, the district sought to substantially reduce the number of bused students and make neighborhood schools a more prominent feature. "The city now has many more naturally integrated neighborhoods than it had in the past," announced the Redesign proposal. "The desire to have students who live in naturally integrated neighborhoods attend schools near their homes [was a reason] for proposing a revision of the racial/ethnic guidelines."[20]

Educational Redesign did away with Horseshoe's primary- and intermediate-level grade structure and reinstituted predesegregation neighborhood school boundaries.[21] Redesign also adopted a new standard to determine whether a school was desegregated—the standard of racial unidentifiability instead of racial balance. A school met the racial unidentifiability standard if it enrolled students from any four of the nine racial and ethnic subgroups recognized by the district and if no subgroup exceeded 45 percent of the total enrollment. This new standard meant that twenty-two elementary and eight secondary schools would be deemed naturally integrated—in other words, enrollment could be entirely composed of students from the school's neighborhood.[22] Most of these schools were in the Sunset and Richmond Districts—middle-class neighborhoods in the western part of the city with pockets of strong opposition to school integration.[23] Zuretti Goosby, a former member of the school board, suggested in the *Chronicle* that part of the aim of Educational Redesign was in fact to curb the flow of middle-class students living in western neighborhoods leaving the district for private schools.[24]

With these changes, the district projected a 44-percent reduction in the number of K–5 students needing transportation (Table 9).[25] This was a significant cutback. However, approximately 7,800 students would still need transportation to the forty elementary schools that were located in neighborhoods that were not naturally integrated.[26] These schools, located primarily in central and eastern neighborhoods (for example, Chinatown, Western Addition, and Bayview-Hunters Point), required students to be bused in from neighboring areas.[27] The district carved small satellite feeder zones of several blocks, each with a demographic profile that would help maintain an otherwise racially concen-

Table 9. Transportation for K-5 Students, Pre- and Post-Educational Redesign

	Spanish Surname	Other White	Black	Chinese	All Others
Total Enrollment (K-12)	9,134	18,267	14,116	11,561	10,794
1977-1978 School Year (bused)	2,086	2,758	4,998	1,820	2,338
1978-1979 School Year (proposed bused)	1,114	1,637	3,022	977	1,054

Source: "Educational Redesign: A Proposal," January 1978, box 1, RFA/HIA.

trated school's racial balance. Some schools needed only one feeder zone. Other schools required multiple feeder zones. For middle school, boundaries were constructed by combining groups of nearby elementary schools. Similarly, groups of middle schools served as high school feeders.[28] Although most schools in the district had attendance areas, alternative schools and programs were open to San Francisco students regardless of where they lived.

The Burden of Busing

The role of the neighborhood school in the district's student assignment policy generated tension that ran both across and along racial lines. During the 1978 public hearings, when the final phase of Educational Redesign was presented to parents, opposition was strong among community advocates who viewed the district's plan as unfairly distributing the burdens of busing. Horseshoe, with its requirement that all elementary students be bused for one of the two elementary school levels—primary (K–3) or intermediate (4–6), distributed the burden of being bused evenly across the district's student population. At least in theory. The practice of Horseshoe proved to be more complicated. The district had a number of "double bus" students (in other words, students who were bused for both primary and intermediate levels; these students were more likely to be Black) as well as some "double walk" students.[29]

Calling for a more equitable system, the Bayview-Hunters Point Community Coordinating Council took the issue up with Mayor George Moscone, writing: "We are not criticizing 'busing' but we are concerned over the fact that it is being administered unfairly. Many of our children are bused out of this community with few coming back into the community. There should be an equality in busing in order that our schools will not be 'short changed.'"[30] Educational Redesign only exacerbated the sense of inequality harbored by many parents. The Redesign boundaries were drawn in a way that created heavy rates of busing from students living in the predominantly Black neighborhoods of Bayview-Hunters Point, Oceanview, and Western Addition; the largely Latino neighborhood of the Mission; and Chinatown.[31] While the overall number of students able to walk to their neighborhood school increased under Redesign, Black students continued to be the subgroup bused in the largest numbers.[32] And in contrast to the Horseshoe plan, which was designed such that all students would be bused for part of their schooling, Redesign required busing only for those students residing in feeder areas designated by the district. In other words, students residing within a school's feeder area were bused through the entire gradespan of that school, and students not residing within a feeder area could walk to their designated neighborhood school for the entire gradespan.

Standing before the school board in 1978, Owen O'Donnell, a White father living in the predominantly Black Western Addition, testified on the uneven geographic distribution of feeder areas by stating, "One wonders why it is the children in the Western Addition are going to 16 separate schools and why those in the Sunset and the Richmond and Pacific Heights—areas that are politically active—are not." O'Donnell suggested that Educational Redesign was a "racist document."[33] Parent J. S. Hunt similarly complained, "It's not fair that some children in some districts be bused all the time and others not at all."[34]

The district strategically used a drastic population change taking place to bolster support for Redesign. A steep postwar increase in the number of public school students produced an enrollment of over 93,000 by 1965. But by 1977, the district enrolled less than 64,000 students. "The school district has lost 27,000 students in the past seven years because of a change in the city's demographics, the declining birth rate, and the shift to private schools by parents who don't want busing," stated Superintendent Alioto. "The district projects a loss of 9,000 more students by 1981 and insists it does not need all the schools to operate."[35] In addition to the apparent fiscal benefits, shuttering schools increased the district's ability to integrate. The enrollment decline allowed the district to propose consolidating and closing several underenrolled schools and schools with low "walk" populations of students from the neighborhood.[36]

By closing schools, the district was able to redirect educational dollars away from underutilized buildings and toward the establishment of several new alternative and magnet programs. Among the instructional changes Redesign proposed was a high school program focused on business and commerce, an academically rigorous middle school in the eastern blocks of the Excelsior neighborhood, a "complex" of schools with a creative arts focus, and new reading, counseling, and media centers. By augmenting instructional spending and instituting new programs and schools, Alioto hoped to increase the student population. And by strategically locating these programs throughout the city, Alioto sought to integrate "racially identifiable" schools in the central and eastern neighborhoods. "Each of these programs is designed to meet special areas of interest," Alioto wrote. "The concept behind alternative education is the recognition of the fact that in a diverse, pluralistic student population specialization in areas of curriculum and teaching styles is essential."[37] But families did not want to lose a school or program in their neighborhood, and teachers were fearful of job loss and school transfers.[38] Resistance to the school closure and instructional components of Educational Redesign was particularly robust in three communities where the proposed changes would have a substantial impact: Treasure Island, Bayview-Hunters Point, and the Mission District.

Treasure Island and Bayview-Hunters Point

To comply with racial balancing expectations laid out in Educational Redesign, the district anticipated needing to bus 1,637 White elementary students. Nearly 40 percent of these children were not permanent San Francisco residents. They belonged to military families, many of whom were temporarily stationed at Treasure Island Naval Air Station.[39] The district's plan was to bus elementary students living on Treasure Island, half of whom were White, to three schools in the Bayview-Hunters Point District—Sir Francis Drake, George Washington Carver, and Dr. Charles R. Drew.[40] For middle school, the plan was that the mostly Black students of

Bayview-Hunters Point would be bused to Treasure Island Annex, a district-run elementary school built with federal funds for military families that would be converted to a middle school.[41] To make the busing scheme more palatable to parents, the schools were designated the "Traditional School Complex," a community of schools emphasizing the "3 Rs" that would receive additional resources and technical assistance from the central office and the district's community partners.[42]

Attempting to make his case to the parents of the island, Superintendent Alioto argued, "Your school has one of the lowest concentrations of Black students in San Francisco. In Bayview-Hunters Point, they have the largest concentration of Black students in the city. That's the problem. You want to know what the logic is for matching these two communities? Well, that's it."[43] Treasure Island parents, backed by the United States Navy, vigorously resisted the district's efforts to integrate their children with the children of Bayview-Hunters Point. A spokesperson for the commandant of Treasure Island described the district's plans as "discriminatory to the military family," and an alternate proposal was advanced by a staff judge advocate that called for the establishment of a K–8 magnet school on the island.[44] Bayview-Hunters Point parents responded in turn by announcing that Treasure Island students were not welcome to their neighborhood. Standing in front of an "uncomfortable" audience of Treasure Island parents and teachers, community leader Julia Comer spoke out: "I give you a hearty welcome from Bayview-Hunters Point. I want to you to know that we are people over there. I wasn't born in Africa. I was born in the United States, but I can understand your frustration. . . . Now listen to me. If you don't want our kids here, we don't want you over there. It's no harder for your kids to travel over that bridge than it is for our kids. . . . If you don't want to come to us, keep your rear end home!"[45]

As Comer's statement demonstrates, busing had its detractors among the largely Black Bayview-Hunters Point residents intended to be desegregation's primary beneficiaries. The neighborhood was home to many parents dissatisfied with the implementation of busing under Horseshoe, and many families and community leaders decided to cast their lot with neighborhood schools. In 1978, Black students were 29 percent of San Francisco's elementary enrollment, yet they were projected to account

Figure 5. Treasure Island PTA president Gene Mattingly addressing parents angry over Educational Redesign, December 29, 1977, *San Francisco Examiner* (Southard). Fang family *San Francisco Examiner* photograph archive negative files, BANC PIC 2006.029:144680.04.12--NEG, box 1722. Copyright the Regents of the University of California, Bancroft Library, University of California, Berkeley.

for 39 percent of the busing population under the Educational Redesign proposal.[46] American Indian students were to be bused at a rate proportionate to their districtwide population. All other subgroups were to be bused disproportionately less.[47] "Why should we be bused to your schools when we have good schools here?," proclaimed LaVert James, a fourth grader at Drew Elementary. "Why should we be bused to your schools while none of your kids are bused here to ours?"[48] To validate neighborhood schools, proponents pitted busing against academic achievement. Framed as a mutually exclusive choice (either busing or academic achievement), racial integration could be expressed as a value, but not at the expense of academics. "We're not going to let our kids be bused— White, Black, purple, or whatever," stated Goldie Judd, a White parent who served as president of the Visitacion Valley PTA. "What we're worried about is the quality of the educational programs for everyone." Echoing this sentiment was Idaree Westbrook, a Black parent of public schoolchildren: "I don't care if the schools are not integrated. The key thing I want Blacks to look at is the education plan."[49]

The contention between Treasure Island and Bayview-Hunters Point parents illustrates the tremendous difficulty school district officials had integrating largely Black and largely poor schools. After failed attempts to convince families to go along with this part of Redesign, the district acquiesced, dropping its plans to bus students to Bayview-Hunters Point and preserving the Treasure Island Annex as a K–5 school. The district had no workable alternative. Consequently, Redesign, as approved by the school board, excluded the schools in Bayview-Hunters Point from the district's integration plans, leaving them with high concentrations of Black students (Table 10). While the concession satisfied many parents, the school board's "decision to rescind the desegregation of Treasure Island elementary school because of the opposition of the White parents and personnel of the United States Department of the Navy" was central to the SFNAACP's cause of action.[50]

Table 10. Black Student Enrollment in Bayview-Hunters Point Schools (Percent)

	1977–1978	1978–1979 (projected)	1983 Consent Decree
Dr. Charles Drew Elementary	82.4	80.6	Conversion to an academic middle school with increased counseling.
Sir Francis Drake Elementary	52.4	91.3	Computer science focus and a new attendance area to achieve racial balance.
George Washington Carver Elementary	86.0	90.5	San Francisco State University lab school with a new attendance area to achieve racial balance.

Source: Special plan for Bayview Hunters Point, Consent Decree, SFNAACP, 576 F. Supp. at 54–56; and Civil Rights Action for Declaratory and Injunctive Relief, 20, *SFNAACP v. SFUSD* (DF1, 6/30/78).

From 1978 to 1982, during which the parties—the SFNAACP and the SFUSD—lumbered toward a settlement, Educational Redesign remained in place, with Bayview-Hunters Point left out of the busing provisions meant to create racially balanced schools. As an alternative to busing, the district sought and received private foundation grants directed toward improving the instructional programs at the three Bayview-Hunters Point elementary schools.[51] Associate Superintendent for Integration Stanley Schainker conceded, "The real key . . . was trying to avoid forcing (teachers and administrators) to work at Bayview-Hunters Point and parents to send their kids to Bayview-Hunters that didn't want to. We have consistently said we weren't going to force-bus people into Hunters Point."[52]

Because Bayview-Hunters Point had been excluded from busing, when the consent decree was adopted in 1983, it included a special plan for the neighborhood.[53] In order to entice parents from other parts of the city to send their kids to Bayview-Hunters Point schools, the consent decree specified that four neighborhood schools would be converted to magnet schools and schools with enriched programs. Pelton Middle School was to become a new academic high school. Dr. Charles R. Drew Elementary would be converted into an academic middle school with increased counseling and a goal of preparing its graduates for Lowell, the city's flagship academic high school. Sir Francis Drake Elementary would integrate a computer science curriculum into its program, and Dr. George Washington Carver Middle School was to receive specialized technical assistance from San Francisco State University.

Despite these reforms designed to desegregate schools and improve academic outcomes, the consent decree generated considerable friction within the city's African American community—pitting the SFNAACP against Bayview-Hunters Point residents. Organized efforts against the proposed gradespan conversions of Drew and Pelton were particularly strong. "Our children must not be singled out as the pawns that make this unreasonable agreement functional," demanded Drew parents in a petition delivered to the court. "Our community *did not* request conversion to a middle school."[54] The court also received over three hundred signatures of residents who regarded the proposed changes to Pelton "unfair to the students, the parents, and the community."[55] In response, Judge Orrick wrote, "The Court understands that the children at Drew School and Pelton School to some extent are being asked to make sacrifices, but it believes that the changes mandated in the decree ultimately will redound to their benefit."[56] By the summer of 1983, a citizens advisory committee headed by prominent community advocate Reverend Cecil Williams urged the SFNAACP and the district to withdraw from its plans to convert the Bayview-Hunters Point schools.[57]

The consent decree also called for Bayview-Hunters Point schools to be reconstituted—an organizational strategy whereby all school staff and administrative positions would be vacated and then refilled. The SFUSD and SFNAACP determined that reconstitution would provide the flexibility necessary to hire new personnel that would best fit the new instructional offerings. In some cases, employees, after reapplying to their old positions, would be rehired. In other cases, new staff would fill vacant positions. A group of mostly African American parents—concerned about the potential impact reconstitution would have on students from the neighborhood—formed the Bayview-Hunters Point Coalition for the Preservation of Our Community Schools and filed a motion to intervene in the court case.[58] "We cannot understand why these employees will be removed from their positions and forced to interview to come back next year and do the same things that they are already doing successfully right now," declared Julia Comer, the Bayview-Hunters Point community leader. "I know full well that this will be used as a power play by Superintendent Robert Alioto to pick only the people who are complacent and compliant with his wishes."[59] The SFNAACP dismissed the group by arguing that turning the case into one centered on labor issues would not best serve students, and in the end, the motion to intervene was denied by Judge Orrick.[60]

The consent decree's special plan for Bayview-Hunters Point was inconsistent with calls made by some desegregation proponents for a systemwide solution. The only way to fully desegregate the school district was to compulsorily bus students who were not Black into the neighborhood. Because of the prejudices of many parents, inducements like supplemental resources and specialized programs were unlikely to work. Speaking to a reporter from the *San Francisco Examiner,* school board member Richard Cerbatos decried the special plan. "I firmly believe what has happened is people have refused to go to school out there," said Cerbatos, referring to Bayview-Hunters Point. "We've had this system of allowing people to get out of it."[61] Furthermore, the additional funds and technical assistance provided to just four schools in the neighborhood meant that only a subset of the city's Black population would receive its benefits and that the many African American families living in Western Addition, Potrero Hill, Oceanview, and elsewhere would be left out. The attention to these schools also left out those Bayview-Hunters Point residents who would be bused to schools outside of the neighborhood. Making this point was Barbara Holman, past president of the San Francisco Parent Teacher Association and a former member of the parents' group that advised the district on the Horseshoe plan. In a statement submitted to the court, Holman said, "A system-wide desegregation problem exists in San Francisco, it affects 100% of the schools. The Decree applies a solution to 7% of the students."[62]

In the months leading up to its proposed start date, the special plan for Bayview-Hunters Point was jeopardized by the reality of the state appropriations process. The costs for implementing the consent decree were eligible for reimbursement by the state.[63] But rather than reimbursement, the district was able to convince the California Legislature to approve an up-front appropriation of nearly $8 million ahead of the 1983–1984 academic year. However, Governor George Deukmejian decided to remove the earmark from the final state budget. The line-item veto led the school district to announce a delay in the implementation of most of the consent decree, including the planned conversions of Drake, Carver, and Pelton schools.[64] Furthermore, the district used the governor's action to convince the court and the SFNAACP that converting Drew into an academic middle school would be too costly. Rather than allowing a racially segregated school to continue operating, the district and the SFNAACP decided instead to close Drew and bus its 220 students to schools in other neighborhoods.[65] This was particularly offensive to Bayview-Hunters Point residents because Drew was one of the newest schools in the city and had been the first school in San Francisco to be named after an African American—the distinguished physician and scholar Charles R. Drew.

For weeks following the start of the new school year, Black parents and children protested, preventing buses from transporting neighborhood students to schools across town; some carried signs reading "Where is the NAACP? Out to lunch!" and "Don't bus me out!"[66] "We always have to trade off and our children are not happy where they are going," complained Sylvester Brown of the Bayview Hunters Point Coordinating Educational Committee and Coalition. "Whites don't want to come here, and we can't care less. But now they are forcing us to their schools."[67] Led by

Reverend Cecil Williams, protesters accused the district and the NAACP of relying on one-way busing to integrate the schools. "I have no qualms with the busing situation," said Mildred Burford, "[but] if they're going to bus . . . they should bus some kids *in* to our neighborhood. I want equality. I have no qualms with integration, but I want two-way busing." Essle Webb of the committee demanded that the Bayview-Hunters Point community be included in the negotiation of the consent decree, remarking, "[The SFNAACP] can't act on our behalf." Brenda Brown, also of the committee, echoed, "We have a right to say where our kids will be bused."[68] SFNAACP officials responded by stating that the consent decree was crafted to provide quality education throughout the city and that Drew was shuttered because its educational program was inferior.[69]

The mobilization of Bayview-Hunters Point residents in support of their neighborhood schools led the SFNAACP and SFUSD to renegotiate the consent decree. Under the revised terms, approved by the court in November 1983, Drew reopened as a magnet early childhood development center in January 1984 and the parties agreed to find a new location for the academic middle school previously planned for the Drew facility. The revised decree also included modifications to the planning and implementation deadlines for various other aspects of the original consent decree, including a push back of the opening of the new academic high school to September 1984.[70]

Mission District Intervention

The consent decree offered an opportunity for the SFNAACP and the school district to reach consensus without a trial. But it also effectively locked out other community advocates from participating in the process of devising San Francisco's desegregation plan. This included advocates for San Francisco's large and multifaceted Latino community. To compound matters, the consent decree required San Franciscans to be informed of its terms and conditions, and while notices were published in the *San Francisco Chronicle* and the *San Francisco Examiner,* none were published in any of the city's Spanish-language publications. The Mexican American Legal Defense and Educational Fund (MALDEF), which at the time had its headquarters in San Francisco; REAL, a coalition of organizations based in the Mission District; and other Latino-serving organizations supported the general structure and goals of the consent decree.[71] In fact, MALDEF had been counsel on behalf of Latino students in desegregation cases in Texas, Colorado, and Illinois. But while advocates for San Francisco's Latino students supported the SFNAACP's efforts to desegregate the schools, they also demanded a stake in the process. Conveying a "great dissatisfaction" from members of the Latino community, MALDEF wrote to the court, "Latino students were unfairly burdened by the settlement while receiving nothing such as the enhancement programs provided by the terms of the settlement for the schools in the Bayview-Hunters Point area."[72] MALDEF's letter to the court commended both sides for crafting a "promising and worthy" consent decree to remedy the denial of equal educational opportunities for the city's African American students.[73] But MALDEF described the decree as "a cipher," at best, compelling Latino students "to take it on faith that the parties' [i.e., the SFNAACP and the school district] future implementation efforts will fully protect and vindicate their rights."[74]

Among the concerns outlined by advocates was a consent decree provision affecting nineteen historically segregated schools. Five schools enrolled mostly Black students, five enrolled mostly Chinese students, and nine were Mission District and Bernal Heights schools that enrolled large numbers of Latino students. The provision in question placed caps ranging from 37 percent to 44.9 percent just for the predominant subgroup in each of these schools.[75] For instance, the Mission District's Hawthorne Elementary School (subsequently renamed César Chávez) had a 40 percent cap on "Spanish Surname" students and the standard 45 percent cap for all other subgroups. While the court regarded this special provision as "an example of the comprehensive nature of the proposed remedy," advocates for the Latino community argued that it placed an "unfair burden" on those schools and communities.[76]

Advocates also worried that the district would place Spanish bilingual programs in Bayview-Hunters Point and bus Latino students in from the Mission District. The Bilingual Community Council pointed to the district's past practice of placing Chinese bilingual programs in the Mission and Spanish bilingual programs in Chinatown. In addition to the burden of busing this created for Chinese and Latino families, the strategy led to racial isolation within schools. A by and large racially and ethnically homogenous group of English learners would take separate classes from the rest of the student population. "Although the schools' ethnic balance was integrated on paper, in reality children rarely saw each other except at lunch time," observed Irene Dea Collier, a community educator and the chair of the Bilingual Community Council. "Since we do not believe that merely housing a bilingual program on a school site promotes integration, we hope that this will not happen in the Bayview-Hunters Point area."[77]

A related issue was the potential impact of the consent decree on the academic achievement of Latino students. Bilingual education advocates were concerned that if they were not involved in the desegregation process, San Francisco could inadvertently deprive English learners of the resources and professional support necessary for success. MALDEF called for an assurance that the effectiveness of any "bilingual or language development program in existence" would not be weakened by the busing scheme proposed.[78] This was principally a concern that school-level race and ethnicity caps could prevent the enrollment of a requisite number of English learners for a robust bilingual education program at any given school.

Alongside the particular needs of English learners, MALDEF called for a strategy to increase the enrollment of Latino students at Lowell High School. The consent decree provided for increased counseling staff and the establishment of a course development committee at Drew Elementary with the expressed purpose of preparing students for Lowell. "Entrance to Lowell is particularly important since it opens a number of postsecondary opportunities," wrote the attorneys for MALDEF, who noted that Latinos constituted only 7 percent of the school's enrollment (compared to a districtwide enrollment of 17 percent). "The proposed Decree contains a specific provision to increase Black students' access to Lowell, but nothing for Hispanics."[79]

Underlying these concerns was the belief that the class definition approved by the district court was too broad. After the court ruled that the class of all children of school age "who are, or may in the future become, eligible to attend that public schools of the SFUSD" was adequately represented by the SFNAACP, advocates in the Mission District urged the court to exclude "Hispanics" from the class definition so that they would not be bound to the terms of the consent decree.[80] The consent decree, wrote MALDEF, "now forecloses and detrimentally affects Hispanic students who seek an equal educational opportunity in the San Francisco Unified School District."[81] Myra Kopf, a school board member and long-time parent activist, concurred: "To assume that the plaintiffs in this case, no matter how well versed, are representing all parents, and are experts on the educational needs [of all school children] is at best very disturbing, and most unrealistic."[82] The court responded by stating that MALDEF's objection "reflects a basic misunderstanding" about the lawsuit and the decree: "This is a school desegregation action, and the gravamen of plaintiffs' claim is the alleged unlawful racial segregation of children in the District. The remedy sought, and the remedy proposed is systemwide desegregation. This is *not* an action to establish an entitlement to a certain standard of academic excellence or to a right to certain programs to meet specific needs."[83]

Neither MALDEF nor any other community advocate was given a formal role when the district court approved the consent decree in May 1983. Rather, the court relied on assurances by the school district that a good faith effort would be made to seek out the participation of Latino advocates and to develop measures aimed at improving the quality of education for Latino students.[84] Over the summer, representatives from various Mission District organizations representing the Latino community formed an ad hoc committee, led by MALDEF, to discuss and monitor the implementation of the consent decree and address needs to the school district.[85] MALDEF was granted amicus status, and, partly because of their efforts, when the consent decree was modified in November 1983, a special plan was approved for Horace Mann, a middle school in the heart of the Mission District. It was to be reconstituted and then transformed into an open enrollment magnet school emphasizing second-language acquisition.[86]

The desegregation of San Francisco schools—like other large urban school systems—required widescale busing. There was no feasible alternative. Although the city as a whole was diverse, many of its neighborhoods were not. And not enough White (or, for that matter, Asian or Latino) families were wooed by the lure of magnet schools and specialized programs in schools and neighborhoods that were largely Black. The desegregation plan adopted by the district in order to settle *Johnson v. SFUSD* was one that sacrificed comprehensive desegregation in favor of maintaining aspects of a neighborhood school system. Even with this concession, many families exited the district following its implementation. Educational Redesign attempted to integrate the district under a racial unidentifiability framework. However, the plan was not entirely successful. Parents and their advocates leveraged resonant ideas pertaining to the legitimacy of neighborhood schools in order to rationalize their resistance to busing into and out of Bayview-Hunters Point. Collectively, these activities helped thwart the desegregation of the school district throughout the 1970s and early 1980s. The following chapter completes the story of San Francisco's transition from racial balance to racial unidentifiability by addressing the role of school choice.

CHAPTER 3
Choosing Schools, Preserving Segregation

In rationalizing the need for Educational Redesign, Superintendent Alioto noted the district's failure to desegregate the schools in the seven years it was under the Horseshoe and Operation Integrate plans. Despite the court's long-standing and unambiguous ruling in *Johnson*, the number of racially imbalanced elementary schools had steadily increased over the years. In other words, contrary to what was required under Horseshoe/ Operation Integrate, San Francisco had an increasing number of schools in which the percentage of pupils from at least one recognized subgroup differed by more than fifteen percentage points from the districtwide subgroup percentage. For the 1973–1974 school year, fifty-nine of ninety-eight elementary schools met the court's expectation of racial balance. Four years later, only thirty-six of ninety-one elementary schools were balanced (Figure 6). The district fared no better in the upper grades. By the 1978–1979 term, only eleven of twenty-eight secondary schools were racially balanced. The steady resegregation taking place was due in large part to the school enrollment choices parents made through the Temporary Attendance Permit (TAP), the district's alternative enrollment program.

This chapter examines the increasing legitimation of school choice. Early on, providing parents the opportunity to choose from an array of public schools, whether in their neighborhood or outside of it, was only appropriate in particular circumstances—students needing specialized academic programs, students with certain ailments, or students in situations that would otherwise warrant attendance at a nonassigned school. It was an option to be exercised by a small number of families; most would enroll their children in the school assigned by the district. In practice,

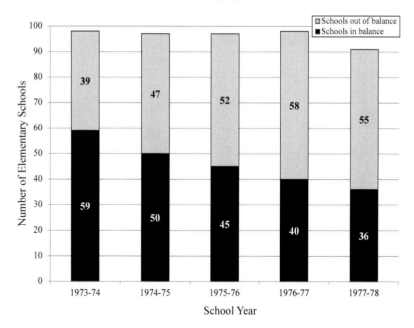

Figure 6. Racial imbalance in elementary schools, 1973–1977. Source: Data from first four columns from Report to Federal District Court Regarding Elementary School Desegregation, June 24, 1977, *Johnson v. SFUSD* C-70-1331 SAW, RG21 NARA. Fifth column from "Educational Redesign: A Proposal," 30, January 1978, box 1, RFA/HIA. Note: Racial balance measured by ±15 definition of acceptable racial balance. Imbalanced schools were predominantly imbalanced (i.e., too many or too few students) by Black (25), Spanish Surname (25), and Chinese (23) subgroups. Nine schools were imbalanced by White students. Several schools were imbalanced across multiple subgroups.

once Horseshoe was in place, TAP was a means of bypassing desegregation. It soon became a fundamental segregative mechanism. Throughout the 1970s, the SFNAACP challenged the legitimacy of school choice. In crafting Educational Redesign, the district attempted to close the loophole created by TAP by enforcing a provision that allowed transfers out of assigned schools only in situations where the racial unidentifiability of both the sending and receiving school would be unchanged. Although the SFNAACP remained concerned about the role of school choice, it eventually agreed to the provision. Choice would become an even more salient and dominant logic in the decades to come.

TAP was established to provide relief to those students with "just cause" to transfer to a school other than the one to which they were assigned. As the program was designed, central office administrators would evaluate each TAP application individually on its merits within the context of the district's desegregation goals and the transfer applicant's impact on the racial balance of both the sending and receiving school.[1] There were various ways for students to justify a transfer. For example, following *Lau v. Nichols*—the Supreme Court ruling requiring school districts to provide equal education opportunity to limited and non-English speakers—the San Francisco Board of Education adopted a resolution permitting students to transfer to a school with a bilingual or ESL program if one was not provided at the assigned school.[2] In addition, the district operated an assortment of alternative schools, including a year-round elementary school, a school with multigrade groupings, and an experience-based work program for high school students with nontraditional schedules. Students residing anywhere in San Francisco could enroll in these alternative schools; the schools either had no attendance area or they provided a means for students outside of the attendance area to petition for entry.[3] The district also allowed students to transfer to the school attended by an older sibling. Each of these just causes to transfer from an assigned school complicated the district's desegregation efforts.

Beyond justifiable transfers, the TAP program was also widely understood and exploited as a loophole for families who simply were unhappy with their school assignment. Transfers were awarded for reasons that were acknowledged as trivial and not relevant. In a 1980 deposition, Albert Cheng, the district's affirmative action officer, described the types of justifications parents submitted: "Some of the things I listened to were asthma problems. I remember there were some complaints of motion sickness. The children were not able to ride on buses because of motion sickness."[4] The conclusion drawn by the SFNAACP and other proponents of desegregation was that many parents were employing excuses such as these for no other reason but to bypass busing, and thus TAP was an unjust segregatory policy. Margery Levy, chair of the district's Affirmative Action Review Committee and the former director of the district's Desegregation and Integration office, testified that TAP had "done the greatest damage to the effective implementation of San Francisco desegregation plans." In asserting that the district's alternative enrollment program was more detrimental than any other factor, Levy faulted the school board for allowing exceptions for "almost any reason" such that the number of permits granted each year ran into the thousands. In a declaration submitted to the court, Levy stated, "The effect was that there were approximately more students attending a school site outside their school of assignment than there were attending their school of assignment."[5] TAP was not the first post-*Brown* school choice program that exacerbated segregation. It had a predecessor in Optional Areas, a program that exempted families residing in certain geographic zones throughout the city from attending their designated neighborhood school. The program was pegged as segregatory because some neighborhoods were excluded. A 1961 letter to the district from the National Lawyers Guild warned that the program "compounds the problem of segregated schools because said optional areas were found usually to be populated by Caucasians."[6] Although TAP was not discriminatory in the sense that all parents were eligible to request a transfer, its existence—and the extent to which it was utilized—presented a substantial obstacle to the goal of systemwide desegregation.

TAP transfers were so abundant and disruptive to desegregation efforts at the elementary level that during the SFNAACP's negotiations with the school district over the desegregation of secondary schools, it made closing TAP loopholes one of the conditions that would prevent legal action.[7] Operation Integrate would be "worthless" otherwise, argued an attorney for the SFNAACP.[8] Among the suggestions were curtailing the processing of permits during the summer months and ensuring that school sites verify all transfer requests. But TAP continued unabated and there was such heavy use of transfer requests and sufficient leniency in the approvals made by staff that by the 1977–1978 school year, one-third of the district's approximately sixty-four thousand students attended a school other than the school they were assigned to for desegregation purposes (significant, albeit less than Margery Levy's estimation).[9] Not surprisingly, TAP was a core issue for the SFNAACP. Its 1978 complaint charged the school district with establishing and operating the TAP program in a manner that created, maintained, and increased racial segregation, in violation of the federal court injunction established under *Johnson v. SFUSD*.[10]

To help counteract the segregative aspects of TAP, Educational Redesign included a recommendation to close eight schools. School transfers exacerbated segregation because transfer preferences often fell along racial lines. Fewer schools meant fewer open seats, and so less opportunity to transfer. But a more fundamental change to limit choice occurred under Educational Redesign. The "Temporary Attendance Permit" was rebranded as the "Optional Enrollment Request" (OER) and stricter controls over the process of reviewing and approving applications were promised. "One of the goals of Educational Redesign is to provide more educational options for students," announced the district. "The student assignment proposal is designed to provide an opportunity for students to choose the program which best suits their needs."[11] Like TAP, OER applications were to be approved so long as space was available at the receiving school and the racial unidentifiability of both the sending and receiving school would not be adversely affected. To prevent misuse, Superintendent Alioto promised to closely monitor the OER process and to report monthly to the school board on the racial balance of every school. The district described the OER process as its "primary voluntary desegregation" effort for years to come.[12]

Choice in Bayview-Hunters Point

Drew, Drake, and Carver Elementary Schools in Bayview-Hunters Point were severely segregated. In September 1978, approximately 80 percent of Drew's students were Black and just over 90 percent of Drake's and Carver's students were Black.[13] Because Educational Redesign's proposal to bus students from Treasure Island had fallen apart, the district pushed back its goal to integrate the schools by three years. In the meantime, each school had an assigned attendance area as well as open enrollment options for students throughout the district. In order to entice students from outside the neighborhood and thereby alleviate racial identifiability, the district promised extra funding and support.[14] In addition, Bayview-Hunters Point families unhappy with their neighborhood school assignment had the option of sending their children to school in Glen Park, with the district providing transportation. These families could also choose some other school in the district through the regular OER process.[15]

The school district's special plan for Bayview-Hunters Point was immediately attacked by the SFNAACP as segregative and unconstitutional.

In a 1978 court filing, the SFNAACP drew parallels between the district's plan and "freedom of choice" plans in the South that subverted the intent of *Brown*:

> The defendants have offered discredited "Freedom of Choice" plans by means of which the burden of desegregating these schools will be placed upon the very victims of the past illegal misconduct of these officials, the students. The Supreme Court has decisively stricken such voluntary or part-time desegregation efforts as inadequate, with the command that desegregation is to be undertaken through the most effective means capable of achieving the maximum results consistent with educational considerations.[16]

In a case that reached the Supreme Court in 1968, New Kent County in Virginia allowed families to choose in which of the county's two schools to enroll their children.[17] In three years of implementation, no White family chose to enroll a child in all-Black Watkins school and only a small number of Black families chose to enroll in predominantly White New Kent school. This pattern was consistent throughout the South and was enforced through coercion and terrorization. A 1967 report by the United States Commission on Civil Rights that drew from field investigations in southern and border states revealed "violence, threats of violence and economic reprisal by White persons" on Black families who enrolled or attempted to enroll their children into previously all-White schools under freedom of choice plans.[18] The commission concluded in a later report that "freedom-of-choice is an almost totally ineffective method of desegregating elementary and secondary schools in the Deep South."[19] The Supreme Court ruled that schools were required to racially mix to a degree greater than what would occur merely as a result of ending discrimination and ordered New Kent County to consider assigning students based on geographic zones or other measures that would force desegregation.

Like New Kent County, school districts throughout Mississippi had used freedom of choice plans to comply with mandates to desegregate without actually desegregating. Lower courts allowed this to persist by applying a liberal interpretation of *Brown II*'s declaration that desegregation occur not immediately but "with all deliberate speed."[20] In a 1969

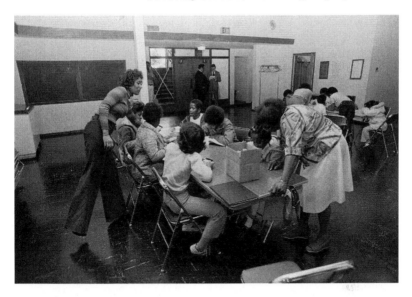

Figure 7. Black churches were used as classrooms during a school boycott over the failure to desegregate Bayview-Hunters Point schools, May 24, 1978. *San Francisco Examiner* (McLeod). Fang family *San Francisco Examiner* photograph archive negative files, BANC PIC 2006.029:144891.07.12--NEG, box 1735. Copyright Regents of the University of California, Bancroft Library, University of California, Berkeley.

case concerning Mississippi schools, the Supreme Court replaced the *Brown II* standard with an order to "terminate dual school systems at once and to operate now and hereafter only unitary schools."[21] Although the ruling forced immediate desegregation in school systems across the country, many communities remained segregated because of White flight to private schools, including to so-called segregation academies.

As the SFNAACP noted in their court filing, rather than placing the burden of desegregation on school systems—what the *Brown* rulings had required—freedom of choice placed the burden on Black families. The Commission on Civil Rights had long acknowledged that under freedom of choice plans in the South, Black families who wanted an integrated school had to make this affirmative choice, placing "a large share of the burden upon those least able to carry it."[22] The SFNAACP argued that similar to school districts throughout the South, if San Francisco merely provided families the choice to bus into or out of Bayview-Hunters Point schools, the racial imbalance of those schools would remain. Because of its choice components, and especially the choice components for Bayview-Hunters Point, the SFNAACP sought a temporary restraining order to prevent the implementation of Educational Redesign. "Despite the efforts of these defendants [i.e., the state and local defendants, including the SFUSD] to somehow suggest that racial segregation might be a preferred or better mode of schooling for the Black children at Hunters Point, it is clear that such arguments have been singularly unpersuasive in the federal courts," argued the SFNAACP. "The warehousing of the Black students at Hunters Point will only make easier their isolation from the other students, and will more greatly guarantee that they will be forced to attend schools which are both separate and unequal."[23]

Despite its vigorous opposition, the SFNAACP was unable to delay the implementation of Educational Redesign.[24] The school choice provisions just for Bayview-Hunters Point remained in place until the 1983 approval of the consent decree, which called for the mandatory assignment of students to Drake and Carver and the closing of Drew for the purpose of desegregation.[25] Beyond the special arrangement for Bayview-Hunters Point, the SFNAACP was troubled by the districtwide OER program. Considering it to be overly permissive, the SFNAACP insisted that the program be terminated. The district refused.[26] The resulting compromise was to dial down the "trigger point" for granting OER requests from 43 to 40 percent of the applicant's racial/ethnic subgroup at both sending and receiving schools.[27] A lower trigger point for transfers made racial unidentifiability across schools more likely.

Parental choice, whether as a loophole under TAP or as a "voluntary desegregation" effort under OER, was recognized by the SFNAACP to be segregatory. Choice would always counter desegregation efforts as long as families chose schools along race and ethnicity lines. Even with controls in place, the opportunity to undermine or bypass the district's court mandate to desegregate was considered a genuine threat. The OER was a central component of Educational Redesign so the district steadfastly sought to preserve it. The SFNAACP, unable to succeed at eliminating OER, in the end, was forced to agree to a minor modification. Choice was a powerful idea that resonated with many parents, the SFNAACP's concerns notwithstanding, particularly since desegregation plans were often framed as the transfer of choice from parents to the government. While

residents (of certain means) formerly chose schools by buying into preferred neighborhoods with their preferred neighborhood schools, they
lost this option under forced desegregation plans. School board member
and parent activist Myra Kopf advised the court to attend to "the needs
of parents and students for self-determination and the ability to make
choices which affect their lives" when considering the district's student
assignment plan.[28] Many agreed with Kopf. And as desegregation evolved
in the years to follow, choice became an ever more prominent logic—a
logic that moved from the periphery to the center—structuring how student assignment was framed and understood.

"On a Long Road . . ."

A public hearing to determine the fairness of the proposed consent decree was held on February 14, 1983—exactly five years after Redesign was
approved by the school board. It must have been a powerful moment
when Grandvel Jackson stood before Judge Orrick to speak. In 1959, five
years after the Supreme Court ruled on *Brown,* Jackson was serving as
president of the San Francisco branch of the NAACP. He recalled:

> "Old" Pat Brown was governor. And he sent his envoy down here to
> work with me and to establish whether or not there was really seg-
> regation in the San Francisco schools. And it was that effort that I
> believe that started us on a long road, twenty years and more, try-
> ing to find some resolution to this problem.[29]

Jackson, who had been at the forefront of school desegregation efforts
since that time, went on to express his strong support for the goals and
objectives of the settlement. "My many years of experience with attempts
to desegregate the schools of San Francisco have led me to conclude that
the best hope the children have for an integrated quality education is
through the development of the plans and procedures outlined in the
Consent Decree," he stated. "In addition, I feel strongly that this Court
must stay actively involved with the implementation process so that the
goals of the Decree become a reality."[30] Current NAACP branch president Jule Anderson proclaimed, "This is an historic moment for the children of San Francisco. We look forward to the speedy implementation of
the goal." But Anderson cautioned that the decree "can only be considered

fair when in practice the district acts affirmatively to fulfill the promises of better educational programming and restores the confidence of the Hunters Point family that they are in fact an integral part of the school district."[31]

Despite the laudatory tone struck by the SFNAACP, the consent decree drew concern from some proponents of integration upset with the compromise that had been made. Barbara Holman, the past president of the San Francisco Parent Teacher Association and former member of the parents' group that advised the district on Horseshoe, stated:

> The Consent Decree is a sad culmination of ten years of litigation between the NAACP and the SFUSD. Thoughtful people of many races are saying, "It is just a way for both parties to save face, and it will mean nothing to most of the students." . . . To those of us who put our children on the buses 10 years ago with hopes for *real* integration and academic improvement, this is a bitter ending. The Consent Decree is a pale substitute for what is really needed. The SFUSD should be satisfied. I hope the NAACP is embarrassed. The time, energy, and legal fees should have resulted in a plan that would serve *all* of the students affected and disadvantaged by segregation practices.[32]

Referring to the new definition of desegregation put forth in Educational Redesign—racial identifiability instead of racial balance—and now affirmed in the settlement, Margery Levy, chair of the district's Affirmative Action Review Committee and the former director of the district's Desegregation and Integration office, urged the court to "hold the SFUSD to the spirit of this Consent Decree and not permit the SFUSD to maintain all non-White schools [which goes against] the spirit of the Consent Decree calling for system-wide desegregation."[33]

Why did the SFNAACP agree to a consent decree that preserved so much of Educational Redesign? Although they went to trial on the basis that Redesign would result in resegregation, Judge William Orrick, in his order and memorandum denying plaintiffs' motion for partial summary judgment, had signaled the difficulty plaintiffs would have proving segregatory intent in a trial. The school district continued its assignment system largely intact while the SFNAACP was able to secure concessions for Bayview-Hunters Point. For all parties, the consent decree avoided what would have been a long, expensive, and racially charged trial. "It was certainly far better to resolve these matters among professionals, who know what they're doing, rather than in a two- or three-month trial, reported daily, which would have not only been tedious for those concerned, but would have been very detrimental, I think, to the well-being of the school district," observed Orrick following the submission of the proposed settlement in December 1982.[34] Several months after the fairness hearing, on May 20, 1983, Orrick issued an opinion finding that the consent decree was fair, reasonable, and adequate. He ordered that the parties immediately begin its implementation.[35]

Robert Alioto began his tenth year as superintendent in July 1984. The district was on an upswing. Enrollment and average daily attendance numbers were up. Six new alternative schools opened. The district offered an expanded summer program. Schools had recently been equipped with computers. During her State of the City address, Mayor Dianne Feinstein, quoting the superintendent, proclaimed, "our schools have weathered the challenges of the 1970's and through higher achievement have returned academic respectability to San Francisco." The mayor continued, "City schools are holding their own among the top 18 urban districts in California, and our third graders are ranked Number One."[36] She thanked teachers and administrators for "doing a tough job well."

In addition, the district was successfully meeting the expectations laid out in the consent decree. For the 1984–1985 school year, all regular schools had at least four racial and ethnic subgroups and only George Washington Carver had a subgroup comprising more than 45 percent of its student body. Among the district's alternative schools, only two, New Traditions and Dr. Martin Luther King Jr. Academic, had subgroups over 40 percent of its student body.[37] As specified by the settlement, the district's efforts were supported with desegregation funds from the state, and by the end of the decade, the annual reimbursement to the district was well in excess of $25 million a year (Table 11).[38] "The Consent Decree is the charter, the constitution," Judge William H. Orrick advised the

Table 11. SFUSD State Reimbursement for Desegregation, 1982–1990

School Year	Desegregation Costs (SFUSD)	Final Audit Report (CDE)
1982–1983	$285,942	$105,959
1983–1984	$2,859,423	$2,467,172
1984–1985	$7,710,382	$6,586,293
1985–1986	$16,162,164	$15,233,053
1986–1987	$23,848,651	$23,139,265
1987–1988	$24,621,372	$23,340,180
1988–1989	$28,176,087	$26,091,903
1989–1990	$27,148,880	$26,812,763

Source: Local Defendants' 1997–1998 Annual Report, *SFNAACP v. SFUSD* (DF873, 7/31/98)

parties to the case in 1984. "And it is, and shall remain, inviolate until such time as it comes to the attention of the court, after due process, that some of the sections should be changed, or some new plan adopted. But for now, that's it."[39]

PART II
Desegregation and Diversity, 1983–2005

CHAPTER 4
From Race Conscious to Race Neutral
The Multiracial Politics of Education in San Francisco

I believe that the highest priority is for the Chinese community to get into the game. The deal over integration cannot be left to the NAACP.

—LESLIE YEE TO ROLAND QUAN, SEPTEMBER 3, 1988

In the fall of 1988, school district integration officer Carlos Cornejo circulated an internal proposal to change the district's student assignment policy. The 1983 settlement produced a consent decree that required the district to draw attendance boundaries so that schools had representation from at least four of nine recognized racial and ethnic subgroups, with no subgroup exceeding 45 percent of total school enrollment. This was required for all but fourteen alternative schools, which had a stricter 40 percent enrollment cap.[1] If any school exceeded the enrollment cap imposed by the consent decree, the district was required to restrict entering classes so as to gradually move the school into compliance.[2] Cornejo's proposal was to bring all schools down to a 40 percent enrollment cap. The enrollment patterns in the district were such that if implemented, the new cap would be especially felt within the Chinese community. The district would be forced to reassign Chinese students from three popular comprehensive neighborhood high schools.[3] The proposal would also require the reassignment of Chinese students from Lowell, the district's premier academic high school and among the highest regarded public high schools in the nation.[4]

With Lowell, two school district priorities were at play—desegregating its schools and operating an elite college preparatory high school. As with

91

every other school in the district, Lowell was held to the desegregation standard laid out by the consent decree. But unlike other schools, Lowell students were required to apply for admission. Applicants were ranked based on an index score that combined standardized test results with seventh- and eighth-grade performance. Balancing these two priorities led the district to maintain minimum scale scores for admission that differed by race and ethnicity subgroup. Cornejo's proposal to lower the subgroup cap would mean that the minimum scale score for Chinese students would increase.

For years, community members brought up the fact that Lowell's student body was not fully representative of the racial diversity of the city (Table 12). Responding to these concerns, Superintendent Ramon Cortines had committed to seeing that the school was "reflective of all the city's kids."[5] But denying admission to Lowell for Chinese students who would otherwise qualify based on academic performance solely because their subgroup had reached the 40 percent limit was politically fraught. School board candidate Leland Yee condemned the plan as "especially unfair to those Chinese American students who have excelled in their studies only to learn that because of their ethnic background, they cannot enter Lowell High School."[6] The *San Francisco Chronicle* referred to the proposal as "a new Chinese Exclusion Act."[7]

Table 12. Student Enrollment, Lowell High School vs. Districtwide, 1986

	Lowell High School	Districtwide	+/−
Chinese	0.43	0.22	+0.21
White	0.24	0.16	+0.08
Filipino	0.08	0.09	−0.01
Hispanic	0.07	0.18	−0.11
Black	0.06	0.21	−0.15
Korean	0.03	0.01	+0.02
Japanese	0.03	0.01	+0.02
Other Non White	0.05	0.12	−0.07
American Indian	< 0.01	< 0.01	

Sources: Diane Curtis, "Top-Rated Lowell a Pressure Cooker," *San Francisco Chronicle*, June 11, 1986; San Francisco Unified School District, Research, Planning, and Accountability Department.

As Cornejo's proposal to modify student assignment came to light, members of the local Chinese American Democratic Club (CADC) took note. The CADC formed in 1958 to support Democratic candidates and issues. By the late 1970s, it had achieved success with the political appointment and election of several CADC members and allies.[8] While these efforts continued, the membership began to work on issues of civil rights and empowerment as a means of strengthening the organization's bonds with its community base.[9] Education became a core area of work.

The CADC was concerned about the impact Cornejo's proposal would have on Chinese American students. But it was not at all clear what its response should be. As a start, club president Roland Quan called on the superintendent to "clear the air" by publicly vetting Cornejo's proposal at the Board of Education.[10] But CADC members soon began to encourage a much more proactive response. Leadership weighed the political cost of confronting Cornejo's proposal—and the consent decree itself—against any potential benefits that might have been gained. Louis Hop Lee, a longtime CADC officer, was among a handful of members who, from the very beginning, strongly advocated involvement in the issue. "I clearly remember making many an impassioned argument over many months and at many meetings to get the majority of CADC to endorse taking a formal position and providing political and other support," he recalled. "Eventually they did, but it took maybe six to nine months and even then, all throughout the support was mostly tepid."[11]

Early on, CADC members focused on the disadvantaged position Chinese students were placed in with regard to White students—lowering the enrollment cap was understood to be a means of replacing Chinese students with White students in the city's top schools. "There is both a negative impact and a negative purpose," wrote Leslie Yee, a club officer. "The schools are being pressured by Whites to open up prestigious high schools for Whites. Whites send their kids to private schools and then if they can get into Lowell or Wallenberg, they go there. If they can't get in, they stay in the private schools. This is purposeful discrimination. Kicking Chinese out to make room for Whites."[12] Among the proposed solutions CADC considered was to maintain an enrollment cap only for White students and to admit minimum numbers of underrepresented subgroups. "No maximum limit on minority admissions should be applied at Lowell" was the argument circulated by the club; however, "ethnic representation to achieve diversity in the student body at Lowell is desirable. Black and Hispanic representation at Lowell is extremely low and should be increased."[13] A campaign began to take shape.

During this time, Chinese for Affirmative Action (CAA), an organization founded in 1969 to promote equal opportunity in education and employment, had also been investigating the impact of the consent decree and Cornejo's proposed changes on Chinese American students. In 1987, CAA helped establish the Chinese American Parents Association, a group created to encourage parental participation and involvement in the public school system. A key issue for members was the enrollment cap, particularly as it pertained to admission into Lowell. Parents worked to encourage the district to establish additional academically competitive schools to handle the demand, enlisting the support of school board member Ben Tom and the Association of Chinese Teachers (TACT). Chinese students "have studied hard and taken the test to qualify," remarked CAA executive director Henry Der. "That shows how much further this school district has to go."[14] By 1991, the CAA board had voted to oppose the higher cutoff scores imposed on Chinese applicants, while still supporting "affirmative action efforts to increase the representation of African American and Hispanic students at Lowell."[15]

In 1991, in order to maintain compliance with the desegregation standard laid out by the consent decree, the minimum test and grade index score for Chinese applicants to Lowell was set at fifty-nine out of sixty-nine possible points. For Black and Latino students, the cutoff score was fifty-four. For all other subgroups, including White students, the cutoff was fifty-seven. A two-point difference on this scale was equivalent to a letter grade difference in one eighth-grade class.[16] Because of changing demographics and school preferences, by 1993 Chinese applicants were required to score a near perfect sixty-six points, while the cutoff was fifty-six for Black and Latino students and fifty-nine for all other subgroups. As the difference in cutoff scores across subgroups increased, the admissions process at Lowell became the lightning rod of the consent decree. It was hard to defend, and it struck some people as very unfair, recalled school board commissioner Steve Phillips. People felt that "if you test better than any other students, you should be able to get in, period. You shouldn't have to get a higher test score number."[17]

A Coalition of Intervenors

The consent decree, which dictated how students were to be assigned to schools, went into effect in 1983 as the settlement for *SFNAACP v. SFUSD*. By the end of the following school year, the district was able to report that nearly all its schools met the decree's standard for desegregation.[18] In addition, the parties agreed that desegregation required "continued and accelerated efforts to achieve academic excellence."[19] At the six-year mark, at the end of the 1988–1989 term, the district pointed cautiously to signs of academic improvement, particularly for African American and Latino students enrolled in schools that had been targeted for special assistance.[20] Describing gains that appeared to make San Francisco Unified the most improved urban school district in the nation, the editorial board of the *San Francisco Examiner* praised the commitment of district officials and community members to turn around the schools and declared, "There is good reason for San Francisco to look forward with pride to the beginning of another educational year."[21] The consent decree also provided for desegregation funding, and by the early 1990s, reimbursements flowing from Sacramento to support the city's desegregation activities approached $30 million annually.[22]

The SFNAACP and SFUSD were, by and large, working together as partners. In the fall of 1991, the consent decree monitor, Gary Orfield, informed the court that "all parties are grateful for the long period of generally peaceful cooperation, the ability to settle virtually all issues by negotiations, and the many new programs and additional school resources provided under the decree."[23] But while there presently was no crisis, the parties had raised questions on various facets of the consent decree. "In a very complex and rapidly changing city, it is not at all surprising that there should be a continuing discussion of ways to improve on the plan," wrote Orfield, a prominent school desegregation scholar. "I know that there were a number of elements that those who designed the plan thought could be further developed as experience accumulated."[24] In response, the court appointed a committee of experts to conduct the first comprehensive review of the consent decree. "The Decree worked well for the first eight years when it was addressing the problems for which it was fashioned. Drastic demographic changes, however, have occurred in San Francisco and the rest of California," stated the court. "It is fair to say that as a result of these changes parts of the Decree are obsolete and that the Decree should be reviewed in light of the changes that have taken place."[25] Following an investigation spanning several months, the committee of experts produced a report (referred to as the "Experts' Report") containing dozens of findings and recommendations but providing no suggestion to modify the decree in ways that addressed the changing racial demographics of the student population.[26]

But the conditions placed on the assignment of students to schools specified by the consent decree were becoming increasingly untenable for many parents and advocates. The SFNAACP had been certified as class representative of all students in the district rather than just African American students, and this had long been a source of contention. Many advocates expressed doubt that an organization predominantly concerned with Black civil rights could adequately represent Latino and Asian subgroups.[27] During the second half of 1992, as the court and the district were considering the findings and recommendations of the Experts' Report, an advocate-led mobilization effort on behalf of these two communities emerged.[28]

The submission of the Experts' Report to the court provided an opportunity to once again address the issue. The Latin American Teachers' Association (LATA) recruited Multicultural Education, Training, and Advocacy (META), a language-rights advocacy organization, to represent pro bono a coalition of stakeholders seeking to formally intervene in the process that, to date, had exclusively involved the SFNAACP, the school district, and a handful of additional government entities.[29] The coalition of intervenors included respected community organizations Mujeres Unidas y Activas/Coalition for Immigrant and Refugee Rights and Services, Alianza, Padres Unidos en Contra de la Violencia, and Chinese for Affirmative Action. "Through this intervention, the applicants seek to ensure that the needs of the largest ethnic/racial groups in the San Francisco Unified School District are adequately addressed through the Decree," declared META.[30] "[Chinese] parents feel that they do not have a voice in influencing educational policies and Consent Decree–funded programs," echoed Henry Der. "[CAA believes] that by intervening . . . we can ensure that the unique needs of the Chinese and Asian communities of San Francisco are adequately addressed."[31]

By early 1993, intervenors presented the court with a range of issues important to San Francisco's Latino and Asian communities. In addition to concerns specific to the Latino community, intervenors noted that according to the Experts' Report, Chinese American students maintained "a strong record of academic achievement."[32] This troubled advocates who understood the ramifications of the frequently applied "model minority" label. META directed the court's attention to the report's lack of recommendations for Asian American students:

> The issues are more complex. . . . While the applicants for intervention do not dispute the fact that a substantial percentage of Asian students in the District are performing well academically, it is short-sighted to ignore those Asian students who are not achieving academic parity. This approach fosters an ethnic stereotype of Asian Americans as the "model minority" who, unlike other racial and ethnic groups, can overcome ethnic and racial barriers without any assistance. As a result, assistance is not made available to many Asian students who are in dire need, especially newly arrived immigrants and those who are low-income.[33]

Noting that no assertion had been made that the consent decree was unlawful or otherwise impermissible, SFUSD, at the behest of the school board, opposed META's motion to intervene.[34] The consent decree was the remedy settling all prior allegations of intentional segregatory acts. The district argued that if the META intervenors intended to allege new or different segregatory acts, an entirely new complaint was warranted. The school board opposed the motion on a split vote, with a minority of board members arguing that intervention would be an opportunity to bring more community input into the process. "Multi-racial cooperation is most effectively built when all minority groups are equally empowered to share in decision making. When only one community group . . . is asked to speak for all Asian American, Latino and African American communities, the other communities are disenfranchised," declared school board commissioner Angie Fa in support of META's motion. "In situations like the SFUSD where there are three major minority groups . . . each group should be given an equal voice in anything as important as the Consent Decree."[35]

Striking a more strident tone was Leland Yee, who had since been elected to the school board. "The consent decree was not intended to serve only African American and Latino students, but all children in San Francisco," wrote Yee in a letter to the head of the district's Integration Department. "However, the neglect of other students, such as Asian Americans, was intentional. It was deliberate and planned. Few individuals would argue that the Chinese have paid a heavy cost in this integration consent decree. They have been adversely impacted because their high numbers have prevented them from entering schools of their choice in the school district."[36]

While the initial school board vote opposed META's motion to intervene, in the face of strong community opposition, two board members subsequently reconsidered their stance. The board ultimately voted to instruct its counsel to support the intervention.[37] "Integration is not a Black/White issue in this City," wrote Commissioner Tom Ammiano. "Under painful re-examination of the case made for intervention by the Chinese and Latino communities and in speaking to members of the African American community who support the intervention of those represented by META, it is my opinion that the needs of all students are better met by their intervention."[38] Similarly, Commissioner Steve Phillips stated that he learned soon after his initial vote that it had been perceived as inconsistent with his efforts to "involve racial and ethnic coalitions of parents and groups at the decision making table."[39] Phillips declared that upon reflection he realized that he had not made the connection between his legal position to oppose intervention and the limitation of parents and "groups such as Alianza and Mujeres Unidas to have meaningful and formal input into the development and implementation" of the consent decree.[40]

The intervenors were in a difficult position. While they supported the consent decree's desegregation goals and the means put in place to achieve them, they were seeking to formally intervene in the lawsuit, thus exposing a rift within the local community of advocates that previously had been aligned on civil rights issues. The central argument to intervene laid out by META was that without the formal participation of Latino and Asian parents and advocates, the needs of this increasingly sizeable community would continue to go unmet.[41] Binding the intervenors together was the perceived lack of linguistic and cultural competence on the part of the SFNAACP. "My interest is not adequately represented by the present plaintiffs in this action," declared public school parent Sui-Ming Wan to the court. "The educational neglect suffered by my children and other Asian and immigrant students is in many ways similar to the historical abuse experienced by African American children, but the needs of my children also differ as a result of differences in language and culture."[42] While limited English–proficient students were as much members of the class represented by the SFNAACP as Black students were, META noted that the parties appeared reluctant to tackle the issue of academic achievement for English learners. META referenced *Lau v. Nichols*—a Supreme Court case brought on behalf of students with limited proficiency in English that generated its own separate consent decree involving the SFUSD—in arguing that the parties to the desegregation consent decree "quickly dismiss the educational needs of these class members by sweeping their needs under the ever-expanding *Lau* rug."[43] While conceding that the SFNAACP had not only refused to incorporate META's suggestions but also lacked expertise in the area of bilingual education, the district court reiterated that

> Bilingual education is the subject matter of *Lau,* not of this case. The subject matter of this case, the desegregation of the schools with respect to all races, is an interest the NAACP shares with the proposed student and parent intervenors.[44]

By the court's estimation, intervention by META was therefore not appropriate. "The NAACP is certainly capable of representing the interests of non-African American school children," wrote the presiding judge. "It assumed the responsibility at the start of this litigation, and the prospective intervenors do not seriously attempt to criticize their past representation. The NAACP insists that it is capable of doing so in the future as well."[45] While denying the motion, the court did grant amicus curiae status to the community organizations and parents involved in META's intervention, creating what was termed the "Latino Group" and the "Asian Group."[46]

Contributing to the growing dissatisfaction with the consent decree and the SFNAACP's role as class representative were the sweeping demographic changes the student population had undergone in the years

Table 13. SFUSD Student Population by Subgroup (Percent), 1982–1992

School Year	TOTAL	L	OW	AA	C	J	K	AI	F	ONW
1982–1983	60,476	17.3	17.0	23.2	19.2	1.1	1.0	0.6	8.7	11.8
1983–1984	61,369	17.3	17.0	22.5	19.9	1.1	1.1	0.6	8.7	11.9
1984–1985	63,215	17.4	16.7	21.9	20.8	1.1	1.1	0.6	8.6	11.9
1985–1986	64,164	17.8	16.1	21.0	21.5	1.0	1.2	0.6	8.9	12.1
1986–1987	64,500	18.3	15.4	20.4	21.9	1.0	1.2	0.6	8.9	12.2
1987–1988	64,263	18.2	14.8	20.0	23.0	1.0	1.3	0.6	9.0	12.2
1988–1989	63,390	18.7	14.7	19.4	23.2	1.0	1.2	0.6	8.8	12.4
1989–1990	62,780	19.3	14.5	18.9	23.7	1.0	1.2	0.7	8.3	12.5
1990–1991	63,506	19.7	14.3	18.9	23.7	1.0	1.1	0.6	8.1	12.5
1991–1992	63,806	19.6	14.3	18.7	24.3	1.0	1.1	0.6	8.1	12.2

Source: San Francisco Unified School District, Research, Planning, and Accountability Department.

Note: The nine subgroups recognized by the district during this period: Latino (L), Other White (OW), African American (AA), Chinese (C), Japanese (J), Korean (K), American Indian (AI), Filipino (F), Other Non White (ONW). Note the decline in the percentage of White and African American students and the increase in the percentage of Latino and Chinese students.

since the consent decree took effect. In 1983, African American and White students together accounted for just under 40 percent of SFUSD enrollment, while Latino and Chinese students comprised just over 37 percent. By the 1991–1992 school year, African American and White students made up just 33 percent of the district, while Latino and Chinese students accounted for nearly 44 percent of the district (Table 13).

The Experts' Report suggested that the city's demographic trends might actually work to facilitate school desegregation:

> The District is not experiencing the kind of rapidly growing proportion of segregated African American and Hispanic students so common in other large central cities. Nor is there a major drop in the proportion of students from the more educationally successful groups in the city schools; the largest growth came among Chinese students, a group with a strong record of academic achievement. Nor is residential segregation expanding. In fact, some of the historically segregated areas, including Hunter's Point, have experienced significant growth of residential desegregation. The demographic

trends suggest that it may be possible to maintain educationally beneficial school desegregation while gradually reducing mandatory busing.[47]

While the Experts' Report took an optimistic stance, it failed to anticipate the political contention the enrollment caps would cause. The consent decree set the racial balance threshold at 40 or 45 percent of a school's population, regardless of subgroup. When the presiding judge approved the consent decree settlement, African Americans were the largest subgroup and the cap often served to prevent racially isolated Black schools. But this changed within a few years.

The demographic transformation of the city meant that school attendance boundaries were no longer compatible with the consent decree (Table 14). Chinese students living in the city's western and northern neighborhoods endured the greatest impact.[48] The district was forced to raise the prospect of an expanded busing system to comply with the court mandate, but the growth of the Chinese population was so extensive that even the schools that were designated to handle overflow students were themselves reaching the court-imposed limit.[49] "It isn't as easy as it appears," remarked Carlos Cornejo. "The Chinese group is the most populous group in all those schools without exception. If the Chinese students are dominant here and down here, you can't take them from one school and move them to the other, because it doesn't do anything."[50]

Table 14. Schools Affected by Enrollment Caps, March 1993

Race	Schools within 6 points of cap	Percent of total schools	Percent of affected schools
Chinese	30	28	44
African American	14	13	20
Spanish Speaking	21	19	31
All Other Subgroups	4	4	5
Total	69	64	100

Source: Declaration by Amado Cabezas on Behalf of Chinese American Democratic Club, *SFNAACP v. SFUSD* (DF751, 4/22/93). Cabezas obtained data from SFUSD Planning and Research Department.

By 1989, the district began working on a new desegregation plan. But there was no option that would not be politically fraught. Redrawing attendance boundaries would be difficult. Parents with children assigned to a less preferable school than before would be understandably angry. The alternative to redrawing attendance boundaries was requesting that the court grant an exception to the racial balance threshold such that Chinese students would not be subject to the enrollment cap. But this was a nonstarter for the SFNAACP. "We're not going over 45 percent," said chapter president Lulann McGriff, referring to the cap. "[District officials] need to come up with a plan. Until they do that, we're not going to entertain increasing another percentage point."[51]

The disparity in admissions standards at Lowell High School was incorporated into META's motion to intervene. "We see no rational reason why Chinese students should be differentially treated," argued attorneys for META. "To maintain the status quo only serves to penalize an ethnic minority community which has long been victimized by ethnic and racial discrimination and harassment in this city and throughout California."[52] CAA's declaration in support of the motion for intervention noted that Chinese parents felt they did not have a voice in influencing desegregation policies in the district. These parents, dissatisfied with the "higher academic requirements imposed on Chinese student applicants seeking admission to Lowell," supported intervention on their behalf.[53] The alternative advocated by CAA was to have only two cutoff scores, one for African American and Latino students and another for all other subgroups, and then to hold a random lottery that would admit students in such a way that would maintain the consent decree subgroup enrollment caps.[54]

CADC sought a different outcome. In February 1993, its membership voted on the strategy it had been considering for some time—calling on the school board to terminate the portion of the consent decree that imposed enrollment caps and instead institute a system requiring minimum subgroup enrollment across schools in order to achieve integration. To build public support, CADC "hit all the bases, personally talking to all important elected officials, political groups, the media, the school board, community leaders, Chinese American groups, everyone who was anyone," recalled Louis Hop Lee, then a CADC board member.[55] CADC members spoke with over seventy students and organized parents to attend school board meetings en masse.[56] Former school board commissioner Steve Phillips remembered the political mobilization that took place as coordinated and strategic:

> They would have a team of people to meet with [school board commissioners], try to lobby this around, making the case for their situation. It became a litmus test issue: *Would you get the endorsement of CADC?* They would try to impact any other endorsements that they could, to make it something that was on the minds of candidates running for office.[57]

CADC followed up its lobbying effort with a brief of objections to the fairness of the consent decree filed with the court. But these efforts did not carry them far. By and large, the response CADC received from the local political elite was that school integration generally, and the consent decree in particular, were not to be touched.[58]

By April 1993, CADC had announced the formation of a consent decree task force whose objective was to "provide equity for Chinese American students, to enhance educational opportunities for underachieving students of all ethnicities, and to promote quality education for all students." Addressing admissions at Lowell remained a focal point, and the task force demanded that the cutoff score for Chinese students be the same as it was for White students. All the while, the task force remained supportive of efforts to maintain or increase the number of Black and Latino students at Lowell and to augment educational opportunities for underachieving students of color districtwide. "CADC's position is very simple," declared the *Fiery Dragon News,* its monthly newsletter. "Individual students should not be denied admission to Lowell, or any other public school, on the basis of race."[59]

Despite concern from Lowell's principal and Parent Teacher Association that the school was already overcrowded, CADC's appeals convinced Superintendent Waldemar "Bill" Rojas to lower the cutoff score for Chinese students from sixty-six to sixty-one in the spring of 1993. Although this was still two points higher than the cutoff for White students, it was positively received by Chinese parents. The change allowed an additional 153 Chinese students to enter Lowell the upcoming fall, but it also necessitated the admission of additional non-Chinese students in order to comply with the consent decree's 40 percent subgroup enrollment cap. The SFNAACP struck a skeptical tone over Rojas's promise to open up spaces for non-Chinese students at the school. "We won't be satisfied until we see whether he has allowed the other students in," cautioned Lulann McGriff.[60]

Both CADC and CAA were against maintaining higher cutoff scores for Chinese American students. But in contrast to CADC, CAA did not believe the subgroup enrollment caps were discriminatory toward Chinese students. The starkly different approaches the two organizations advocated for was indicative of the divide within the Chinese American community on the issue of school integration. The rift, framed at least in part as one that ran along class lines, only deepened as CADC's campaign grew increasingly more effective and prominent in the years to follow. In a news article that exposed the schism to the broader public, CAA director Henry Der dismissed CADC's complaints as little more than "middle class angst." Middle-class Chinese parents were benefiting from the system, Der argued. "What [CADC members] say is racially divisive and is not very progressive at all. They want basically single-race schools."[61] The comments infuriated CADC members. "We are extremely disturbed that [Der] blames children and parents for the discrimination they suffer," stated a CADC press release. "Blaming the victim only fuels racial prejudice."[62] The two organizations held a series of meetings and exchanged letters soon after in order to work through their differences. CADC and CAA had been close partners, with overlapping membership, interlocking boards of directors, and mutually supported fund-raisers. But tension between the two groups over the consent decree remained and would strain (though not destroy) relations for years to come.[63]

To this point, while some within CADC supported the dissolution of the consent decree in its entirety, the organization's public stance—to its members, the school district, the court, and the general public—was nuanced. CADC recognized the value of affirmative measures to increase diversity in schools and the workplace. Race-conscious efforts that afforded a preference to Black and Latino students were acceptable. This stance aligned with past CADC campaigns that sought affirmative action in, for example, contracting for city services and hiring in the school district. What was offensive was not the race-conscious system of student assignment, it was that White students were admitted to Lowell with lower scores than Chinese students, a group that had endured school discrimination in the past. "What has occurred is that Chinese American students have the highest rejection rate by far for entrance to all High Schools," wrote CADC members Louis Hop Lee and Juliet Gee in a brief to the court. "At Lowell High School, Chinese American students bear the *only* burden of desegregation as defined by the Consent Decree."[64] Such was where things stood in the summer of 1993. Within a year, however, as a new strategy surfaced and the pace of the campaign quickened, the race-conscious position within CADC became vulnerable.

The Development of a Legal Campaign

Over the spring and summer of 1993, the district tried to recruit new Black and Latino students to Lowell as a means of offsetting the superintendent's decision to admit additional Chinese American students. The district was only partially successful. At the start of the 1993–1994 school year, the Chinese subgroup comprised nearly 43 percent of the school—over the 40 percent subgroup limit for alternative schools like Lowell. From the very start, the SFNAACP carried out the role of consent decree watchdog. Primarily because of the tenacity of chapter president Lulann McGriff and attorney Peter Cohn, district leaders and school board members were forced to remain mindful of the goals of the consent decree on a constant basis.[65] The possibility of starting the school year with Lowell out of compliance generated an angry reaction from the SFNAACP, which vowed that the district would not be given a "pass" on the issue.[66]

With pressure mounting to resolve the Lowell issue, the superintendent convened a twenty-one-member panel of Lowell parents, teachers, students, and alumni as well as community advocates—including representatives from SFNAACP, CADC, and CAA—to advise the district on Lowell's yet-to-be-determined admissions policy for the 1994–1995 school year.[67] The CADC consent decree task force submitted recommendations to the panel that sought to lower the percentage of Chinese students at Lowell by redoubling district recruitment and retention efforts for Black, Latino, and White students. But a central concern for CADC remained the effect of the 40 percent enrollment cap on qualified Chinese applicants. The group proposed creating a secondary pool of applicants to be admitted through a "race-blind merit-based" process and revisiting the consent decree "with a view of adapting the racial guidelines to changing demographics."[68] The SFNAACP, however, continued to regard the maintenance of enrollment caps as nonnegotiable.[69]

It became increasingly clear to CADC that a new tactic was required. Talk shifted to mounting a legal assault on the consent decree.[70] "After exhausting political remedies for two years, we finally turned to lawyers," stated CADC member Amy Chang.[71] The idea of a lawsuit was not new. Years earlier, Leslie Yee called for a lawsuit, declaring that "some Chinese organization, for example, CADC, must sue the school board to get into the game."[72] The idea had been bandied about since then. But up to this point, a lawsuit was always a "'Plan B' because of the expense and uncertainty" of such a campaign.[73] In search of expertise, the CADC task force organized a legal luncheon in early December 1993 for "partner-level Chinese Americans" at prominent San Francisco law firms and attorneys from public interest firms, including Asian Law Caucus and American Civil Liberties Union.[74]

A week or two prior to the luncheon, Daniel Girard and Anthony Lee, colleagues at a well-known San Francisco class action law firm, were flying back from a trip to Texas. Their conversation turned to the use of race in student assignment. Lee's wife had brought up the issue to him, having learned about the consent decree through her friend, Amy Chang. "Somebody should bring that legal challenge," mentioned Girard. When Lee heard about the luncheon, he invited Girard to attend. The luncheon "was a very memorable thing because, I remember, there were a number of lawyers in there from big firms, and I think everybody had a sense this case was going to be a very, very high-profile case that would attract a lot of attention," recalled Girard. "These lawyers were saying they could sort of help out but not really do it because they might get in trouble with their firms, and that it was viewed as a very politically unpopular case that was going to draw down a lot of pressure from powerful people in the community."[75] At the luncheon was David Levine, a professor at University of California's Hastings College of Law with expertise in federal civil procedure and institutional reform. Girard had not known Levine, but he immediately recognized him as "a guy who could make the difference" as a complement to Girard's class action expertise.

Following the luncheon, Girard attended several follow-up meetings sponsored by CADC in which parents would discuss their frustrations with the student assignment system. It was a powerful experience for him: "Sometimes they were parents who had been here for several generations, other times they were recent immigrant parents, but everybody's common sense was that this was contrary to the basic fabric of what it is to be American, that you couldn't have people discriminating against you based on your ethnicity or your race." Girard arranged to have a group of parents speak to partners at his firm. Although the consensus from Girard's colleagues was that a case challenging the consent decree had merit, they were upset when Girard agreed to represent the parents. "The phrase that I remember is: It's going to offend powerful people in the community that we can't afford to offend," recalled Girard. Shortly thereafter he left to strike out on his own. But he kept the case and enlisted Levine and Lee. Together, the three comprised the core legal team that would work for the next eight years on the consent decree challenge.[76]

By spring 1994, the search for plaintiffs was well under way.[77] CADC put out a citywide call for students "turned down by Lowell because of the higher education standards for Chinese applicants" as well as students turned down by other schools because of their Chinese ancestry.[78] But internally, the possibility of a lawsuit placed a strain on CADC's membership. Although the organization as a whole endorsed the consent decree campaign, "it was still pretty obvious that there were elements within CADC that were very resistant to rocking the boat and trying to pursue the remedies that we [i.e., the CADC Consent Decree Task Force] thought were right," recalled Lee Cheng, a 1989 graduate of Lowell High School who had since gotten involved in CADC's consent decree campaign.[79] Echoing this sentiment, Henry Louie remarked that in fact, "there were a number of people within CADC who felt that the consent decree was necessary to desegregate."[80] To resolve the issue, CADC spun off the task force into a separate organization, the Asian American Legal Foundation (AALF). The two organizations remained aligned throughout the duration of the lawsuit, with AALF existing as a vehicle to channel donations and structure the political and community aspects of the consent decree campaign apart from CADC.[81] With regard to the lawsuit, a "double prong" approach developed: While Girard, Levine, and

Lee would handle the case proper, AALF would focus on the political and community aspects of the campaign.[82]

By the summer of 1994, three class representatives with compelling stories had been recruited: Because of the enrollment cap, five-year-old Brian Ho was unable to attend schools in the Sunset District, the westside neighborhood where he lived. Similarly, Hilary Chen, aged eight, was denied a transfer from her former school to a school in the Sunset District where her family had recently moved. A third student, Patrick Wong, was denied admission to Lowell because his combined test and grade index score was fifty-eight, which fell below the cutoff for the Chinese subgroup. However, the score was high enough to gain admission for every other recognized subgroup, including the White subgroup. The three students (referred to collectively as "Ho" after the first named plaintiff), represented by lead attorney Girard, sued the SFUSD and the California Department of Education on July 11, 1994, alleging that the district, by assigning students based on its system of racial classifications and enrollment caps, violated the Fourteenth Amendment.[83] The students sought declaratory relief and an injunction on what they believed to be the unconstitutional portion of the student assignment system. "After exhausting all attempts to effect satisfactory reform within the established political system, the plaintiffs are turning to the judiciary to protect our Constitutionally guaranteed rights to be free from discrimination," read the statement released by CADC.[84]

Understandably, there was considerable interest from within San Francisco's Chinese American community in the run-up and immediate aftermath of the lawsuit. "It is reasonable that Asian parents in San Francisco are against ethnic quotas," began a typical sentiment expressed in the local Chinese media. "Schools should open their doors to all students regardless of students' racial groups, and enroll students with equity."[85] But the assignment system did enroll students equitably, argued SFNAACP attorney Peter Cohn. "The desegregation plan assures that no school will ever again become a one-race school. It affirmatively opens the door of opportunity to all San Francisco school children."[86] Aubrey McCutcheon, the school district's lawyer, agreed. "There have been African American students turned away from schools because they're African American, and some because they're Latino. No student is guaranteed to attend any particular school."[87]

Early on, the local and state defendants were confident the student assignment system would not be changed.[88] "It's going to be more than an uphill battle to topple" the consent decree, remarked Barry Zolotar, counsel for the California Department of Education. But as the case progressed, it become clear to the parties involved that the district's use of racial classification would in fact put the assignment system in jeopardy. The next fifteen months were occupied primarily by the defendants' motion that the case should be dismissed because the issues brought up by the Ho plaintiffs had been decided in the 1983 settlement that resulted in the consent decree. The motion was denied by the court since conditions had "changed since the consent decree was approved" and Ho plaintiffs, unlike the SFNAACP, "intend to focus on the operation and effects of the consent decree, and not whether the [school district] is segregated."[89] This was followed by the certification of plaintiffs as class representatives for "all children of Chinese descent of school age who are current residents of San Francisco and who are eligible to attend the public schools of the San Francisco Unified School District."[90] However, in the earlier lawsuit, *SFNAACP v. SFUSD,* the SFNAACP was still the certified class representative "of all the school children, heretofore, now or hereafter eligible to attend the public elementary and secondary schools of the SFUSD," a designation that of course includes children of Chinese descent.[91] It was left unclear to what extent the SFNAACP was no longer representing Chinese American students.[92]

The new guidelines for Lowell High School were finally approved for the fall 1996 incoming class. All applicants whose combined score was sixty-three or higher were guaranteed admission. This would account for 70 to 80 percent of an entering class. To fill the remaining 20 to 30 percent of an entering class, some students who scored just below sixty-three were admitted on a "value-added" basis. For this group, a selection committee took into account elements such as leadership, coursework, artistic talent, and family need. The guidelines required Lowell's selection committee to also give special consideration to underrepresented applicants "recognizing the historical racial discrimination against these communities" and the need to comply with the consent decree.[93] The practical effect of the special consideration component was that the superintendent admitted all Latino and African American applicants who scored above fifty points. Although the plan was celebrated by the selection committee chair as providing "equity at last" and was essentially what CADC had asked prior to filing the lawsuit, it was viewed differently by the Ho plaintiffs. "It's still race conscious and it's still illegal," proclaimed Girard, who vowed to move forward with the case.[94]

Earlier in the summer, Girard filed a motion for summary judgment on the grounds that the district's student assignment system did not meet contemporary constitutional standards and that there was "no factual dispute as to the SFUSD's use of racial criteria" in its student assignment system.[95] The motion was denied.[96] The court determined that Ho plaintiffs were bound to the consent decree because the SFNAACP had been certified as class representative for all students. However, the court agreed with the attorneys for Ho that SFUSD students were subject to race-based classifications by a state actor. This came despite testimony from the superintendent that he had "not assigned or authorized the assignment of students to schools in San Francisco based on their race or ethnicity."[97] But the core issue—whether the assignment plan at present was constitutional—was one that the Ho attorneys had failed to show and would thus require a trial.[98] "Any time a single child is denied an opportunity to pursue educational opportunities due to their ethnicity is wrong," said Amy Chang after the ruling. But Alex Pitcher, Lulann McGriff's successor as chapter president of the SFNAACP, argued that without the consent decree, "we'd be back in the 1950s, when the schools for Black children in San Francisco were at the bottom rung of the ladder." The presiding judge recognized that while the SFNAACP and the Ho plaintiffs had come to different conclusions on the consent decree, they both were working on behalf of "the same right—the right of children to attend public school free from invidious discrimination."[99] The attorneys for Ho filed an appeal in what would mark a critical turning point in San Francisco's student assignment system.

Desegregation and Affirmative Action Jurisprudence

As *Ho v. SFUSD* proceeded through the judicial system, jurisprudence was changing in important ways. Following the 1973 decision in *Keyes v. School District No. 1, Denver*, judicial conservatism gradually led to a more restrained application of court-mandated desegregation. In a 1974 case, *Milliken v. Bradley*, the Supreme Court disallowed an interdistrict "metropolitan" plan that sought to desegregate the Detroit public school system and counteract White flight by busing students from dozens of outlying suburban school districts.[100] While the Detroit Board of Education was found to have engaged in segregatory acts, there had been no such finding on the part of the suburban districts. The court's ruling limited desegregation remedies, including the busing authorized in an earlier case, *Swann v. Charlotte-Mecklenburg Board of Education,* to just those districts that had committed constitutional violations, even if what results is an essentially Black central-city school system surrounded by essentially White suburban school districts, as was the case in Detroit.[101] In clarifying the limits of school districts, the court reminded the respondents that "desegregation, in the sense of dismantling a dual school system does not require any particular racial balance" across schools, grades, or classrooms.[102] In addition, judicial oversight was not meant to remain in perpetuity. By the early 1990s, the court set about providing guidance on determining the point at which school districts should be released from supervision.[103] A three-part test was developed. If (1) a school district adequately complied with its desegregation mandate, (2) judicial control was no longer necessary to achieve compliance, and (3) it could be shown that a good faith effort to eliminate "the vestiges of past discrimination" to "the extent practicable," school districts could be classified as unitary.[104]

Relying heavily on these rulings, the Supreme Court cast doubt on a desegregation plan developed for the Kansas City, Missouri, School District (KCMSD).[105] In addition to redistributing students within KCMSD, the district court's remedy involved a comprehensive program of capital, instructional, and curricular improvements designed to attract White students from outside of the district. This was an interdistrict goal, wrote Chief Justice Rehnquist in delivering the opinion of the court. "In effect, the District Court has devised a remedy to accomplish indirectly what it admittedly lacks the remedial authority to mandate directly: the interdistrict transfer of students." Also at issue was the duration of the court's involvement with the school district. "Sixteen years after this litigation began, the District Court recognized that the KCMSD has yet to offer a viable method of financing the 'wonderful school system being built,'" stated Rehnquist in reminding the district court that its end purpose included returning control of the school system to state and local authorities. It was a divided ruling. The dissenters disagreed with the majority's opinion that the courts had no authority to mandate improvements that might in fact help recruit new students.[106] "Today, the Court declares illegitimate the goal of attracting nonminority students to the Kansas City, Missouri, School District," wrote Justice Ginsberg in her dissent. "Given the deep, inglorious history of segregation in Missouri, to curtail desegregation at this time and in this manner is an action at once too swift and too soon."

Judge Orrick's order refusing to dismiss the *Ho* case came on the heels of the Supreme Court ruling. Like KCMSD, San Francisco's plan combined desegregation with a concerted effort to improve academic achievement. The Supreme Court's ruling strengthened an argument made by the Ho plaintiffs that California should be freed from permanently funding the consent decree, particularly given the indeterminable effect the hundreds of millions of dollars in state desegregation funding had had on increasing academic achievement.[107] The *San Francisco Chronicle* editorialized that with this ruling, the Rehnquist court "took a lurching step backward in reversing school desegregation efforts." Foretelling the future direction of desegregation, the newspaper warned that "the worst may be yet to come" and that if the court remained "true to form," *Brown v. Board of Education* could be endangered.[108]

While the court's role in desegregation was increasingly limited, the use of racial classifications in student assignment as a means of remedying past segregatory acts had not been jeopardized by these cases. However, a separate line of jurisprudence developed over the years that did view racial classifications as constitutionally suspect. Allan Bakke, a White applicant who had been denied entry to the University of California, Davis medical school first in 1973 and again in 1974, argued that the school's affirmative action efforts violated his right to equal protection under the Fourteenth Amendment. Through its "special admissions program," the medical school set aside a fixed number of spaces for students who were economically or educationally disadvantaged or were members of a recognized racial minority group. The trial court determined that the program operated as a quota system.[109] While special admissions applicants had the opportunity to compete for every seat in the class, applicants who did not qualify for special admission were barred from competing for the set-aside seats.[110] On appeal, the California Supreme Court declared: "No college admission policy in history has been so thoroughly discredited in contemporary times as the use of racial percentages. Originated as a means of exclusion of racial and religious minorities from higher education, a quota becomes no less offensive when it serves to exclude a racial majority."[111]

The U.S. Supreme Court considered the *Bakke* case in 1977, and it attracted what court officials thought to be the largest number of amicus briefs ever filed, the most prominent coming from the Justice Department.[112] Griffin Bell, President Carter's attorney general, cast doubt on whether a quota existed at the school and advised the justices that "racially conscious" admissions plans were constitutional.[113] The following year the court delivered a nuanced set of opinions that would have lasting effect.[114] Justice Lewis Powell stood at the center of two opposing pluralities that, taken together, affirmed the California court's ruling that the special admissions program at UC Davis was unlawful but reversed its restriction from any consideration of race in its admission process. Speaking on the need for diversity, Powell wrote, "The State has a substantial interest that legitimately may be served by a properly devised admissions program involving the competitive consideration of race and ethnic origin."[115] Summarizing the case, the *New York Times* editorialized: "Minorities may be helped through the doors of opportunity but not through a separate door that is racially reserved for them alone."[116]

Bakke was followed by rulings that required all government use of racial classifications to be assessed under the highest standard of judicial scrutiny.[117] "Whenever the government treats any person unequally because of his or her race, that person has suffered an injury that falls squarely within the language and spirit of the Constitution's guarantee of equal protection," declared Justice O'Connor, writing for the majority.[118] Therefore, regardless of the race of those "burdened or benefited," racial classifications "must serve a compelling governmental interest, and must be narrowly tailored to further that interest."[119]

Petitioners in school desegregation and affirmative action lawsuits sought relief under the Fourteenth Amendment in different ways. The NAACP claimed that school district practices violated (primarily) Black elementary and secondary students' right to equal protection, while plaintiffs in affirmative action lawsuits argued a violation of the right to equal protection held by those who do not qualify for such programs, including White university students and White-owned contractors. In contrast to the "racially conscious" means employed by school desegregation plans, in the mid-1990s, affirmative action jurisprudence promoted a "colorblind" ideal, where racial classifications are employed as a last resort, only after "consideration of the use of race-neutral means."[120] These divergent lines of jurisprudence would materialize in the *Ho* case.[121] The admissions process for Lowell High School was perceived as much more egregious than the general admissions process for the rest of the SFUSD schools. Admissions at Lowell, similar to university admissions, was a selective process that hinged on academic achievement. This was distinct from the typical desegregation process of sorting students across district schools. The national debate over affirmative action in higher education, generally, and the meaning and use of racial quotas, in particular, resonated with local observers of San Francisco's student assignment system.

A National Dialogue on Affirmative Action

California was entrenched in the debate over affirmative action. In June 1995, Governor (and presidential candidate) Pete Wilson ordered an end to all state affirmative action programs not mandated by law or court decree.[122] "Today we begin a new chapter in the journey toward a colorblind society that protects the rights of every individual and offers equal opportunity to all Californians," stated Wilson.[123] The following year, voters approved a first-of-its-kind ballot initiative amending the state constitution by prohibiting discrimination and preferential treatment "on the basis of race, sex, color, ethnicity, or national origin" in public education, employment, and contracting.[124] The affirmative action ban was backed by the artfully named California Civil Rights Initiative, cochaired by Ward Connerly, a University of California regent well known for sponsoring a policy change that ended race, ethnicity, and gender preferences across the university system.[125] "Tonight, my friends, we celebrate," a euphoric Connerly proclaimed on election night. "In our hearts and minds we dance not in the darkness but in the warm sunshine to the sweet music of equal treatment for all and special privileges for none."[126]

Affirmative action was a prominent and closely observed topic of concern across the nation. Following a five-month administrative review concluding that affirmative action remained "a useful tool for widening economic and educational opportunity," President Clinton forcefully defended the institution in a landmark speech delivered at the National Archives. "We should reaffirm the principle of affirmative action and fix the practices," urged Clinton. "We should have a simple slogan: Mend it, but don't end it."[127] By 1996, Texas became another flash point in the debate. In a controversial ruling, the Fifth Circuit determined that the University of Texas Law School erred in using race as a factor in its admissions process. The Supreme Court declined to hear the case and so higher education affirmative action programs were presumed unconstitutional, at least throughout the Fifth Circuit's jurisdiction.[128]

But the gravitational center of debate remained California, and over the summer the Senate Committee on the Judiciary held a hearing on the matter.[129] The committee chair, Utah senator Orrin Hatch, both condemned the Clinton administration's "pervasive politics of preference" and extolled the actions of Governor Wilson and Ward Connerly. Among the witnesses was Lee Cheng, the Lowell High School alumnus working on the CADC/AALF consent decree campaign. "I will never forget the shock and disappointment that I felt upon discovering that Chinese American applicants had to score quantifiably higher on the admissions index than any other applicants for the sake of ensuring diversity," testified Cheng. "But being subjected to higher standards because of my race wasn't enough. Even worse was having the school district hierarchy tell me that the discrimination was not only legal, but, in fact, was a good thing. That was my first encounter with institutional racism."[130]

The following year, and just days after President Clinton issued a call for a "constructive national dialogue to confront and work through challenging issues that surround race,"[131] the Judiciary Committee held a hearing ominously titled "State-Sanctioned Discrimination in America."[132] Speaking on behalf of the minority side, Democratic senator Richard Durbin reminded the committee that "any fair appraisal of State-sanctioned discrimination might start with the document that created this Nation [i.e., the Constitution]." The affirmative action and school desegregation programs to be discussed at the hearing "are a response to the legacy that was created by many bad decisions made at the inception of this great democracy—State-sanctioned discrimination against Blacks and women," argued Durbin. Invited to speak before the Committee was Charlene Loen, the mother of Patrick Wong, among the named plaintiffs in *Ho v. SFUSD* who was denied admission to Lowell in 1994. "Under the consent decree, hard work and good grades are not always enough," stated Loen. "My son, Patrick, found out the hard way."[133] Wong's combined index score was high enough for a student of any racial and ethnic subgroup except "Chinese" to gain admission to Lowell. She subsequently tried, without success, to enroll her son into his second-, third-, fourth-, and fifth-choice schools.[134] Loen teared up as she recounted her plight:

> By treating people as members of racial groups rather than as individuals with the same rights before the law, the consent decree has dashed the hopes of children, denied my son and many others the right to opportunities they earned through hard work and diligence, condemned children to needless busing, prevented parents from being involved in their schools and holding school administrators accountable, and divided the people of San Francisco.[135]

Loen's story was compelling, and it would be recounted numerous times over the ensuing months by several nationally prominent political figures.[136] Back in San Francisco, her testimony was perhaps the defining moment in the case, at least in the mind of Daniel Girard. Girard traveled to Washington, D.C., with Loen and assisted in the preparation of her statement. "I knew that it was going to be powerful footage because she was so articulate and presents very well," recalled Girard. "It was on MacNeil-Lehrer that night when I got back to my hotel . . . and later that week, Judge Orrick got us [i.e., the *Ho* attorneys] all on the phone and wanted to know what she was doing on TV and how this had all happened. And I think he was pretty shaken by it all—the presentation to him of the decree as being a source of this injustice."[137]

By the fall of 1997, the California State Board of Education realigned its position to that of the Ho plaintiffs: "In opposition to the maintenance of racial quotas as ordered pursuant to the Consent Decree."[138] The move followed a request by Governor Wilson to the president of the board that it "take a leadership role in ridding California's public schools of an invidious form of racial discrimination that limits students' educational opportunities solely because of their race."[139] At the time, the California Department of Education, the State Board of Education, and the State Superintendent of Public Instruction were named defendants, along with the SFNAACP and the school district, in the *Ho* lawsuit. The state board, composed entirely of appointees of the Republican governor, moved quickly to find outside counsel.[140] But the reversal was met with opposition from State Superintendent Delaine Eastin, a Democrat, who asserted that the consent decree "has worked to prohibit racial isolation of all students and to provide academic achievement of all students."[141]

This was an extremely thorny issue for CADC. While support from the state was certainly welcome, it came about for the wrong reasons. San Francisco's student assignment system "demonstrates the perversity of the affirmative action mind-set," wrote Governor Wilson.[142] "I don't agree with that," remarked CADC President Roland Quan. "Our group has never been for dismantling affirmative action and in fact we are supportive of affirmative action."[143] Indeed, CADC had worked on campaigns in support of race-based remedies to increase Chinese American representation in government contracting and civil service positions, including in the area of public education.[144] But these Republican efforts to latch onto the case clouded the argument made by the Democratic Club. "Many groups have tried to piggyback on our case and interpret it to fit their agendas," complained Quan. "We want to emphasize that this case is about ending discrimination and not at all about ending affirmative action."[145]

The distinctions between the affirmative action programs supported by the CADC and the desegregation program institutionalized by the consent decree had been a point of focus for their opponents, particularly the SFNAACP and CAA, throughout the course of the campaign.[146] CADC anticipated the association that might be made. "We are not against affirmative action for disadvantaged students," stated a 1994 press release announcing the lawsuit. "In fact, we are strongly committed to ensuring opportunities for disadvantaged students. The quotas used by the SFUSD are not only fixed and arbitrary ceilings, but in reality provide admissions preferences to non-disadvantaged groups and individuals" (in other words, White students).[147] "It's sort of an intellectual disconnect sometimes," remarked Henry Louie. "CADC at that time and continues to this day to be strong advocates of affirmative action."[148] Indeed, former CADC board member Doug Chan recalled his experience delivering auto parts for his father, who "knocked his head against the wall trying to sell spark plugs and shock absorbers to the City and County of San Francisco." Chan saw affirmative action as "a necessary and valid tool to pry open opportunities for previously disenfranchised or excluded groups, racial minorities, and women, to assure that public activities and opportunities are allocated with reference to a relevant standard of parity, but that such remedies need to be narrowly tailored."[149] This commitment to affirmative action was embedded in the programmatic work of the organization for years. "That's where I was very critical of them," recalled Henry Der. CADC supported the consideration of race when it meant submitting a government bid, "but they're certainly not going to have any race consideration when it comes to the schools."[150]

Ninth Circuit Appeal

The two campaigns led by SFNAACP and the Ho plaintiffs had been working on behalf of the same right yet sought different outcomes, and they would soon collide in a decisive manner.[151] The appeal of the district court's order denying summary judgment was argued before a three-judge panel of the Ninth Circuit Court of Appeals in April 1998. Plaintiffs were joined in the appeal by the California Board of Education, following its vote to oppose the consent decree. In June, the appeal was dismissed for lack of jurisdiction.[152] The panel majority's opinion might have ended there. However, it went on to detail two issues left for trial regarding the so-called Paragraph 13 Requirements—the section of the consent decree that described the racial and ethnic subgroup caps: "Do vestiges remain of the racism that justified paragraph 13 of the consent decree in 1982? Is paragraph 13 necessary to remove the vestiges if they do remain?"[153]

Citing recent Supreme Court desegregation and affirmative action cases, the majority opinion reminded the parties that racial classifications are suspect and subject to strict scrutiny, a standard of judicial review used to determine the constitutionality of a law or policy. The strict scrutiny standard is a three-part test. In order to use racial classifications, (1) there must be a compelling government interest (it cannot be for some arbitrary or inconsequential purpose), (2) it must be narrowly

tailored (tailored to the compelling government interest and not expan-
sive), and (3) it must be the least restrictive means (if there exists a race-
neutral method that achieves the same goal, that method must be employed). The majority opinion stated that racial classifications may only
be used by the government if "its use is found to be necessary as the way
of repairing injuries inflicted on persons because of race."[154] While the
SFUSD had asserted that vestiges of racism did remain, the majority
panel determined them to be conclusory (an assertion lacking evidence).
At trial, defendants would need to provide concrete evidence that tied
back to the discriminatory practices justifying the consent decree in the
first place. Once this was shown, defendants would need to prove that
paragraph 13 was "a remedy fitted to a wrong"—a narrowly tailored policy serving a compelling government interest.[155]

"The gamble at the appellate court had paid off handsomely" for the
plaintiffs, observed David Levine.[156] Although the appeal by the Ho plaintiffs was dismissed, thus upholding the district court's denial of the motion for summary judgment, the majority panel's opinion did not auger
well for the defendants. The circuit court determined that racial balancing efforts by the SFUSD could only be used "if necessary to correct the
effects of government action of a racist character" and that the district
would need additional (nonconclusory) evidence beyond what had been
previously presented.[157]

The circuit court ruling came amid a budget crisis for the school
district. While Sacramento legislators were haggling over a surplus of
funds, the SFUSD was preparing for cuts nearing $20 million on an ap-
proximately $500 million budget.[158] The consent decree provided a sig-
nificant source of revenue that the district had come to rely on. With the
district incurring well over $30 million in desegregation program ex-
penses each year, much of it reimbursable by the state, the *Ho* action
and its impact on the ultimate fate of the consent decree was an added
concern—in addition to racial segregation and the achievement gap—for
local observers.[159]

Following the ruling from the circuit court, parties prepared for a
September 1998 trial.[160] However, during a status conference in late August
it became apparent to the presiding judge that the "defendants were ut-
terly unprepared."[161] The trial was subsequently moved to February 1999.
At the August conference, the school district offered a glint of hope by

informing the court that an agreement was within reach. After Governor Wilson's letter urging the California State Board of Education to align itself with the Ho plaintiffs, Delaine Eastin, state superintendent of Public Instruction, sought separate legal representation for herself and the California Department of Education.[162] Over the summer, her new attorneys began to explore settlement options with counsel for each party. Following these exploratory discussions, a compromise position took shape. Although the consent decree continued to be necessary, it was no longer narrowly tailored, as required by law.[163] In a law review article assessing the case, David Levine identified three requirements for settlement: (1) The elimination of racial classifications as required by the Ho plaintiffs; (2) a release from court supervision in the near future; and (3) the avoidance of racial isolation and identifiability as required by SFNAACP and the school district.[164] Upon hearing from the district the possibility of a settlement, the court appointed a longtime San Francisco attorney with arbitration experience as special master to oversee discussions.[165]

In October, the SFNAACP, the SFUSD, and the state superintendent proposed two sets of modifications to the consent decree. The first modification provided for an "orderly transition to unitary status" by proposing the submittal of sections of the consent decree to the court for dismissal by the 2000–2001 school year and that a unitary status hearing be held by 2003, with a final deadline for dismissal of any remaining portions of the decree by 2005.[166] The second, more controversial set of modifications proposed a new student assignment system to be implemented no later than the 2000–2001 school year. Students would be assigned on the basis of "geographic distribution, residence, socio-economic status, and OERs" (optional enrollment requests), with each school having at least six racial/ethnic subgroups represented in its student body.[167] While race or ethnicity "shall not be the sole consideration in determining such admission criteria," argued the defendants, "district officials may consider many factors, including the desire to promote racial, residential, geographic and ethnic diversity in all schools."[168]

The attempt to modify the consent decree was described by Levine as an "end run" around the Ho plaintiffs, who had recently filed a motion to immediately halt the execution of paragraph 13. Defendants used the proposal to contend that plaintiffs' preliminary injunction was not necessary.[169] The court described the proposal as "vague and incomplete."[170] More importantly, by requiring that schools enroll no less than six subgroups, the proposed modifications preserved racial classifications that were questioned by the circuit court. "The parties must demonstrate that such a system meets strict scrutiny under the Equal Protection Clause of the 14th Amendment of the United States Constitution," admonished the court. "The parties have not attempted to meet this burden."[171] The court consequently rejected defendants' request to modify the decree.

The fateful year ended with a second appeal by the Ho plaintiffs. "One of the key legal disputes in this action was over the burden of proof," explained the presiding judge. "With each party arguing that the opposing party bore the burden of proof."[172] The issue had been clarified back in June with the Ninth Circuit's opinion, but defendants maintained that it was inconsistent with Supreme Court case law, and that plaintiffs, in fact, bore the burden. The presiding judge was concerned that the dispute was preventing the preparatory work to be done: "developing an adequate factual record to ensure that the trial in this action would be based on facts, rather than on an absence of facts."[173] To move things along, the court reappointed a special master in November to oversee the drafting of a report to the court on "discriminatory acts, policies and practices by state actors, at or prior to the time of the adoption of the Consent Decree in 1983."[174] The attorneys for the Ho plaintiffs regarded the district court's move as an unwarranted interference with the adversarial process. "It appeared that the court, confronted with the defendants' failure to prepare for trial, had decided to appoint a special master to do a substantial portion of what the defendants had not done to prepare the case," wrote Levine.[175] Plaintiffs went back to the circuit court seeking an emergency petition for a writ of mandamus (a judicial remedy), which was granted in short order. The Ninth Circuit allowed the special master to give his report to the parties. But from that point forward, the defendants, ill-prepared though they were, carried the burden of gathering evidence.

Settlement

Over the final few days before the bench trial was to begin, the parties made one last push to settle. On the eve of the trial they still remained at an impasse, but in a last-minute breakthrough, a settlement was negotiated the following morning. On February 16, 1999, less than an hour after the trial was scheduled to begin, lawyers agreed on the final sticking points to a settlement.[176] As was the case in 1983, the parties were able to avert what surely would have been a racially charged trial.[177] "The NAACP and the District, as well as the Superintendent of Public Instruction, worked night and day with Mr. Girard . . . to come up with a viable and, at this stage, proper solution," declared the presiding judge, in announcing the terms of the settlement.[178] The consent decree would continue but with significant amendments.[179] The central stipulation was that:

> District officials may consider many factors, including the desire to promote residential, geographic, economic, racial and ethnic diversity in all SFUSD schools. However, race or ethnicity may not be the primary or predominant consideration in determining such admission criteria. Further, the SFUSD will not assign or admit any student to a particular school, class or program on the basis of the race or ethnicity of that student.[180]

In addition, the racial or ethnic subgroup identification of students would no longer be required and enrollment forms would include a "decline to state" option.[181] With these provisions in mind, the school district would develop a new student assignment plan that would include the replacement of paragraph 13 of the consent decree.[182] The plan would be reviewed by the SFNAACP and the Ho plaintiffs before being submitted to the court for approval. The parties agreed to terminate the consent decree before 2003, barring an extenuating circumstance.

The fairness hearing took place on April 20, 1999. That morning, outside the federal courthouse, the Coalition to Defend Affirmative Action By Any Means Necessary (BAMN) held a press conference and rally in opposition to the settlement. To the chants of "Equal quality education! We will fight for integration!," speakers from CAA, Lowell High School's Black Student Union, and other organizations expressed fear that the settlement would lead to the resegregation of schools.[183] It will be "disastrous" for African American students, worried Lowell senior Jamaal Marshall. "I feel my race is not welcome at Lowell. When you can fit all of the school's African American students in one classroom, you have a problem."[184] Inside the courtroom, most of the speakers opposed the settlement but were unable to challenge its legality. "If this settlement were approved, it would be even harder for Black and other minority students to get into Lowell," wrote Rahel Tekste, an African American student at Galileo High School petitioning the court to be heard in opposition of the settlement. "It would also result in my school becoming more segregated. That would hurt the quality of education for minorities and all students."[185]

A coalition of advocates for the Chinese American community led by CAA registered their opposition to the settlement, arguing that "schools must remain integrated to provide high quality education and to meet the needs of limited-English proficient students."[186] The settlement "closes a chapter in San Francisco public education," wrote Diane Chin, executive director of CAA. "It has been a sad chapter: one that pitted one minority group against all others and divided that minority group." Beyond the obvious changes the consent decree would bring, it would lead to the characterization that Chinese Americans do not value integration, Chin feared. "Once again, Chinese Americans are being used as a proxy for anti-affirmative action and anti-integration viewpoints, which ultimately increase discrimination against our community. Lost in this debate have been the many Chinese Americans who spoke out for integration."[187]

A month prior to the settlement, the Consent Decree Advisory Committee lauded the community-wide cooperation that distinguished San Francisco's desegregation plan: "Almost all of the efforts since the early 1980s has been directed toward finding solutions, not battling over history."[188] The collaborative nature the consent decree fostered allowed for a plan designed by educators that was achieving positive results, both in desegregation and academic achievement, argued the committee.[189] But the settlement proposal, and in particular, the exclusive process undertaken to determine its scope, troubled committee chair Gary Orfield: "I would certainly not have spent a great deal of time working on very complex issues of educational inequality had I thought that there was any chance that the entire effort would be junked without a hearing by a group of lawyers who did not even bother to address the urgent issues of denial of equal education we documented or consult with us on the feasibility of resolving them within the arbitrary deadline set in this decree"[190]

Despite the opposition to the proposed settlement, the presiding judge, finding it to be fair, reasonable, and adequate, approved it in July

1999. Responding to the "misunderstanding" brought up by the students organized by BAMN (and by Gary Orfield in comments to the court) that San Francisco's schools would now be on a path toward racial resegregation, the court pointed to paragraph C of the proposed settlement, which allowed the district to promote racial and ethnic diversity in all SFUSD schools.[191] In fact, David Ely, an expert for the state superintendent, was prepared to testify at trial that devising a student assignment system "using a combination of individual and census-derived socioeconomic factors to assure reasonable socioeconomic diversity at each school" would not result in racial or ethnic resegregation.[192]

The time frame set by the court was aggressive. For the 1999–2000 school year, a temporary "default" plan was to be implemented. The SFUSD would modify its student assignment system by eliminating the enrollment caps of paragraph 13 and assignment priority given to African American and Latino students. Beyond this, enrollment would be consistent with prior procedure—students would be given their assignments based on home address or optional enrollment requests through a process of random selection, allowing for certain nonracial priorities (e.g., a sibling preference), by grade and program at each school.[193]

By early August 1999, the court ordered parties to submit a modified consent decree that incorporated the changes outlined in the settlement agreement, and by October, a new student assignment plan for the following school year was to be provided. Ely's prepared testimony and early drafts provided by the SFUSD student assignment committee gave the attorneys representing the Ho plaintiffs a sense of what the district's plan for the 2000–2001 school year might entail. "The expectation was that the committee would propose to redraw school attendance zones, as the state superintendent's expert suggested, in order to maximize diversity and use a race-neutral lottery system to assign students within the zones," wrote David Levine. "Second, the school district committee would test a variety of socio-economic factors to determine what sort of a mix would best achieve the racial and ethnic diversity the school district wanted to maintain."[194]

The consent decree began in 1983 on a hopeful note. But early gains made at eliminating racial identifiability were severely curtailed starting in the 1990s. Resegregation started during the first phase of the consent decree, under Rojas, and did not slow following the *Ho* settlements. Resegregation took place during a period of renewed attention on student assignment. The population of White and Black students had been in decline since the 1970s. Conversely, the population of Chinese and Latino students had grown rapidly. These demographic changes created an opening for stakeholders seeking to intervene in the process through political and legal means. Beyond San Francisco, the decade saw fundamental changes in federal desegregation and affirmative action jurisprudence. As the Supreme Court clarified the limits of government use of racial classifications, the nation was engaged in a dialogue on race with considerable attention focused on California and its so-called color-blind policies. San Francisco's student assignment system and, in particular, its impact on Chinese American students received national exposure and was held up by opponents as a symbol of the failings of race-conscious policy.

META's motion to intervene on behalf of Latino and Asian students, although supported by the board of education, was denied by the court. While Judge Orrick acknowledged that the SFNAACP lacked expertise on issues affecting English learners, he determined that school desegregation "with respect to all races" was an interest it could adequately represent. With no serious criticism leveled on SFNAACP's representation, intervention was not permitted. Had META been allowed to intervene, it is entirely possible that a compromise solution would have been crafted that CADC found acceptable.

Outside of the court, and apart from META's intervention, CADC mobilized its members and directed resources toward the consent decree issue. Although advocacy efforts aimed at the school board generated some attention, there was no indication that the board possessed the political will to challenge the consent decree outright. CADC shifted to a legal strategy, secured a team of attorneys, and identified class representatives. Unlike earlier desegregation lawsuits, in *Ho v. SFUSD,* the SFNAACP was aligned with the school district and the state representatives. As with any school discrimination lawsuit, the *Ho* action led to divisions in the community, as stakeholders aligned with either the Ho plaintiffs or the SFUSD and SFNAACP defendants. After nearly five years of pretrial work and the gradual realization by defendants that the law could no longer hold up the consent decree as it was currently composed, the parties agreed to amendments that eliminated the use of racial classifications in student assignment. Over the next two chapters, I complete the story of court-mandated desegregation in San Francisco. Chapter 5 chronicles the gradual acceptance of choice as a means of achieving diversity and chapter 6 describes how the idea of neighborhood schools persisted through the 1990s and 2000s.

CHAPTER 5
Creating Diverse Schools through Choice

With the introduction of Educational Redesign in 1978, school choice became a much more prominent and legitimate feature of San Francisco's student assignment system. Through Redesign, the Temporary Attendance Permit (TAP) component of Horseshoe was rechristened Optional Enrollment Request (OER), and several new alternative schools and alternative programs within traditional schools were established and made available to all students, regardless of where they lived. In an attempt to close the loophole that TAP had created, Superintendent Alioto promised to closely monitor and strictly enforce the provision requiring that any approved OER request not adversely affect the racial balance of both the sending and receiving school. While the SFNAACP regarded TAP as a segregatory mechanism, Alioto's promise allowed the district to tout OER as its "primary voluntary desegregation" effort and a key component of Educational Redesign that assisted in the creation of a racially and ethnically diverse school district.[1] When the consent decree was approved in 1983, school choice was extended even further with a special provision that gave students residing in Bayview-Hunters Point an option to attend any other school in the district, with transportation provided.[2]

OER was a nine-month process that required a fair amount of planning. The district's Educational Placement Center (EPC) received requests during the winter and notified students of their placement by spring for enrollment in the fall. Two types of school choice requests were handled by the EPC—students wishing to enroll in an alternative school or program and students wishing to transfer out of their assigned school.[3] In random order, students were matched to their schools of choice until the racial and ethnic subgroup enrollment caps were reached. Following this, new assignments were made only if space became available, within the constraints of the caps. Preferences, each with their own weight, were given. An applicant with a sibling already attending the requested school was given the highest priority. In nearly every case, all applicants with this preference were accommodated.[4] Preferences were also given to applicants bumped from the school designated by their home address,[5] applicants with addresses from certain low-income zip codes,[6] and applicants who identified as Latino or African American. New applicants who did not receive their choice were placed in a school determined by the EPC based on home address and available transportation options. Students who did not receive their choice remained at their current school.

The OER program was popular. By the 1991–1992 school year, SFUSD processed well over eleven thousand transfer requests and approved approximately 60 percent of them. Nearly 40 percent of all SFUSD students were on optional enrollment permits, attending a school other than their designated school. SFUSD's 1992 annual report to the court proclaimed: "These numbers attest to the magnitude of the District's program of allowing maximum student and family choice within desegregation guidelines."[7] And although the district was now led by Ramon Cortines, the second superintendent since Alioto was forced out in 1985, the racial balance controls originally put in place by Alioto remained. During the first decade of the consent decree, only a handful of schools had been deemed racially identifiable (i.e., a racial or ethnic subgroup comprised greater than 45 percent of the student enrollment). This was a far cry from Horseshoe, when between one-quarter and one-third of the schools were racially identifiable, and even more so from the pre-desegregation era of the late 1960s, when more than three-quarters of the schools were racially identifiable (Table 15).

But OER was not without its faults. Although it was a widely accessed program, the district had trouble reaching some immigrant and Latino parents. Among the principal concerns of several community advocates brought to light during META's motion to intervene was the "lack of a concerted organized effort on the part of the District to meaningfully explain to Latino parents . . . OER procedures and to make the process accessible to them."[8] These concerns were echoed several years

Table 15. Percent of SFUSD Schools with at Least One Racial or Ethnic Group >45%

School Year	Total Number of SFUSD Schools	Number of Racially Identifiable Schools	Percent of Racially Identifiable Schools
1965–1966	81	69	85.2
1968–1969	83	65	78.3
1971–1972	85	27	31.8
1974–1975	91	25	27.5
1977–1978	94	25	26.6
1980–1981	94	22	23.4
1983–1984	101	11	10.9
1986–1987	104	2	1.9
1989–1990	103	3	2.9
1992–1993	102	1	1.0

Source: Declaration of Donald I. Barfield, Attachment C-5, C-7, *SFNAACP v. SFUSD* (DF1228, 4/11/01).

later by the court monitor, Stuart Biegel. "Too often, it is the parents with more money and more time who can obtain additional information regarding the OER process and alternative schools in general," wrote Biegel. "These realities raise issues of equal access that cannot and should not be ignored."[9] In addition to the need for better outreach, OER was still considered by many stakeholders to be a loophole—though not as large as TAP—for parents wishing to "game the system." Several stakeholders interviewed cautioned that "ethnicity on paper didn't mean the same in reality." As Mark Sanchez, a former teacher and two-term school board member, recalled, "You'd go in a school and you could see that it was eighty percent Black. But on paper, it wasn't. It was forty percent Black." Sanchez attributed this phenomenon in part to parents intentionally misidentifying the subgroup to which their child belonged so as to secure a more favorable assignment. Another charge was that families, including some living outside of San Francisco altogether, would falsely claim a home address in one of the priority zip codes.[10]

The share of students on optional enrollment permits steadily increased during the 1990s such that by the end of the decade, just over 56 percent of the district attended a school other than the one designated by home address.[11] In addition, the decade witnessed a gradual loosening of the once tightly controlled consent decree enrollment caps. Although some political observers consider longtime superintendent Bill Rojas to have been an active supporter of the consent decree, and while there is evidence to support this claim, the number of racially identifiable schools rapidly increased during his tenure.[12] For the 1992–1993 school year, the first complete term with Rojas as superintendent, SFUSD had only one racially identifiable school. However, by the 1998–1999 school year, the district reported thirty-four racially identifiable schools (see Figure 8).[13] Despite the resegregation taking place, Superintendent Rojas supported optional enrollment to the very end, describing it as a way to attract students to all corners of the district, as long as the schools were rigorous, well resourced, and of superior quality.[14]

The spring and summer months of 1999 were extremely demanding for the school board and central office staff. In addition to the Ho settlement, which produced the most significant change to San Francisco's student assignment system since the consent decree was first approved in 1983, SFUSD faced several other challenges. In March, the California State Assembly called for an external audit in order to investigate questionable spending practices of the Rojas administration.[15] In April, the *San Francisco Examiner* raised the possibility that the district manipulated standardized test score results.[16] And by May, the school board was embroiled in its perennial predicament of balancing the district's budget, this time with an expected shortfall of $17 million. Amid all of this, Superintendent Rojas resigned in order to take the helm of Dallas Independent School District. "This news couldn't have come at a worse time," remarked Kent Mitchell, president of the teachers' union. "We have to deal with assignment policy for next year, budget cutbacks, possible layoffs—issues that take leadership." School board member Jill Wynns agreed. "We are entering a period of high drama and anxiety," she remarked. "Board members have a tremendous responsibility to try to make this major transition go smoothly."[17] Even with the yearly increase in the number of racially identifiable schools on his watch, Rojas had been an ally of the SFNAACP. "We believe that Dr. Rojas showed leadership and went forward in an educationally sound manner," praised SFNAACP attorney Peter Cohn. "He was regularly working on equality

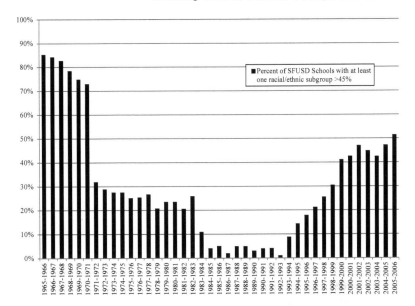

Figure 8. Racial identifiability in SFSUD schools, 1965–2006. Source: School years 1965–2001 from Exhibit, Declaration of Donald Barfield, Attachments C-5 and C-7, *SFNAACP v. SFUSD* (DF1228, 4/11/01). School years 2001–2006 from Research Planning and Accountability Department, SFUSD.

in the curriculum."[18] The departure of Rojas immediately led to questions about how the next superintendent would work with the various constituencies of the school district. A deputy superintendent filled in on an interim basis for the 1999–2000 school year before the district hired Arlene Ackerman, chancellor of D.C. Public Schools, to run the district beginning August 2000.[19]

Proposed Settlement, Phase II of the Consent Decree

David Ely, the state's expert, claimed that a student assignment system "that utilizes primarily, or entirely, socio-economic factors should not result in resegregation of the SFUSD schools," as long as there was sufficient monitoring and oversight.[20] The testimony Ely planned to present in court indicated to many that the district would propose a permanent student assignment plan for the 2000–2001 school year (and beyond) that would find a substitute for race and ethnicity in order to meet both the court's proscription on racial classifications and the district's goal of racial diversity.[21] And in fact, early drafts of the proposed new student assignment plan (tentatively called PNSAP) did just that. But as the plan developed, the district reported that such a system would be undesirable:

> Originally, it was theorized that using socio-economic status (SES) as a primary singular criterion and developing district guidelines using SES instead of race/ethnicity, would result in racially/ethnically diverse student populations. This did not actually happen. The District has concluded that, at this point in time, race/ethnicity must be considered as a part of the criteria used to assign students to schools to prevent schools becoming increasingly racially/ethnically segregated.[22]

The PNSAP that was ultimately submitted to the court proposed an index of diversity comprised of four characteristics that "describe students, and particularly may be indicators of specialized student learning needs."[23] Indicators assessing poverty level, academic achievement, and English language proficiency were to be combined with an applicant's racial and ethnic classification to create one of 624 possible diversity profiles.[24] Each school in the district would have a Composite Diversity Index (CDI) derived from the diversity profiles of the existing student population. For every open seat in a school, the assignment system would place the student that would best contribute to that school's CDI-calculated diversity. A new CDI score would be calculated after each additional new student was added. "There are no set percentages, caps, or guidelines for race and ethnicity that act to prevent the placement of any student," read the plan submitted to the court. "Rather, every student is considered for every seat every time a placement decision is made."[25] Assignments would occur over several rounds. For each school, siblings of current students and students needing special programs offered on-site would be assigned first.[26] Then, students living within a chosen school's "geographic proximity area" or in a district-designated preference zone would be assigned. Finally, if open seats remained, any other student who requested the school would be considered.[27] The PNSAP made no changes to Lowell High School's admission system. The policy of admitting students below Lowell's cutoff score on a "value-added" basis that included special consideration for underrepresented students of color would remain in place.[28]

With PNSAP, school choice became the central mechanism to place students in schools. Under former assignment systems, students were initially assigned to a school designated by home address. Only those applicants seeking an alternative school or wishing to transfer out of their designated school went through the OER process. In contrast, the PNSAP would not make an initial assignment based on address. Rather, all applicants were expected to choose up to five schools.[29] "The idea is that everyone should be proactive about choosing the schools they want, whether it's their neighborhood school or another one," remarked Jennie Horn, the district's enrollment supervisor.[30]

In the fall of 1999, when the district submitted PNSAP to the court, it noted that the previous student assignment system "defines diversity only in terms of race and ethnicity," while "the new plan defines diversity from a multidimensional perspective."[31] Since race and ethnicity classification was but one of four diversity factors, the district assured the court that the plan conformed to the consent decree settlement and was constitutional. The attorneys for the Ho plaintiffs disagreed. From their perspective, any use of racial and ethnic classification in the assignment of students was disallowed by the settlement. Furthermore, the Ho attorneys doubted that the PNSAP would pass the strict scrutiny standard.[32] On the issue of compliance with the consent decree settlement, paragraph C was the source of the dispute. Although district officials were permitted to consider many factors, including racial and ethnic diversity, in setting criteria for admissions, it could not "assign or admit any student to a particular school, class or program on the basis of the race or ethnicity of that student, except as related to the language needs of the student or otherwise to assure compliance with controlling federal or state law."[33] In other words, SFUSD could have the goal of racial and ethnic diversity, but the means by which it would achieve that goal could not include the assignment of students on the basis of racial classification.[34] On the issue of strict scrutiny, the district argued that a lesser legal standard applied.

In December 1999, a frustrated Judge Orrick rejected the PNSAP because it "expressly considered the race of each student in violation of the Equal Protection Clause" and thereby "violated the terms of the settlement agreement."[35] With school assignments due in the spring, the district was now facing a difficult situation. "It's showtime. And we've got

65,000 school children and their parents not clear about what school, particular schools their children are going to," remarked Orrick. "And the court is not disposed to defer decisions any longer on this matter."[36] Rather than revising the PNSAP so that it was entirely race neutral, the school board decided to continue the default plan for another year, even though doing so would likely increase racial identifiability at several schools. "The judge seems to think you can address the effects of segregation without considering race. Try as we might, we haven't been able to come up with a mechanism that will allow integrated schools" without using race and ethnicity, observed school board member Dan Kelly. "So in the interest of continuity, we're going to go with the plan we used last year, though the impacts are very negative."[37] The decision was derided by the SFNAACP as "throwing in the towel."[38]

Although the use of racial classifications had been removed from the July 1999 settlement, the original goal of the consent decree remained intact:

> A major goal . . . shall be to eliminate racial/ethnic segregation or identifiability in any S.F.U.S.D. school, program, or classroom and to achieve the broadest practicable distribution throughout the system of students from the racial and ethnic groups which comprise the student enrollment of the S.F.U.S.D.[39]

Additionally, the settlement did not address how academic achievement gaps would be handled under the PNSAP. The parties to the consent decree, recognizing that reaching its goal of desegregation would "require continued and accelerated efforts to achieve academic excellence throughout the S.F.U.S.D.," compelled the district to address student achievement in a concerted manner.[40] This was regarded as an essential component of the decree.[41] However, as David Levine observed, "what was particularly discouraging about the PNSAP was its utter lack of attention to educational quality."

Following Superintendent Arlene Ackerman's arrival in August 2000, the work to devise a new student assignment system was folded into a larger effort to develop a comprehensive plan that sought to address both diversity and academic achievement. By spring 2001, the plan, titled Excellence for All, was adopted by the board of education and formally introduced to the public.[42] "We are focused on our children's success," stated Ackerman. "This comprehensive plan is a blueprint for success."[43] The plan outlined three ways to achieve diversity: a new student assignment system, a more robust recruitment strategy, and the strategic placement of programs (for example, language immersion was a popular program that had potential to draw a wide variety of students from across the district to schools that would otherwise be disfavored).[44] Excellence for All became the district's interpretation of the court mandate. "Compliance with the consent decree equals compliance with Excellence for All," remarked Matt Kelemen, special assistant to the superintendent.[45]

Despite Judge Orrick's ruling against the PNSAP, the district's assignment plan once again proposed the use of race. In this version, seven race-neutral factors would first be used to assign students. However, if an incoming class was not diverse enough, students would be reassigned using race as an eighth factor. "How can you look at diversity without considering race?," wondered Ackerman. "We believe we will achieve real diversity by using the other factors. Race will be used only as needed."[46] The plan faced immediate criticism from the Ho attorneys. "Even though they're saying race is a last resort, the plan is in violation of the agreement and is unconstitutional," stated Levine.[47] In April, Judge Orrick appointed Thomas Klitgaard as special master to facilitate negotiations among attorneys for all parties.[48] After two and half months, they reached a preliminary settlement, referred to as the "2001 settlement."[49]

Following a fairness hearing in the fall, Judge Orrick required the district to address concerns raised by recently released reports of the consent decree monitor and the consent decree advisory committee. In addition, Orrick approved three amendments to the consent decree.[50] One, the termination date was pushed back to December 31, 2005, with desegregation funding from the state continuing through the end of the 2005–2006 school year.[51] Two, the allocation of desegregation funds from the state would be more closely tracked and targeted to the specific goals of the decree.[52] Three, the parameters regarding student assignment would read, in part: "The SFUSD shall not use or include race or ethnicity as a criterion or factor to assign any student to any school class, classroom, or program, and shall not use race or ethnicity as a primary or predominant consideration in setting any such criteria or factors."[53]

Excellence for All, Diversity Index Lottery

In compliance with Orrick's order, Excellence for All was revised in January 2002 and students were assigned based on a new system, the "Diversity Index," for the 2002–2003 school year.[54] Along with the change in student assignment was a change in court supervision. The two cases— *SFNAACP v. SFUSD* and *Ho v. SFUSD*—were reassigned to William H. Alsup in January 2002 following the retirement of Judge Orrick at the end of 2001.[55] Similar to PNSAP, school choice was at the heart of the Diversity Index. All students changing schools would submit an application listing up to five choices. "SFUSD maintains an enrollment process that enables parents to express preferences regarding which schools, in addition to their attendance area school, they would like their child to attend," stated the district's plan.[56] If there were sufficient seats to accommodate all applicants for a particular school and grade, those applicants would be assigned without consideration to the effects the assignment might have on a school's diversity. However, if there were more applicants than seats available at a particular school and grade, the system would assign students through what was called the Diversity Index Lottery. Under the lottery, a diversity profile was created for each applicant through six binary indicators: an SES indicator based on the student's family's participation in the free or reduced lunch program, CalWORKs (California's public assistance program), or public housing; an academic achievement indicator based on the student's standardized test scores for third graders and above, the student's kindergarten assessment score for first and second graders, and whether the student attended preschool for incoming kindergarteners; and four additional indicators based on whether a student's mother attended college, the student was proficient in English, the sending school of the applicant was above or below the 40th percentile in California's accountability measure (Academic Performance Index), and the student's home language was English.[57] The system would be modified over the years. For the 2004–2005 term, applicants could choose up to seven schools, rather than five. In the 2006–2007 school year, the language proficiency factor was eliminated, and the following school year the mother's educational background factor was eliminated and an extreme poverty factor was added in its place.[58]

As with the prior system, a "preassignment" preference allowing siblings to be placed at the same school was given. Similarly, students with specialized learning needs had priority to those schools with an appropriate program (for instance, English learners exiting a newcomer program and entering a bilingual program and special education students in Special Day and Inclusion classes).[59] This was not an insignificant group of students. In 2002, at least 40 percent of all elementary students were English learners and approximately 12 percent of the entire district enrollment was classified as special education.[60] Traditional schools would first consider applicants who lived within its attendance zone. Alternative schools would consider all applicants at once. As in PNSAP, the applicant contributing the most to the overall diversity of the school would be assigned to each available seat, and after each individual assignment, the diversity index would be recalculated.

Excellence for All also introduced a new plan for Lowell High School. Admissions would occur through three "bands." Band One assigned 70 percent of Lowell's available seats and was based on grade point average (GPA) and standardized test scores.[61] Band Two assigned 15 percent of available seats. Students who met the GPA requirement but did not gain entrance through Band One could be nominated based on factors including extenuating circumstances, community service, and leadership. Under Band Three, the remaining 15 percent of seats were assigned to applicants from underrepresented feeder schools that received a nomination from their principal.

Almost immediately, it became apparent that the Diversity Index would be unable to meet the consent decree's goal of reducing racial and ethnic identifiability. Beyond the restriction on using race and ethnicity as factors in student assignment, the sorting mechanism only went into effect in situations where there were fewer spaces than applicants. In other words, the mechanism that sought to create diversity through race-neutral means affected only a subset of students and schools rather than all students and all schools. During its initial year, the Diversity Index was not a factor in the assignment of students to 17 percent of the district schools, including 24 percent of the district's middle schools.[62] An additional challenge was that a substantial number of students did not participate in the school choice process. These students, who tended to be among the more educationally disadvantaged in the district, were "assigned by default" by the EPC and often were used to fill seats in underenrolled, underperforming schools.[63]

Stuart Biegel, the consent decree monitor, warned that the district was rapidly resegregating. Thirty-four of the district's 114 schools were severely segregated (defined by Biegel as a school in which 60 percent or more of the enrollment in a grade came from a single racial/ethnic subgroup) during the 2002–2003 school year, up from 20 schools three years before. After an additional two years, the number of schools severely segregated at one or more grade levels would reach 43.[64] "There is an apparent lack of congruence between the current Diversity Index factors and the goals of Paragraphs 12 and 13," wrote Biegel, referring to the sections of the consent decree that required the elimination of racial and ethnic identifiability.[65] The schools that were most severely segregated on the basis of race and ethnicity were also the schools determined to be the most diverse, based on the six diversity indicators of the index.

"School Reform Begins with Enrollment"

In the fall of 1999, amid mounting concern and disillusionment with the SFUSD, a group of three hundred parents gathered for the kick-off event of Parents for Public Schools-San Francisco (PPS-SF).[66] The newly formed organization had embarked on a campaign to recommit parents to the local public school system. "Schools are not isolated islands in a community. They need the support of the whole community in order to succeed," wrote PPS-SF founders Sandra Halladey and Deena Zacharin. "We value public education as a community enterprise. We are organizing to promote and focus attention on the public schools and to work for improvement. We want excellent public schools for all our children."[67] Earlier in the year, Halladey attracted attention to her cause with an op-ed excoriating the *San Francisco Chronicle* for presenting a skewed depiction of the city's "beleaguered" public schools. "We need to stop scaring people away from the public schools and, instead, support efforts to improve them," she urged.[68] Shortly thereafter, the Zellerbach Family Foundation provided funding for Halladey to attend a conference sponsored by Parents for Public Schools, a national organization founded in Jackson, Mississippi, with local chapters throughout the country.[69] Soon after the conference, the San Francisco chapter was established. For Halladey, her work with PPS-SF was informed by her personal politics. "I really believe strongly that public education is the foundation of democracy, and if we have good public schools, then a lot of the other problems kind of go away later," she stated. "It might be a little bit naïve, but I think it's a very political decision. And I was *really* disturbed that in progressive San Francisco so many people that were really 'right on' politically and wearing their politics on their sleeves would then send their kids to very expensive private schools, and I just saw such a disconnect in that."[70]

As it was founded just as the district was transitioning from a student assignment system based on race-conscious subgroup enrollment caps to the race-neutral Diversity Index, much of the work of PPS-SF involved helping parents understand and navigate the student assignment process so that they could make the best possible choice for their children. The group also pushed the district's Educational Placement Center (EPC) to make its work more parent friendly. These efforts addressed some long-standing issues with the amount of time required by parents to navigate school choice systems. For years, the procedure to enroll children had been labor intensive. In the past, rather than employing a more orderly process, alternative schools considered new students on a rolling basis. This led parents who had the means to do so to camp overnight on school grounds days before registration began.[71] But even after the EPC eliminated the practice, between identifying schools, visiting them, and filling out the OER application, parents were required to devote countless hours of work to the enrollment process.[72] In addition, advocates criticized the EPC for not doing enough outreach and education to parents. "There was no desire to really recruit families into the public schools," said Halladey.[73] The OER program, though widely used by many parents, remained a mystery for others because of language barriers and insufficient community education. According to Hydra Mendoza, a former school board commissioner and former executive director of PPS-SF, the Diversity Index created its own tension once in place because its purpose was ambiguous and the implementation unclear for many parents.[74] In addition to an opaque application process, the consensus among San Franciscans was that SFUSD had only a handful of good schools, when at least in the minds of district officials and PPS-SF members, there were many good schools that operated under the radar of parents.[75] "I just knew that there was a huge opportunity and potential to recruit families into the public schools and explain the application process, because there was so much confusion about it," recalled Halladey. "So, I was just sort of like a squeaky wheel, saying, 'You need to do this. You need to do that.' And no one was listening."[76]

The task was clear. "We needed to really change the public perception of our public schools and really get people to start enrolling their kids," recalled Deena Zacharin. "The first step to school reform, really, was everybody embracing the schools and sending their kids" to public schools.[77] The organization set out to identify "hidden gems" in the district—schools that were on the rise academically but that parents might otherwise overlook. In time, PPS-SF grew into a well-regarded intermediary between the district and parents. On behalf of the district, the organization promoted public school options to parents and helped them with the application process. On behalf of parents, the organization provided information to the school board and the district on the concerns and priorities of the community. With this scope of work, PPS-SF saw itself as a "critical friend of the district," working to catalyze improvement rather than merely serving as its publicity arm.[78]

Very early on in the organization's history, Sandra Halladey's personal view of student assignment shifted. The lack of support among many of her neighbors for the local public school initially led her to establish PPS-SF. "We should have neighborhood schools," Halladey recalled thinking. "Why are there people from my neighborhood (there's ten kids on the street) why aren't they all going to Alvarado [Elementary School]? Why are they going to Rooftop or Claire Lilienthal or Clarendon or this private school or that private school? Why aren't we all going to our local school?"[79] But as she began to examine the issue "from an education policy standpoint," she came to a different conclusion:

> I realized that it's not fair to have neighborhood schools, and realized that it can't just be about where you can afford to live. So, I really changed. And then, I met people all over the city who really wanted to have choices. So, I actually changed, really changed my position a lot once I got to know more about the subject. I think it's a very easy call to say "we want neighborhood schools" if you're not really looking at the whole picture.[80]

Halladey's shift in position was solidified at the PPS national conference where she met some Black community organizers from the South. She recalled a conversation where they advised her: "You know, you shouldn't be talking about neighborhood schools, that's segregation. You really need to get educated on this." PPS-SF professed a desire that school quality improve. But rather than advancing a strict neighborhood school rationale for student assignment, PPS-SF set its sights on improving school quality districtwide with the recognition that choice—including the choice for a neighborhood school—was an important value for parents.[81]

Over time, public school choice became a legitimate and increasingly central component of student assignment in San Francisco. Under Horseshoe, the Temporary Attendance Permit was understood to be a loophole, exploited by parents as a means to bypass the district's desegregation effort. With Educational Redesign, school choice along with the addition of several new alternative and magnet schools enabled the district to tout a voluntary desegregation complement to its designated schools system. While students were assigned to schools based on home address (primarily neighborhood-based, but with several "jump zones" in order to ensure compliance with the enrollment caps), Optional Enrollment Requests (OERs) allowed parents to choose alternate schools. In the first decade of the decree, during the 1980s, enrollment caps were tightly enforced. OERs were not to be approved if they had an impact on either the sending or receiving school's racial identifiability. But in the second decade of the decree, the constraints of the enrollment caps were much looser. With the second phase of the consent decree, under the Diversity Index, choice became the centerpiece of student assignment. No initial assignments were made, and all students were expected to choose the schools they wished to attend. Choice was constrained by nonrace diversity factors in order to comply with the consent decree's still-in-effect mandate to eliminate racial identifiability. But choice was the central component, nonetheless.

In 2004, reflecting on the history of student assignment, Henry Der lamented the limited success of the SFUSD in integrating its schools. Because the "forces of resegregation" may be too difficult to overcome, the district must instead determine how to make the best of the situation. Choice has a role, he offered, if San Francisco could figure out how parental choice could be "leveraged" to create strong schools throughout the city.[82] Former PPS-SF executive director Ellie Rossiter agreed, remarking: "Every parent will say that they prefer to have a quality school in their neighborhood, but if they don't, they'd rather choose something else. And it doesn't matter what neighborhood or what parent you're talking to, almost every single one of them will choose that. Those who say they want neighborhood schools are also choosing, they just happen to be choosing their neighborhood school. So, choice is a big priority for families."[83]

CHAPTER 6
The Enduring Appeal of Neighborhood Schools

I think everyone agrees it has to work better, but the simplest thing to do is not going to be the best thing for kids, in the board's opinion and in my opinion. Right? Neighborhood schools. I mean, it's not even that simple, because there's lots of neighborhoods that have way more kids than school space, there's a lot of neighborhoods that have way more school space than kids. And so, someone's going to get juggled in there somewhere.

—RUTH GRABOWSKI, PARENTS ADVISORY COUNCIL

It's a sort of bread and butter issue—it's like apple pie and the American way. You say neighborhood schools, and it resonates with everybody.

—ARLENE ACKERMAN, SUPERINTENDENT OF SCHOOLS

The position of the attorneys for the Ho plaintiffs and the court was that the actual crafting of a new student assignment system rested with the district.[1] As long as the conditions laid out by the revised consent decree were met, the district could determine a system of its own choosing. The solution—the Diversity Index—relied on six race-neutral diversity factors that would, ideally, achieve the goal of eliminating racial segregation or identifiability throughout the system. While settlement was an appropriate solution for everyone involved in the legal case, it created rifts throughout the broader community, particularly among constituents who favored a neighborhood assignment system and who viewed the Diversity Index as a less than ideal resolution to the enrollment caps called for in the original version of the consent decree. Over time, frustration with the Diversity Index only increased, with a large part of the opposition coming from proponents of neighborhood schools.[2]

Some objected to the Diversity Index by dismissing the six indicators as nothing more than proxies for race.[3] "On the surface this plan is indistinguishable from a program based on race," wrote one such parent in a letter to the court. "I think the result will be to continue denying White children an equal chance to participate in San Francisco schools and create new segments of children denied access, such as Black children who do not qualify for lunch subsidies."[4] This did not pose a concern for the Ho attorneys, though. "I think we were willing to accept fairly obvious proxies for race, because we weren't trying to stop them from having a diverse school system," remarked Daniel Girard. "We were just trying to stop them from assigning students based on race."[5] Furthermore, the court determined that the legal standard for challenging a facially race-neutral plan had not been met. "There is no evidence here that the factors chosen by the District for its diversity index correlate so strongly with race that they cannot be explained as anything but a proxy for race," wrote Judge Orrick. "Each of the factors chosen by the District for use in its diversity index can apply to students of any race or ethnicity."[6]

The decision to settle and the terms of the settlement that allowed for the Diversity Index to be implemented was an issue for debate within CADC and AALF. Contention was, at least in part, generated from the Ho lawsuit's "double prong" approach, whereby first CADC and then AALF would focus on building political and community support, while Daniel Girard and his team of attorneys had final say on the legal strategy that would best serve the class.[7] For some CADC and AALF members, a trial was risky. While in all likelihood, the Ho plaintiffs would prevail and the enrollment caps would be eliminated, a trial win might have jeopardized the state desegregation funds attached to the consent decree. "Cutting off our nose to spite our face," was how CADC and AALF board member Henry Louie described this possible outcome. "The loss of $35 million [would] affect all the students in the district."[8] However, others argued that the state desegregation funding had been misspent and had done little over the last decade and a half to close the achievement gap.[9] In addition, the prospect of proceeding with a trial was appealing to some. "This was always supposed to be a Supreme Court fight. That was the hope. And we had the legal issues to take it all the way there," stated AALF board member Lee Cheng. "Signing off [i.e., deferring to counsel] on settling Ho was probably the biggest regret of my legal career." Cheng continued: "In fact, the legal issues that could have been resolved in *Ho* were not really resolved at all until Seattle and Jefferson County two years ago. And, candidly, I think if we hadn't settled the case in 2000, we could have avoided [the Supreme Court affirmative action cases] *Grutter* and *Gratz*."[10] Girard agrees with Cheng on the import of the case: "I think the Supreme Court would have loved to get their hands on this case."

Support for a neighborhood-based system from CADC and AALF was expressed as a particular sort of choice: parents should be allowed the option to choose the public school their child attends, through their housing choices. Although the Diversity Index asked parents to select up to five (and, eventually, seven) schools, the choice was constrained by the seven diversity indicators. "The proposed enrollment policy overemphasizes diversity and sacrifices parental choice and the integrity concept of neighborhood schools," wrote CADC education committee chair Victor Seeto to Judge Orrick. "The assignment system is not neutral or evenhanded. . . . It is biased against the middle class. Its potential disruptiveness can lead to an exodus of middle class parents from the school as had been demonstrated by the departure of White pupils from the school since the 80s."[11] Similarly, Henry Louie, then vice president of AALF, expressed "grave concerns regarding the District's proposed student assignment plan." SFUSD "is under the misguided belief that its latest machination at social engineering via student assignment by diversity index, will improve the academic achievement of heretofore poorly performing students," wrote Louie to the court. "The District may have social and political motives and agendas to use its Diversity Index plan. However, these agendas and motives should not run counter to widely held and proven pedagogy for educational achievement and excellence: parental choice and parental and community involvement in our children's education."[12]

Apprehension with the Diversity Index emerged from other sectors. Naomi Gray, a parent advocate and president of the Urban Institute for African American Affairs, had worked for years with African American families in Bayview-Hunters Point.[13] Gray, along with prominent community activist Espanola Jackson, Bayview-Hunters Point Democratic Club president Harvey Matthews, and former Parent Teacher Association president for Gloria R. Davis Academic Middle School Diane Mooring, argued for the dissolution of the consent decree because so little had been accomplished to improve the quality of schools in the neighborhood. The parties "failed to get input from the community before deciding to file for an extension," wrote Gray on behalf of the others. "The NAACP has been as negligent as the School District in keeping parents and community aware of the progress or lack of progress."[14] This had been an ongoing issue in the neighborhood. Several years earlier, Gray delivered a statement to the Health, Family, and Environment Committee of the Board of Supervisors severely rebuking the district and the SFNAACP. Despite a consent decree that funneled resources and attention to the Bayview-Hunters Point neighborhood, the situation remained dire.[15] African American students were among "the lowest underachievers in the District," according to Gray, with a mean grade point average of 1.9. "The NAACP is responsible for playing along with the District making the Consent Decree useless," she testified. "It's time to make the Consent Decree meet its mandate by putting extra money in the Bayview to upgrade schools and increase parent participation."[16]

The first cohort of Diversity Index students was assigned in the spring of 2002. Most of the sixteen thousand students (primarily students entering the gateway grades of kindergarten, sixth grade, and ninth grade) received one of their top choices. And many families that requested neighborhood schools were accommodated.[17] "It all worked out," remarked relieved parent Concepcion Segarra to the *San Francisco Chronicle* after successfully enrolling her twins at Buena Vista. "I think we have to remember that we live in a big city and have to deal with bureaucracy at every turn."[18] But many parents were unsatisfied or confused with the Diversity Index. The assignment system developed for the original consent decree adopted neighborhood attendance boundaries, allowing parents to anticipate school assignment (and to request, if so desired, an optional enrollment).[19] Under the default plan, in place from 1999 to 2002, while enrollment caps were eliminated, school attendance boundaries were maintained. For the Diversity Index, applicants to schools with attendance areas (in other words, nonalternative schools) were considered in two waves. Those living within a school's attendance boundary were considered first and assigned as long as seats were available and "the students contribute[d] to the diversity of the school based on the diversity factors."[20] If, after this wave, open seats remained, all students requesting the school would be considered.[21] So while the neighborhood attendance zones were preserved, the ability to anticipate school assignment was lost, particularly for the top-scoring, popular schools in the west side of the city that would receive as many as five applications for every available seat. Unsurprisingly, this upset families who had made housing decisions based on neighborhood school preferences.

After the first cohort of Diversity Index assignments were made in the spring, the consent decree monitor urged the district to provide more clarity on the system and to make the process more user friendly: "Throughout the course of our systematic monitoring efforts this past spring, we found that many district officials, school site administrators, teachers, and parents had great difficulty understanding the basic procedures and requirements of the new system."[22] In particular, accessible information on the Diversity Index had failed to adequately reach many low-income African American and Latino families living in the east side neighborhoods, who disproportionately failed to meet the enrollment deadline, thus limiting their access to popular schools. The monitor urged the district to redouble its community education, outreach, and counseling efforts to improve participation.[23] But variation in enrollment participation rates would remain a troubling issue in the years to come.

During the summer prior to the 2002–2003 school year, pressure from west-side neighborhoods, particularly from Chinese American families, was mounting. At the center of contention was the lack of space available at the two west-side high schools: Lincoln in the Sunset District and Washington in the Richmond District. In a scheme that was described by political observers as "bizarre" and "pandering," Supervisor Leland Yee, who represented the Sunset District and formerly served two terms on the school board, proposed an east-west split of the school district.[24] The resulting small district on the east side, home to the majority of low-performing schools, would enroll predominantly low-income Latino, Asian, and Black students; the resulting district on the west side, with the majority of high-achieving schools, would enroll predominantly middle-class White and Chinese students. "What he is pushing is transparently racist, reprehensible and un-San Franciscan," wrote Al Magary, former president of the Lowell High School PTA.[25] Yee, a candidate for the California state assembly district that included the west side of San Francisco, initially announced his proposal only to the Chinese-language media.

"Over the last 16 years, give or take a few, the San Francisco Unified School District has been one of the most, if not the most integrated school district in the country," said Michael Harris of the Lawyers' Committee for Civil Rights. "This proposal now going forward would have the opposite effect."[26] Yee's proposal, dismissed in a *Chronicle* editorial as "not worthy of serious consideration," was quickly countered by a resolution carried by Supervisor Mark Leno, himself a candidate for a state assembly district that included the east side of San Francisco.[27] Leno's resolution called on the Board of Supervisors to support "a unified school district, not a divided one," to encourage efforts to "maintain diversity in our schools and achieve educational equity for all youth," and to support "a school district policy of parental choice, allowing all children access to any school in the district when possible."[28] The resolution was unanimously adopted by the Board of Supervisors (even Yee voted for it) and approved by Mayor Willie Brown. Although talk of a split district continued, even Yee eventually acknowledged that such a move would never gain the necessary traction.[29]

The following year, the Diversity Index was tweaked such that students who qualified for multiple schools were assigned to their most preferred school (rather than the school to which they contribute the most grade-level diversity).[30] The district also made a concerted effort to improve its responsiveness and streamline the process of enrollment. But as with the first year of implementation, substantial numbers of students were unhappy with their placement. Throughout the spring of 2003, from March until May, school board meetings took place in front of overflow crowds of parents, advocates, and students. Several times the audience reached into the hundreds, necessitating makeshift overflow rooms. Similar to its debut year, for the 2003–2004 school year, most students were assigned to a school of their choice, and many received their first-choice school.[31] But for some families, the system was still flawed.

As was the case the previous year, the main challengers to the Diversity Index were Chinese American families from the west side of San Francisco. Many felt that, like the enrollment caps before, the current system was discriminatory. "Why is it every year that the people who get hurt are the Asian people," complained Sam Low at a school board meeting. "The Diversity Index is not fair."[32] In agreement was John Shek: "It's 99 percent Asian children that get assigned to schools away from their neighborhood."[33] At an April meeting, the school board made further modifications, including revising assignments so that elementary and middle school students were assigned to schools within two miles of their homes.[34] John Zhao, a parent advocate who for several months was the de facto spokesperson for the demonstrators, was hopeful that if an amenable resolution could be found for the early grades, the district would eventually find one for high school.[35] But the school board made no changes to the assignment policy for high school students. The *Chinese Times* reported on an impromptu gathering of several hundred students and parents immediately following the board meeting. Zhao called on elementary and middle school parents to stand united in protest with high school parents. Discussing what their collective response should be, Zhao asked the gathered crowd if they should submit to the school district's assignments. In response, the crowd shouted, "We do not accept!"[36]

Meeting with a group of Chinese American parents the following week, Superintendent Arlene Ackerman explained: "I understand and I recognize the fact that the placement of the students in various high schools is the issue. I don't know if there is anything I could do to make everyone happy. But I hope we can find a place where the parents are happy with their children's placements."[37] Parents focused on Washington and Lincoln, the two high-achieving high schools in the west side of the city. Both schools had large Chinese American enrollments. While just over one-third of the district's incoming ninth graders were Chinese American, nearly half at Washington and three-fifths at Lincoln were Chinese American.[38] Furthermore, contrary to the complaints from some parents that many students assigned to these schools came from outside the neighborhood, nearly 80 percent of Lincoln's incoming class lived in the school's attendance area.[39] However, not every student could be accommodated. Each of the schools received several thousand enrollment requests for fewer than six hundred spaces.[40]

By the end of April, the situation intensified as positions hardened. At a special school board hearing on student assignment, Zhao's group of parents successfully halted the proceedings. The group silenced several proponents of the new assignment system with chants of "We want neighborhood schools! We want neighborhood schools!"[41] Several incoming ninth graders who were placed at Balboa High School arrived at the meeting to encourage parents of Balboa assignees to attend an upcoming open house, but they opted not to speak because of the intimidating presence of the neighborhood schools proponents.[42] Dana Woldow, an active member of PPS-SF whose son was to speak on behalf of Balboa, remarked: "It is unfortunate that in their single-minded determination to allow only those who shared their viewpoint to be heard last night, the parents prevented those who might have been willing to explore other options from receiving any useful information."[43] Caroline Grannan, also active in PPS-SF, agreed and urged the protestors to "do some soul-searching and rethink their strategy" after her son was shouted down at the meeting.[44]

In May, upon hearing that the school district was planning a $295 million school facilities bond initiative, between seventy-five and one hundred parents who opposed the student assignment system confronted Ackerman at her district office. They pushed past a security guard and demanded an immediate meeting with her and her staff. One angry parent asked, "If my child cannot attend a neighborhood school, why is SFUSD asking us to support education bonds?"[45] The superintendent granted the meeting, which quickly became heated, and accounts of what happened next vary.[46] Ackerman reported that parents grabbed her clothing and yelled at her as she attempted to leave a rapidly escalating situation, while Zhao stated that he never saw a parent touch the superintendent. The police were called, and after board of education commissioners Emilio Cruz and Eddie Chin addressed the parents, the police stayed to monitor the remainder of the meeting. "We understand that they are passionate about [the enrollment process]," a shaken Ackerman remarked. "But the behavior was just so unacceptable and out of control."[47]

While parents may have had their children's interests in mind, there was "an ugly undercurrent of racism from some members of the group," editorialized the *San Francisco Chronicle*.[48] Ackerman labeled a few as racists who opposed their assignments because of negative stereotypes of Black and Latino students. Over the course of the neighborhood schools campaign, "they've said racist things I hadn't heard since the late sixties," Ackerman stated. "Talking about 'In that neighborhood, my child might be raped!'"[49] In the beginning, "it was sort of untethered," recalled former special assistant to the superintendent Matt Kelemen:

> There were people who would come up to the microphone and talk about "those people" on the other side of town and they would talk, there were some really nasty racial insults hurled around. So, people were not very schooled in how to sort of make a case that would be acceptable to a wider audience. . . . By the second year, that was all gone and it was all about just neighborhood and proximity and being a family and caring for elderly grandparents and all the kinds of stories that people had.[50]

"It's there," remarked Ackerman. "Just below the liberal surface there is this sort of insidious racist stuff that goes on around ethnicity." Part of the problem was that the district had not adequately "educated parents about why we have a desegregation plan or about other neighborhoods," said school board commissioner Eric Mar, concerned about the propagation of an unfair characterization of Chinese parents. "This is a culture clash between an African American superintendent who came from outside the district and parents who have concerns about their children's safety, the quality of some of the schools, and who want their kids close to home. I understand that. I live in the Sunset, so I know how far away these other schools feel."[51] Still, Mar opposed a neighborhood schools system: "We still have to deal with the inequities in the system, and neighborhood schools aren't the answer."[52]

Over the summer, Zhao's loose association of Chinese American parents split in two. Several decided to form Parents for Neighborhood Schools Association (PFNSA); others were wary of formal structure and remained with Zhao.[53] Ahead of a school boycott planned by both PFNSA and Zhao's group, Ackerman offered to meet once more with parents who had yet to accept a school assignment offer by the district. Zhao's group accepted the offer and agreed to back out of the boycott. Many of these parents accepted their students' original assignment to Galileo High School, located near Chinatown, once the district agreed to send a school bus to pick up their children. Additionally, the school district extended additional Galileo assignment offers to other parents of Zhao's group, and many of these parents also accepted their amended assignment to Galileo. PFNSA, however, went forward with the boycott, and fifty-eight of their parents vowed to keep their children out of school until space was made available for them at Lincoln or Washington. "We will wait every day until we get our school," PFNSA vice president Catherine Chan promised.[54] A couple dozen PFNSA families sustained the boycott until it was called off in early October following a compromise with the district that sent some students to Galileo and others to charter schools in the Sunset and the Excelsior neighborhoods.[55] Looking back on the campaign, Zhao remarked: "*Brown v. Board of Education* is not applicable in today's San Francisco. It's not a racial issue, it's a fairness issue: [Chinese Americans] are forced out of our own neighborhood."[56]

The STAR and Dream Schools Initiatives

While Superintendent Ackerman was contending with overenrolled schools in the west-side neighborhoods of the city, she was also seeking ways to improve the academic performance of underenrolled schools on the east side. During the first years of her tenure, she implemented several programs, large and small, throughout the Mission, Bayview-Hunters Point, and their surrounding neighborhoods.[57] "There's not one answer to how you improve academic achievement," said Elois Brooks, the district's chief academic officer. "Real change will come when we get the right combination of things."[58] Ackerman incorporated a weighted student formula budgeting system in Excellence for All.[59] There were two key aspects to the plan. First, a dollar amount was calculated for each student. Those that tended to be more expensive to educate—students from low-income households, English learners, and special education students, for example—brought additional funds to the schools that enrolled them. Second, the system afforded some control over school budgets to site councils comprised of principals, teachers, and parents. If an issue arose that was particular to a school (for instance, the need to improve English language arts scores), its site council could more nimbly respond (say, by purchasing additional materials). The program was piloted at Bret Harte Elementary in Bayview-Hunters Point. "The people who are the closest to the kids are given power to make decisions," stated an impressed Cheryl Curtis, principal of Bret Harte. "I don't think parents had ever been treated with such respect." The plan was also welcomed by public education advocates. "I think it's very exciting," remarked Sherrie Rosenberg, president of the San Francisco PTA. "It will be a lot of work for those on the site council, but they will have the ability to decide how funds are spent so that children are well served."[60] And while union leaders may have originally been circumspect, they raised no serious objections to the plan.[61]

A second program component of Excellence for All, Students and Teachers Achieving Results (STAR), sought to "increase student achievement at underperforming schools by providing targeted interventions at the school sites."[62] By 2002, thirty-nine schools located primarily in the eastern neighborhoods of San Francisco had been placed into the program.[63] Some but not all of these schools were also targeted for assistance by the consent decree. "The real distinction, as I see it, is that STAR Schools classifications look at issues of performance whereas the Consent Decree is looking more at vestiges of discrimination," remarked Matt Kelemen, special assistant to the superintendent.[64] STAR schools benefited from supplementary personnel, extra support from the district central office, and various additional resources.[65] STAR was hailed as a successful strategy.[66] But the program did not foster greater interest in these schools from nonneighborhood parents. This concerned Stuart Biegel, the consent decree monitor. "The mandate of the decree has always included desegregation as a strategy for improving education quality as well as maximizing equal educational opportunity," cautioned the monitor. "We urge the members of this taskforce and the relevant district officials to develop and implement forceful, concrete steps that directly address current resegregation patterns."[67]

In March 2004, the consent decree monitor filed a supplemental report to the court describing the failure of the district to meet the desegregation goals of the consent decree. The number of schools severely segregated was larger than previously anticipated, and there was no indication that the trend would reverse in the near future. Data addressing the consent decree's goal of academic achievement was equally startling. The monitor noted that as a group, African American students in San Francisco performed worse than their African American counterparts in other urban districts across the state.[68] In response, Judge Alsup held an evidentiary hearing in August and set a September deadline for parties to propose changes that would increase racial diversity.[69] "But no one came forward with a motion to modify the student assignment plan," stated Alsup. "The same discredited diversity index was left in place."[70]

Instead, the district focused on closing the achievement gap by moving forward on an initiative that had been announced earlier in the year. "Dream Schools" was a controversial program to improve the performance of the most troubled schools in the east-side neighborhoods of the city. The schools implemented so-called back-to-basics efforts, such as longer school days and some Saturday classes, college preparatory coursework, tutoring, and college and career planning services. Parents were asked to sign a contract pledging their support, and students were required to wear uniforms.[71] Dream Schools will give "private school educational opportunities for public school students," Superintendent Ackerman proclaimed.[72] For its inaugural year, three schools in Bayview-Hunters Point were selected.[73] Although children from anywhere in San Francisco could enroll, 70 percent of the students lived in the neighborhood. "She didn't think that schools had to be integrated," longtime district employee and consultant Hoover Liddell surmised. "She felt as though even if they were segregated, if they did get the good education, that kids could learn."[74] In her words to the *San Francisco Examiner*, she stated, "if our children are going to go to segregated schools let them be the best schools we can give them."[75]

Dream School positions were open to staff throughout the district. Akin to reconstitution under the Rojas superintendency, current staff at the three new Dream Schools were required to reapply for their jobs. However, unlike reconstitution, in which displaced teachers had no guarantee to open jobs elsewhere in the district, current staff not hired for Dream School positions would be offered similar positions elsewhere in the district. Officials with the United Educators of San Francisco (UESF) were initially opposed to the requirement. "The teachers are not the problem, and that's the implication of this," stated Linda Plack, vice president of UESF. "It's such a slap in the face to all the dedicated people who go to those schools day in and day out and do a wonderful job."[76] However, the union acquiesced once community leaders and teachers from the neighborhood offered the school board a strong show of support for the initiative. "Where were you when they kept getting low test scores? Where was the union then?," wondered Reverend Carolyn Habersham of Allen Chapel AME Church. "You're talking about teachers being stigmatized. We're talking about our children being stigmatized."[77]

Despite the rocky initial reception, three Dream Schools opened with a flourish in fall 2004, and the initiative was ultimately folded into the consent decree, thus making it mandatory.[78] The initiative will "bring a ray of light back to the community, something families can be hopeful about," proclaimed SFUSD Dream School manager and Bayview native Tamitrice Rice-Mitchell.[79] School board commissioner Dan Kelly remarked, "Some of the most talented children and valuable children in the city live right here in Bayview-Hunters Point. We cannot afford to leave them behind and have them fail."[80] Understandably, proponents of neighborhood schools from the west side also had reason to applaud the initiative. "We're for Dream Schools, Dream Schools are neighborhood schools," testified Ed Jew, a CADC board member and an organizer with Parents for Neighborhood Schools, the advocacy organization for Chinese families in the Sunset District. "There's a commitment from the parents and so the kids could actually build within the community."[81] Jew's point was that with a system of neighborhood schools, families can more easily participate in and support the efforts of the school community. "So what we should do," continued Jew, "[is] make sure that every school is the same as those schools."[82]

Soon after the start of the school year, an additional seven Dream Schools were announced for other east-side neighborhoods.[83] "The significance of the Dream School effort is to provide the same kind of high-quality education that exists in other parts of the city," Mayor Gavin Newsom remarked. "The notion is simple, isn't it? Community involvement, parental involvement and developing a holistic approach to educating our kids."[84] There was excitement over the initiative. But it was not universal. Dream Schools became "political fodder," recalled Carl Barnes, former president and board member of the San Francisco PTA. "It wasn't well-received, so it was kind of hard to take a position on it because any position that you took tended to put you at odds with somebody or make you seem allied with somebody."[85] The top-down imposition of Dream

Schools on the neighborhood did not conform to the organizing model of Coleman Advocates for Children and Youth, an influential organization. "These were not stakeholders from the community that were saying: 'We want a better form of education for our children.' It's different when it comes from community," recalled Sandra Lee Fewer, former director of education policy and parent organizing. "And I think that when you don't have that initial investment, it's very hard. I think it's hard to move things forward, it's hard to get policies passed." She continued, "And it's a different philosophy, maybe, that I think some of us felt about children and particularly Black children."[86]

There were, of course, different perspectives on the issue. Some observers felt that the Dream Schools initiative was, in fact, community-based because many Bayview-Hunters Point residents supported it.[87] Although the UESF did not oppose Dream Schools, it was also not an entirely committed partner.[88] Mere months after the first schools opened, a dispute over the terms of the extended hours required of teachers became a sore point between union and district leaders.[89] Likewise, the school board was divided in its view of Ackerman, with a bare majority backing her agenda.[90] Ahead of the 2004 election, Ackerman described the division of the board. "One vote will determine whether there will be a majority that continues to support the progress that we've made or one that wants to see the district move in a very different direction," she remarked.[91] Support for the superintendent grew tenuous following the defeat of Ackerman proponent Heather Hiles and the reelection of Ackerman rival Eric Mar. The following year, after plans for the second round of Dream Schools were held up by the school board, district spokesperson Lorna Ho observed that the superintendent was "tired of having to deal with all the political infighting."[92] Soon after the start of the school year Ackerman announced her resignation. By then, every Dream School except one was "severely resegregated" at one or more grade levels (meaning a recognized subgroup comprised 60 percent or more of a cohort).[93] Ackerman responded that resegregation was an issue that needed to be addressed wholesale: "We can't solve this issue as a school district without the larger San Francisco community and the governmental agencies and community organizations helping us."[94] With the initiative's champion no longer in office, it quietly fizzled out once the consent decree ended in

2005. "We were trying to do something good by creating the Dream Schools in the Bayview," remembered longtime school board commissioner Jill Wynns. "But I don't think [we] had time to do what it could have done."[95]

In January 2005, the board of education elected Eric Mar president and Norman Yee vice president. As the school enrollment season began, a new coalition of Chinese American families began a renewed call for neighborhood schools. With two Chinese Americans heading the school board and with the consent decree set to expire at the end of the year, the opportunity for something closer to a neighborhood-based system for the 2006–2007 term seemed like a real possibility. This will be "a pivotal year for the Chinese community, particularly Chinese activists who are interested in this issue, to mobilize," pronounced David Lee, executive director of the Chinese American Voters Education Committee.[96] In May, Commissioner Yee, in an unusual move, held a press conference announcing a yet-to-be-voted-on student assignment proposal that would reserve 60 percent of a school's open seats to neighborhood children with the remaining 40 percent allotted based on factors meant to create diversity. "I think Norman is simply pandering to NIMBY attitudes," remarked Commissioner Dan Kelly. "It's a divisive tactic that will only make the task of unifying the school district more difficult."[97] Reflecting on the issue of school assignment broadly, Yee had a different view: "Between the neighborhood and the choice [concepts], there [are] opportunities to create diversity. So, to me, it's just a matter of trying to figure out something that can satisfy both parties."[98] Yee's proposal was similar to a 60–40 plan developed by a school board–appointed community advisory committee on student assignment earlier in the year. Based on simulations conducted for the advisory committee, Yee's plan, depending on the factors used and other details, had the potential of actually creating more integration than the current Diversity Index, despite the former's set-aside for neighborhood students. In fact, community organizations that were in support of integration—Chinese for Affirmative Action, Coleman Advocates for Children and Youth, and Parents for Public Schools—signaled their support for some sort of 60–40 plan.[99]

But hope for any change to the student assignment system, much less a system based on neighborhood schools, diminished over the summer when the school district announced that the Diversity Index would be in place for another school year. And, with approval from the Ho attorneys, the district filed a request to extend the consent decree for an additional eighteen months, to June 2007. With the district still developing a student assignment system to replace the Diversity Index, with the continued expansion of the Dream and STAR schools programs, and with the various other efforts dictated and funded by the consent decree, an extension would allow for "an orderly transition from federal court jurisdiction," argued the school district.[100] The need for an extension became even more apparent after Ackerman announced her resignation. "Educational reform efforts are still in its infant stages and its student assignment process requires modification and further Court supervision in order to succeed," stated Christina Wong of Chinese for Affirmative Action. "Without the Court's supervision, it is highly unlikely that the Board will resolve this issue in a timely manner, especially given Superintendent Ackerman's recent resignation from the San Francisco Unified School District."[101] Advocates for the African American community concurred. "It is important to achieve a fair and inclusive student assignment system," wrote Reverend Calvin Jones, pastor of Providence Baptist Church. "I wholeheartedly support the programs and educational initiatives that further assist our children in achieving an equal educational opportunity."[102] Several parents supported continuing the consent decree not because they felt court supervision was necessary but because they favored the choice aspects of the Diversity Index. "It is because of the diversity index that my son can get in a very good primary and middle school," wrote Sally Sok Man Chan, a parent living in a low-income neighborhood. "If we don't have this diversity index then all the unwealthy families will always have no chance to get into the good school districts and no chance to receive a higher quality education. . . . We should try to give any child to have the same education opportunities regardless of races and wealth."[103]

While parents and advocates representing the greater southeast section of San Francisco argued for the continuation of the consent decree, most of the public comments submitted to the court came from parents from the west-side neighborhoods, "appearing by name to be a further subgroup of the Ho class" (in other words, parents with Chinese surnames who, unlike the Ho plaintiffs, opposed an extension of the decree).[104] These parents demanded the court honor the original expiration date of the consent decree based on their preference for neighborhood schools. However, ending the consent decree did not preclude the district from maintaining (or ending) the Diversity Index. As Judge Alsup explained to a parent:

> You need to be aware, and parents who feel the same way as you, you need to be aware that even if the Federal Court completely is subtracted from this picture, the school board has—and the school district have the perfect right, as far as I can see, to continue with the Diversity Index, if they want. In other words, subtracting the Federal Court from this picture does not mean that you are going to get what you want.[105]

Although school choice became the central means of assignment and racial diversity remained the central goal (albeit through race-neutral means following the 1999/2001 settlements), strong support for neighborhood schools from both community stakeholders and the school district remained an important aspect of the local political landscape throughout the course of the consent decree. The most vocal community proponents of a neighborhood-based system were parents—primarily middle class, primarily Chinese American—residing in the western neighborhoods that were home to the district's most desirable schools. Support for neighborhood schools also emerged among African Americans living in the southeastern neighborhoods that were home to less desirable schools. And while the *Ho v. SFUSD* settlements eliminated the use of racial classifications in student assignment, the agreed-upon student assignment plan, the Diversity Index, left some parents as unsatisfied as they were under the prior enrollment cap system.

Recognizing the potency of neighborhood schools, Arlene Ackerman instituted several programs to improve academic achievement for underserved students in the absence of desegregation. But STAR and Dream were not the first initiatives that focused on the low-performing schools clustered in the east side of town. Bill Rojas introduced the Comprehensive School Improvement Program in 1993 and Robert Alioto developed the special plan for Bayview-Hunters Point, first on an ad hoc basis before it was institutionalized in the 1983 consent decree. "I think integrated schools provide the optimum learning experience in which students learn to get along and get to know each other," said Ackerman. "But the truth is we live in this city, in neighborhoods segregated by race and ethnicity, and many parents want their children to go to schools close to home."[106]

Conclusion
Opportunity, Choice, and Proximity

And so the challenge before us and this court is: How can these assets be most fairly shared for the benefit of all the school children? And having a comprehensive and effective student assignment system can help determine that, because public school educational assets, they belong to all the children of San Francisco.

—PETER COHN, SFNAACP COUNSEL

As the decree has come to be used, the Court must pretend to supervise decisions better left in the hands of education professionals subject to the rough and tumble of local politics and government.

—WILLIAM H. ALSUP, U.S. DISTRICT JUDGE

Resegregation by Consent

"Everybody in this room wants to do what is best for the children of San Francisco—that's a given," observed Judge Alsup during a public hearing held in October 2005 to consider whether the consent decree needed to be extended. But the question comes down to: "Who is best equipped to make that decision—a trained professional like [Superintendent] Arlene Ackerman or a federal judge?"[1] Rather than filing a formal motion, counsel had instead submitted a stipulation and proposed order to the court to amend the consent decree by extending its termination date for a second time.[2] The terms of the proposed settlement would prohibit any adjustments to the Diversity Index prior to fall 2006 and extend the consent decree to June 30, 2007. While all parties—the state, the district, the SFNAACP, and the Ho plaintiffs—agreed to the proposed modifications, Alsup articulated multiple concerns.

No party had ever provided evidence in court that present-day school segregation was a result of prior intentional racial segregation by the district. Indeed, when Judge Orrick approved the 1999 settlement he stated that "none of the parties to the litigation have been able thus far to demonstrate that the current problems in the SFUSD have been caused by the prior governmental discrimination that justified the adoption of the Consent Decree in 1983."[3] The Ninth Circuit made clear that a primary issue for trial was whether or not vestiges of segregation or discrimination remained in the district.[4] But since the parties settled, a trial was never held, leaving the issue unresolved. "A federal judge is trained to make sure that the law is obeyed," said Alsup. "But the anchor for the federal court's involvement in the first place is supposed to be that at some point in the past there was a proven violation of the law."[5]

Despite an absence of proof that the consent decree was justified, all parties participated in its maintenance. The SFNAACP saw the decree as a means toward educational equity, the state defendants had no objection to it, and neither did the attorneys representing the Ho plaintiffs—as long as the student assignment process did not use racial classifications. Furthermore, the SFUSD had come to rely on the consent decree and the mandate it provided. "The school district wants to support it because they like having the 800-pound gorilla to deal with the teachers union, and if it comes to it, the board," remarked Alsup. "I know that's what's going on."[6] The consent decree had drifted too far, the judge argued. Even if it ever had in the past, the consent decree no longer remedied past racism or segregation. As Alsup saw it, the modus operandi had become:

> Counsel broker a deal for their clients. Then they write it into the decree. Then they use the supremacy of the decree to override any opposition from parents, teachers, and other interests not represented in this suit. The checks and balances of the traditional governmental and political processes are short-circuited. Counsel and their clients have become a kind of supreme council able to fast-track educational initiatives of their own choosing and to bypass concerns of those unrepresented herein.[7]

To the court, it would be improper to maintain the consent decree any longer, even if the school reform efforts it mandated were improving the academic achievement and educational opportunities of San Francisco's children. "Excellent as it sounds, this rhetoric has no anchor in the original source of the district court's power to intrude upon local government," wrote Alsup. "What is best for the children of San Francisco should be left to the professionals in the district, subject to the voices of all in the community, whether or not they have a seat at counsel table."[8] Many agreed with Alsup. "We don't need the court's supervision anymore. It should sunset this year," testified Ed Jew, the Parents for Neighborhood Schools organizer. "And I'm sorry to say, your honor, I mean your job is to be judge, but not as a teacher, not as a superintendent not as a faculty member, but as a judge. And it's time that we move on."[9]

But others saw real value in maintaining the decree. Although CADC president Larry Yee acknowledged the burden the Diversity Index placed on families, he announced the CADC education committee's support for the decree's extension because of the stability it would bring in light of the changes taking place in the district: "Within six months to a year the superintendent [Ackerman] leaves. There's also a school board that we are not sure of which way they are going."[10] (Despite the official view of the CADC, there were several members who opposed the extension of the decree.) And Reverend Derrick Eva valued the consent decree as a tool to direct financial resources to schools serving low-income students, proclaiming, "It is a long-standing family, American, and democratic value to see that limited resources are fairly shared with everyone."[11]

Apart from the legal question of whether the consent decree should be maintained was the issue of resegregation. "It has been the greatest disappointment to me over the years," stated Alsup. Because the *Ho* settlements led to the Diversity Index, "you could point a finger at this court and say this district court has caused the resegregation in San Francisco."[12] Stuart Biegel, the consent decree monitor, reported in April 2005 that for the 2004–2005 year, forty-three schools—more than a third of the district—were severely segregated at one or more grade levels. Of these, eleven schools had a race/ethnicity subgroup percentage greater than 80 percent at one or more grade levels. Twenty-seven were severely segregated at the school level.[13] The district had the highest percentage of racially identifiable schools (schoolwide subgroup enrollment greater than 45 percent) since the 1970–1971 term, just prior to the implementation of the Horseshoe desegregation plan. Following the first nine years of the consent decree, under Superintendents Alioto, Cornejo, and Cortines, the district was substantially in compliance with the school-by-school component requiring the elimination of racial identifiability. Beginning in the early 1990s, the district began a steady march back toward a segregated system that accelerated once the Diversity Index was put in place. "The decree has transformed itself into court-ordered resegregation," remarked Alsup. "Parents would buy into the burden if it achieved desegregation, but it doesn't."[14] These were the principal reasons Judge Alsup denied the request for an extension and ordered that the consent decree end on December 31, 2005, as previously stipulated by the parties.[15]

January 1, 2006

After more than twenty-seven years, *SFNAACP v. SFUSD* was finally closed. For twenty-two of those years, the court supervised and approved all public school assignments for San Francisco students through the consent decree. The Supreme Court had noted that "returning schools to the control of local authorities at the earliest practicable date is essential to restore their true accountability in our governmental system."[16] To emphasize the point that San Francisco's time had come, Judge Alsup wrote:

> This action is the oldest case on the entire docket for the Northern District of California. It has spanned more than one-tenth of our nation's existence. It has lasted nearly as long as the combined duration of all major wars against foreign powers by the United States since the Revolutionary War. The consent decree itself has lasted almost twice as long as the period of Reconstruction following the Civil War. The entire educational careers of many students were spent under its regime with their own children under it yet.[17]

Court supervision extended back even further. In *Johnson v. SFUSD*, the SFNAACP charged the district with creating, maintaining, and operating a dual school system. Ruling on the case on July 7, 1971, Judge Stanley Weigel ordered the immediate desegregation of the district's elementary schools. That fall, the district sought to address equal educational opportunity with the launch of its Horseshoe plan.

In the final week of 2005, Judge Alsup received a letter from David Johnson, the named plaintiff in the 1971 case whose daughter Patricia had attended an elementary school that was 75 percent Black. Upon learning that the consent decree was allowed to expire in part because the district was as segregated as it was three and a half decades earlier, Johnson wrote: "I wish to bring to your attention the fact that African American students in San Francisco Unified School District continue to receive an unconstitutional education based on the precedents established in the *Brown versus Board of Education*. I fervently urge you to use your authority to compel the San Francisco Unified School District to prioritize the welfare of its Black students and to explain its [negligence]."[18]

Johnson wrote the letter on the same day Stuart Biegel issued his final report as consent decree monitor. The disparities in academic achievement that had long plagued the district persisted. And a review of fall 2005 enrollment data indicated yet another increase in the number of severely segregated schools. "We note again, as we have in many of our recent reports, that we have found a direct relationship between this resegregation and the disparities in academic achievement," wrote Biegel. "The effect is corrosive and widespread, impacting not only the quality of the education at individual school sites, but also the culture of the community."[19] With the expiration of the consent decree, SFUSD embarked on a new era of local control. Biegel took notice of this and closed his report with a plea to the district's stakeholders to move beyond the political standoffs that stalled past reform efforts: "We look forward to new and creative efforts from local political leaders and from within both the legal community and the education community that can break this stalemate and enable this great city to become the shining example of education success that everyone knows it can be."[20]

Desegregating San Francisco Schools

San Francisco's long and unfulfilled struggle to desegregate its schools in the wake of *Brown v. Board of Education* offers a powerful lesson on the complex politics that can emerge with education reform. The case helps illuminate the interrelated and evolving relationship between jurisprudence and community-based advocacy and activism in the decades-long struggle over equal educational opportunity. Desegregation programs were developed by the superintendent and her or his cabinet and approved by the school board. Preferred alternatives were stipulated by legal parties, originally with the SFNAACP as class representative for African American students, then with the SFNAACP as class representative for all students, and finally with a party representing the subclass of Chinese American students. Under the consent decree, the state directed desegregation funds to the district and created the regulatory environment within which student assignment was confined. Decisions were ultimately made by the federal district court and, in a few instances, the Ninth Circuit. All the while, numerous community stakeholders sought to intervene, formally and informally, through political and legal channels, with varying degrees of success.

Desegregation was a racial project. Under court mandate to desegregate its schools, the district transitioned first from Horseshoe/Operation Integrate to Educational Redesign and then from Educational Redesign to the Diversity Index Lottery. With each transition, the new system embodied a fundamentally different understanding of student assignment and was a source of political contention as different community stakeholders sought to protect or dismantle the status quo system. The use of race and ethnicity subgroup categories in the assignment of students to schools and the end goal of eliminating racial segregation in every school, program, and classroom meant that in a city like San Francisco, both schisms and partnerships emerged within and across community groups representing Black, White, Asian, and Latino constituents. Many families and several community groups in the city supported desegregation and racial diversity in the schools. But their efforts were countered by mobilized groups for whom a desegregated school system was a lesser priority or an alternative that needed to be opposed.

Logics—those sets of ideas, assumptions, practices, values, and rules that constitute patterns of organization and dictate appropriate behavior—matter in the negotiation over policy alternatives. How educational values, priorities, and goals are shaped, framed, and understood—and how they change over time—helps determine which alternatives are taken up by policymakers and which ones fall by the wayside. Logics were stable but not fixed. They were available for elaboration and manipulation by community and district stakeholders. Logics influenced desegregation by constraining and guiding the course and content of student assignment policy. Political contention over characterizations of student assignment led to fundamental policy shifts that altered the educational experience of multiple cohorts of public school students.

To this point, each contentious episode of community mobilization and court action—the transition to Educational Redesign and then the transition to the Diversity Index Lottery—was considered apart from the other. In the paragraphs that follow, I join these two episodes together to explain how logics of opportunity, choice, and proximity shaped desegregation policy over the thirty-four-year span of court supervision.

The Trajectory of Equal Educational Opportunity

From Racial Balance to Racial Unidentifiability

Contention arose over the school district's proposal to replace Horseshoe/ Operation Integrate with Educational Redesign. Throughout most of the 1970s, desegregation had been framed and understood largely as a Black-White issue. Its principal purpose was to correct government racial discrimination of Black students. Consequently, the definition of racial balance was a school in which the ratio of White to Black students was not substantially at variance with the districtwide ratio of White to Black students. To comply, the district adopted the standard that each recognized racial and ethnic subgroup at every school must fall within 15 percentage points of the subgroup's districtwide percentage. Because of the demographics of the district, schools only needed to enroll significant numbers of Black and White students, and not Latino or Asian students, in order to be in compliance. The SFNAACP and its allies vigorously fought to preserve this bimodal (Black/White) desegregation framework.

With Educational Redesign, the district proposed a new standard. Unlike Horseshoe and Operation Integrate, schools would no longer be required to have a fixed ratio of White to Black students. Instead, the goal would be schools in which no racial or ethnic subgroup constituted a majority. To be in compliance, a school would need to enroll at least four of the nine recognized racial and ethnic subgroups, with no subgroup consisting of more than 40 or 45 percent of student enrollment (depending on the school). This amounted to an alternate concept of opportunity, from a bimodal desegregation framework to a multimodal integration framework. Educational Redesign was approved by the school board and the federal district court and went into effect in the 1978–1979 school term. To the disappointment of the SFNAACP and its allies, a school could now enroll no Black students and/or no White students and still meet the definition of racial unidentifiability and thus comply with the court's desegregation mandate.

With the passage of Educational Redesign, contention moved from the board chambers to the courthouse in the form of a legal action by the SFNAACP against the school district and state. As with *Johnson,* the lawsuit was filed on behalf of Black students. But in 1979, the class was redefined to encompass all schoolchildren, regardless of race or ethnicity, "now or hereafter eligible" to attend public schools in San Francisco. After nearly five years of pretrial maneuvers, the parties settled by agreeing to a consent decree. The decree had two goals. First, to eliminate racial identifiability in "every school, classroom, and program." And second, to improve academic achievement, particularly for underserved students. The second goal was to be achieved through a focused effort on African American students, primarily through a special plan for Bayview-Hunters Point. Notably, the strategy offered nothing for underserved students attending schools outside of Bayview-Hunters Point.

With the California Department of Education a party to the lawsuit, the district was all but guaranteed a steady flow of state desegregation funding to offset costs associated with consent decree activities. The consent decree also created a seat "at the decision-making table" for the SFNAACP. The decree was inviolate, observed the court. Any changes the school district wanted to make to its student assignment plan would need to be stipulated by all parties and would need final approval of the court. While the SFNAACP had a formal role in student assignment policy, the consent decree effectively locked out other community stakeholders, including the teachers' union, the PTA, and the numerous organizations representing San Francisco's diverse student communities. With a fast-growing population of English learners, questions soon emerged from MALDEF and other advocates regarding the SFNAACP's ability to adequately and fairly represent all students.

From Race Conscious to Race Neutral

In applying the new definition and standard brought about by Educational Redesign, San Francisco was able to substantially eliminate racial identifiability in the schools for the first eight years or so of the consent decree.[21] But by the 1990s, the district began to resegregate. Starting in the 1970s, the proportion of White and Black students in the district declined while that of Chinese and Latino students increased. These "drastic demographic changes" led the court to order a comprehensive evaluation of the consent decree. The resulting Experts' Report and its potential to leverage efforts to amend or eliminate terms of the decree provided an opportunity for stakeholders seeking to intervene through political and legal means. Beyond these efforts in San Francisco, the decade saw fundamental changes in desegregation and affirmative action jurisprudence as the Supreme Court determined the limits of government use of racial classifications. Across the country, lawmakers, advocates, and everyday people considered California and its "color-blind" policies as they engaged in dialogues and debates about race. The student assignment system San Francisco had in place and, in particular, how the system impacted Chinese American students received national attention and was propped up by opponents as a symbol of the failings of race-conscious policies.

The 1993 motion by META to intervene was endorsed by members of the school board but denied by Judge Orrick. Although the district court conceded that the SFNAACP lacked expertise on the needs of students who were English learners, it determined that school desegregation was an interest it could adequately represent. Intervention was therefore denied. If META's motion to intervene had been approved and advocates for Latino and Asian students were formally involved in the process, observers postulated that a student assignment system might have been crafted that the CADC would find acceptable.

The CADC's early advocacy on the consent decree issue was directed at the board of education. While the political effort generated some attention, it was ultimately unproductive as the school board lacked the will to substantively challenge the consent decree. A legal path forward emerged, and the CADC identified a team of attorneys and class representatives. Unlike in *SFNAACP v. SFUSD*, with *Ho v. SFUSD* the school district and the state representatives sided with the local chapter of the NAACP in support of the consent decree's race-conscious integration scheme. The lawsuit was contentious. The legal challenge divided communities as people and organizations aligned with either the Ho plaintiffs or the school district and SFNAACP. Following close to five years of pretrial activity, defendants determined that the law no longer aligned with the consent decree as it was composed. The parties to *Ho* agreed to consent decree amendments that eliminated the use of racial classifications in student assignment. After an interim period in which a default plan was in place, the district introduced the Diversity Index Lottery in 2002. The new system remained through the December 2005 end of the consent decree (and beyond).

During the first phase of the consent decree, student assignment was based on a race-conscious integration framework first introduced in Educational Redesign. Following settlements in 1999 and 2001, assignment was based on a race-neutral diversity framework. Diversity was broadly defined, allowing the concept to be understood in multiple ways. While the consent decree's original goal of racially and ethnically diverse schools remained, the use of racial classifications was dropped as it would almost certainly have been considered unconstitutional if the case went to trial. So in place of racial classifications, the Diversity Index Lottery sought to create cohort diversity based on socioeconomic indicators. In essence, "race neutral" constrained the means but not the ends of a student assignment that required desegregation.

The 1983 implementation of the consent decree initially led to an increase in racially unidentifiable schools. However, gains were curbed by the 1990s. Resegregation began during the first phase of the consent decree, under Rojas, and did not slow following the *Ho* settlements. By the end of the consent decree in 2005, more schools failed to meet the 45 percent subgroup threshold than at any time since the 1970–1971 school year. A similar claim can be made about the consent decree's second goal. From as early as Equality/Quality in 1970, the district recognized the value of tying desegregation to efforts to improve the academic achievement of underserved students. Over the years, money, specialized programs, and technical assistance were provided to underperforming schools throughout the eastern neighborhoods of the city. With the 1983 consent decree, the goal of improved academic achievement was made explicit. While the achievement gap narrowed during the 1990s, this improvement was short-lived. And by 2005, although SFUSD's districtwide Academic Performance Index ranking exceeded that of other urban school districts, African American students in San Francisco possessed lower achievement scores than their African American peers in San Diego, Los Angeles, Long Beach, Sacramento, and elsewhere.

The Rise of School Choice

In 1971 it would have been difficult to anticipate the looming dominance of a logic of choice in San Francisco. Parental choice was not a formal part of the Horseshoe and Operation Integrate desegregation plans, although it was part of the student assignment system. The Temporary Attendance Permit (TAP) was intended to be used in special circumstances— students needing specialized academic programs, students with particular ailments, or students in situations that would warrant attendance at a nonassigned school. In practice, it was widely understood and exploited as a means of bypassing desegregation. The number of students requesting exceptions grew under Horseshoe such that the SFNAACP declared closing the TAP loophole a condition before they would agree to abandon their desegregation lawsuit targeting secondary schools. TAP requests continued to be granted, however, and by the time Educational Redesign was introduced, fully one-third of the district's students attended a school other than the one to which they were assigned for the purpose of desegregation. Subsequently, in its 1978 lawsuit, the SFNAACP pointed to the district's operation of TAP as evidence of a government mechanism that created, maintained, and increased racial segregation in violation of the law.

With Redesign, TAP was recast Optional Enrollment Request (OER). The district, having recently placed TAP requests under the purview of its Integration Department, promised to maintain the strictest of controls over approvals. Under OER, any applicant could choose a school other than the one assigned for desegregation purposes. But requests would be granted only if the transfer would not adversely affect either the sending or receiving school's compliance with the enrollment cap standards. OER was cast as a voluntary integration component of Educational Redesign. From the 1984–1985 term to the 1992–1993 term, as the district's compliance with the integration aspect of the consent decree indicates, there was a general enforcement of the policy. In time, OER was understood to be a loophole in its own right. Observers charged that parents savvy enough or connected enough to influence the district's

Educational Placement Center would receive favorable assignments at the expense of others.[22]

When the district introduced Educational Redesign, it legitimated choice by incorporating it directly into the plan. OER was the method for students choosing an alternative school or requesting a different traditional school than the one assigned. In time, choice moved from the periphery to become the principal means of student assignment. For the 1991–1992 school year, close to 40 percent of students were on optional enrollment permits. By the end of the decade, the OER share had increased to 56 percent of all students. Along with its increasing popularity, parental choice became institutionalized through the efforts of the San Francisco chapter of Parents for Public Schools. Its founders were originally proponents of neighborhood schools under the premise that schools were community institutions and that middle-class families leaving the public education system could be brought back through a concerted community effort to revitalize neighborhood schools. But the focus of PPS-SF soon centered around improving the choice process. The organization bridged parents and the district, assisting parents navigating the complicated enrollment process so that the best school choices could be made, and assisting the district's efforts to become more efficient, transparent, and responsive to parents.

When the district introduced Excellence for All in 2002, in the absence of assignments based on racial classifications, choice was moved to the center of the student assignment framework. Students no longer received an automatic assignment based on home address. Choice requests were no longer "temporary" or "optional." With the Diversity Index Lottery, all applicants were asked to choose their preferred schools. The district touted the benefits of choice and promised to diversify its portfolio of options by offering a range of start and end times and providing a range of curricular options. Many parents came to appreciate the freedom to choose the school down the block, close to their work, or clear across town. But for some parents, including Chinese American parents who had supported the campaign to eliminate enrollment caps, the Diversity Index was a less-than-ideal solution. While assignment relied on school choice, choice was constrained. For schools with more applicants than available seats, the system enrolled those students who contributed the most to the school's overall socioeconomic diversity. While the language of the district was often centered on programmatic diversity, and the mechanism of assignment focused on socioeconomic diversity, the consent decree's goal of eliminating identifiability made racial diversity an obligation.

Segregated Neighborhoods and Segregated Schools

A third logic governed student assignment in San Francisco, that of proximity. A formalized system of neighborhood schools with defined catchment areas had been a component of the district since the 1930s. But with housing discrimination and housing patterns that fell along race and class lines, a neighborhood school system could not be fully maintained with desegregation as a goal. Throughout the district's era of court supervision, neighborhood schools were never completely abandoned by community stakeholders or by the district. Comprehensive school desegregation was always tempered by neighborhood elements. Horseshoe was explicitly designed as a zone system that retained the "feeling of a neighborhood" by ensuring that students living on the same block would attend the same school. Operation Integrate was built on a similar premise. The district touted a decrease in busing and a return to the pre-desegregation school boundaries as the underlying basis for Educational Redesign. These same neighborhood school boundaries remained largely untouched during the first phase of the consent decree. Even with the Diversity Index, when students were no longer preassigned to schools based on home address, traces of the neighborhood logic remained: Schools filled open seats by first considering neighborhood applicants before applicants from outside the school's catchment area were considered.

San Francisco is defined by its neighborhoods. And a neighborhood's public schools are widely seen as important community institutions. Due to the racial geography of the city (along with factors such as transportation lines, topographic isolation, economic segregation, and housing discrimination), the experience and understanding of student assignment by residents varied across neighborhood boundaries. Bayview-Hunters Point is situated on the edge of the city, but it was always at the conceptual center of desegregation. The lion's share of desegregation resources aimed at improving academic quality targeted Bayview-Hunters Point schools. Resistance to busing into (and in some instances, busing out of) Bayview-Hunters Point became such a flash point in the Educational Redesign proposal that in the end, the neighborhood was left out of the plan's busing provisions. And at times, Bayview-Hunters Point served as a foil for desegregation opponents, whether they were military families on Treasure Island, Mission District language rights advocates, or neighborhood schools activists from the Sunset.

San Francisco is emblematic of the contemporary multiracial city. In recent years, political contention shaped by logics of opportunity, choice, and proximity has influenced student assignment policies in city school systems across the nation, from New York to Chicago to Los Angeles.[23] Opposition to integrating school systems has always been formidable. However, racially diverse schools have been a value that many education policymakers, administrators, teachers, parents, and students maintained, even as desegregation jurisprudence narrowed and desegregation cases languished on court dockets.[24] Although the goal of integration remains central for some, school choice has become increasingly popular. Beyond the choice embodied in the charter school and school voucher methods of reform, many urban districts have employed a system of choice akin to San Francisco's Diversity Index Lottery. And alongside the decline of desegregation and the rise of choice, the neighborhood school has been and continues to be a powerful conceptualization of the most appropriate means of assigning students to schools.

These three logics—proximity, choice, and opportunity—extend beyond student assignment and even public education. They are resonant with broader, societal logics of contemporary America. Neighborhood schools call to mind the localism that is so deeply engrained in American society that it is an ever-present theme that runs throughout our nation's history. School choice has its basis in neoliberalism. Where earlier decades favored high levels of government involvement in social programs, in more recent decades, privileging market-based mechanisms—including competition and choice—as solutions to social problems has gained a foothold in American society. The struggle for equal opportunity in education and in other sectors of society has been a constant. For many, it is through education that opportunity for success in life is realized. Educational opportunity was the underlying basis of the *Brown* decision. In a statement that bears repeating, Chief Justice Warren declared, "Such an opportunity, where the state has undertaken to provide it, is a right which must be made available to all on equal terms."[25]

Acknowledgments

This project would not have been possible without the expertise and guidance of the librarians and archivists at the San Bruno Federal Records Center, San Francisco Law Library, San Francisco Public Library, Stanford University, University of California, Berkeley, and University of California, Santa Barbara. I am especially appreciative of Charles Miller, Wei Chi Poon, Susan Snyder, and Tami Suzuki.

Brenda Huang provided valuable insight into the San Francisco Chinese media landscape. Hai Yang, Claire Kwan, and Qinglian Lu made an important contribution to the project by identifying and translating relevant articles from *Sing Tao Daily* and *Chinese Times*. Much of this work occurred at *Sing Tao Daily*, which generously provided us access to their newspaper morgue.

I owe a special debt to the school district staff, school board members, attorneys, community leaders, and parents who agreed to be interviewed. Several interview participants were kind enough to provide personal papers, organizational records, newspaper clippings, and other artifacts that greatly contributed to the study. I am particularly grateful to Stuart Biegel, Arthur Brunwasser, Douglas Chan, Libby Denebeim, Henry Der, Sandra Lee Fewer, Daniel Girard, Ruth Grabowski, Anthony Lee, Louis Hop Lee, David Levine, Hoover Liddell, Denise Louie, Henry Louie, Miranda Massie, Hydra Mendoza, Ellie Rossiter, Mark Sanchez, and Lorraine Woodruff-Long. Their recollections, stories, perspectives, and insights, along with those of my other interview participants, meaningfully illuminated the archival and media data I collected.

I am thankful for the advice, support, and encouragement over the years from my mentors at Stanford University, University of California, Berkeley, and University of Pennsylvania. My deepest gratitude goes to Anthony Lising Antonio, Luis Fraga, Leah Gordon, Michael Kirst, Milbrey McLaughlin, Debra Meyerson, John Puckett, Francisco Ramirez, Janelle Scott, and Jon Zimmerman.

Jennifer Moore gave me valuable advice and feedback before I brought the manuscript to the University of Minnesota Press. Mercury Meulman provided a careful and exacting eye on the manuscript in its final stages. I am indebted to both of them. Their efforts to clarify my argument and animate my prose have made me a stronger writer.

It was an absolute pleasure to work with Pieter Martin at the University of Minnesota Press. He was an enthusiastic, supportive, and critical editor. His feedback was uniformly insightful. He also assembled a peer-review team that provided extremely helpful criticism. I am grateful to him and everyone else at the press who worked to push the manuscript forward.

Most of all, I am thankful for the patient encouragement from family and friends that helped bring this project to its completion.

Notes on Research Method and Data Sources

My argument results from an analysis of political discourse and action of stakeholders attempting to influence the course and content of San Francisco's school desegregation policy from 1971 to 2005, a period of time during which the federal district court supervised the school district's desegregation efforts. Data were drawn from sources selected to reveal the politics emerging from institutional realms critical to school desegregation—the federal courts, the school district, and local media. Altogether, I drew from thousands of pages of archival documents, hundreds of newspaper articles, and dozens of informant interviews.

Federal District Court Records

I reviewed the docket files from three San Francisco school desegregation lawsuits: *Johnson v. SFUSD, SFNAACP v. SFUSD,* and *Ho v. SFUSD.* Docket files are fertile yet surprisingly underexploited sources of data in studies of the politics of court-mandated education reform. The files contain memoranda, orders, motions, court transcripts, briefs, and other documents submitted to or issued by the court. Particularly for the last two cases (which covered more than a quarter century of student assignment in San Francisco and filled thirty-one cartons in total), the docket files include more than just courtroom activity. As parties prepared for trial, the docket grew to include data and reports from the school district, memos and other correspondence from school board members, superintendents, and district staff, and letters to the court from parents, teachers, and students. These files proved to be the most fruitful source of data for the study. The National Archives and Records Administration, Pacific Region, in San Bruno, California, houses the *Johnson* records; the Federal Records Center, also in San Bruno, houses the *SFNAACP* and *Ho* records.

Organizational Records

I analyzed available documents including meeting minutes, newsletters, press releases, and internal memos from community organizations working on issues related to school desegregation in San Francisco during the focal period. These data were collected from a variety of sources. For example, the California Ethnic and Multicultural Archives (CEMA) at University of California, Santa Barbara, holds records of the Chinese American Democratic Club (CADC), an organization that spearheaded the *Ho* lawsuit against the school district in the early 1990s. Stanford University maintains archived records from Mexican American Legal Defense and Education Fund (MALDEF). The Ethnic Studies Library at University of California, Berkeley, holds newsletters, annual reports, and other files of Chinese for Affirmative Action and the CADC. Records of the Western Regional Office (Region I) of the NAACP are housed at Berkeley's Bancroft Library. In addition, Bancroft holds records the SFNAACP legal counsel compiled in preparation for trial in their 1978 lawsuit against the school district. These records are extensive and contained personal memos, district reports (obtained through discovery), meeting minutes, and other materials relevant to my analysis. In addition, documents from the Coalition to Defend Affirmative Action By Any Means Necessary, CADC, Parents for Public Schools–San Francisco, and a handful of other community organizations were provided to me by former and current organizational leaders.

San Francisco Unified School District Records

I examined school district records, including internal evaluations, superintendent speeches, reports from the SFUSD Office of Integration, district bulletins, and board circulars and memoranda. I also analyzed district documents submitted to the court, including reports on changes to the student assignment policy, district enrollment and population data, and *New Views* (1984–1988) and the *Insider* (1988–1992), two district newsletters devoted to San Francisco's desegregation efforts. The records of the SFUSD are maintained at the Daniel E. Koshland San Francisco History Center at the San Francisco Main Library. At the Hoover Institution Archives at Stanford University, I reviewed miscellaneous papers of Superintendent Robert F. Alioto (1975–1985). Among other items, these records include public comments by Alioto and contemporary San Francisco Civil Grand Jury Reports on school desegregation. I also acquired several documents directly from the school district and board of education, including meeting minutes, historical student demographic information, miscellaneous papers, and various reports and publications on student assignment. The bulk of materials spanned 1965 to 2000. These data help reveal the institutional stance of the school district to students, parents, and the broader San Francisco public.

Mainstream and Community Newspapers

I analyzed just over eight hundred newspaper articles, letters to the editor, and opinion pieces pertaining to San Francisco's school desegregation policies, the use of race and other factors in assigning students to schools, and desegregation lawsuits filed against the district during the study's focal period. Newspapers were a useful source for capturing the political rhetoric employed by stakeholders. While editorials do not necessarily capture community sentiment, they do offer insight into which policy issues are important during a particular period of time, how issues are generally perceived, and, often, the ideas around which political contention are organized. I sought to compile a comprehensive corpus of items from the more prominent of the city's two dailies, the *San Francisco Chronicle*, from 1971 to 2005. I identified items published prior to 1995 using subject indexes. Articles from 1995 to the present are available on the internet and were compiled using the *Chronicle*'s online keyword search tool. To the *Chronicle* corpus, I added several dozen articles from the *San Francisco Examiner, San Francisco Bay Guardian, New York Times,* and several other publications. Articles from these papers were identified using Google's News Archive Search feature, Lexis-Nexis Academic, and the NewsBank, Inc. America's Newspapers database.

To ensure that a full range of stakeholder political rhetoric and activity was captured, I collected articles from several community newspapers. Articles from the *Recorder* and the *Daily Journal,* San Francisco's two legal newspapers were provided to me by a CADC board member. I compiled articles from the Chinese-language *Sing Tao Daily,* the most prominent of the Chinese-language newspapers during the focal period. Most of these articles were collected at *Sing Tao*'s newspaper morgue, which warehouses newspapers from 1993 on. Because there was no subject index available, identifying relevant items from *Sing Tao* required a review, one-by-one, of the main and metro newspaper sections. A list of

date ranges during which some substantive activity relating to desegrega-
·tion took place (e.g., a school board meeting, a court ruling, the first day
of school) was used to narrow the number of newspapers reviewed. More
recent articles (generally, from 2002 to the present) were available
through an online search that took place at *Sing Tao*'s Bay Area headquarters. I also analyzed articles from *Chinese Times,* another local Chinese-
language newspaper. These articles were available through the Him Mark
Lai Collection at the University of California, Berkeley, Ethnic Studies
Library. The identification and translation of relevant articles were conducted by research assistants who were fluent in Chinese and English.
Articles from *Asian Week,* an English-language newspaper, were collected
through both an online search and a microfilm review that focused on
particular date ranges, similar to the *Sing Tao* process. Articles from the
San Francisco Sun-Reporter and the *San Francisco Bay View,* both of which
serve the local African American community, were identified through the
ProQuest Ethnic News Watch, a microfilm review, and an internet search.
I intended to conduct a similar analysis of Spanish-language newspapers.
However, it was suggested to me that this might be less fruitful since for
San Francisco's Spanish-speaking community, desegregation, student assignment, and other education issues were typically addressed through
community meetings, local television, and radio. I was able to incorporate
the perspective of Latino-serving community organizations and leaders
through other data sources.

Informant Interviews

In order to illuminate and inform data gathered from archival and media
sources, I conducted sixty-seven semistructured, open-ended interviews
with organizational leaders, district officials, and other informants inti-
mately knowledgeable of desegregation and student assignment policies
during the focal period. Retrospective interviews are not without problems. What we recall often differs from what actually happened. In order
to minimize the "risks" involved with retrospective interviews, I relied on
this source primarily as a means of enhancing and verifying the data provided by archival materials. Informants include executive staff, board
members, and parent leaders from organizations involved in student assignment and other education advocacy efforts in San Francisco (40),

school board members (17), attorneys involved with the lawsuits and court-appointed monitors/experts (6), and senior school district staff (4). Separate interview protocols were created for the various informant categories. Interviews began with a brief introduction of the interviewer, the purpose of the study, and the other constituent groups that would be interviewed. The core interview questions asked informants to "map out" the political landscape of education in San Francisco by reflecting on the various sides of the debate, the motivations and incentives of community stakeholders, the different ways community stakeholders "got things done," the alliances and partnerships community stakeholders make, and the relationship between civic engagement and the timing, content, and fate of San Francisco's desegregation and student assignment policies. The interviews closed with the opportunity for respondents to share any final thoughts on issues related to student assignment and school desegregation. The average interview was seventy minutes long; interviews ranged from thirty minutes to two and a half hours. All but a handful of interviews were conducted in person, digitally recorded (with permission), and professionally transcribed. In addition, I had thirteen informal conversations with individuals possessing perspectives on and informed knowledge of various aspects of the school desegregation plans. Although these conversations were not recorded or analyzed, they helped to inform my general understanding of the political lay of the land.

Rather early in the data analysis process, three analytical categories—opportunity, choice, and proximity—emerged as the primary logics through which stakeholders framed, understood, and shaped school desegregation and student assignment. The centrality of the categories persisted through subsequent rounds of data analysis. The three analytical categories became the basis for the remainder of the analysis and eventually served to structure the narrative.

Consent Decree

SFNAACP v. SFUSD, Opinion and Order, 576 F. Supp. 34 (1983)

1. The Complaint in this cause, filed June 30, 1978, alleges that Defendants have engaged in discriminatory practices and maintained a segregated school system in the City and County of San Francisco in violation of the constitutions and laws of the United States and of the State of California. The Complaint seeks the desegregation of the public schools of San Francisco, and the conversion of the San Francisco Unified School District (S.F.U.S.D.) into a unitary system in compliance with the Constitutions of the United States and of California and applicable federal and state statutes.

2. Plaintiffs are individual Black parents, proceeding on behalf of their own children, and the San Francisco branch of the NAACP, a civil rights organization which represents its members. Plaintiffs also bring this action, pursuant to Fed.R. Civ.P. 23, on behalf of a class composed of all children of school age who are, or may in the future become, eligible to attend the public schools of the S.F.U.S.D., and who are entitled to do so under circumstances which afford them full and equal protection of the laws.

3. Defendants are (a) the S.F.U.S.D., its Board Members and its Superintendent (hereinafter collectively called the "S.F.U.S.D."), the entity and officials created and/or empowered by the State of California to carry out public education functions, in compliance with State law, within the City and County of San Francisco; and (b) the California State Board of Education and its members, the State Superintendent of Public Instruction, and the State Department of Education (hereinafter collectively called the "State Defendants"), the entities and officials created and/or empowered by the Constitution and laws of California to carry out the State's system of compulsory public education, including the performance of certain regulatory, supervisory, advisory, and oversight functions with respect to local school districts, including the S.F.U.S.D.

4. This Court has jurisdiction over this action and over the parties. This Court has pendent jurisdiction over Plaintiffs' claims under the Constitution and laws of the State of California, including Title 5, chapter 7 of the California Administrative Code. State Defendants concede jurisdiction for purposes of this case only. Venue is properly laid in this Court.

5. The parties have conducted extensive discovery, including numerous depositions and interrogatories and document discovery. The Court has denied motions of the State Defendants for a more definite statement and for dismissal and/or abstention, and a motion of the S.F.U.S.D. for a separate trial on certain issues. The Court has also denied the motion of Plaintiffs for partial summary judgment. In denying that motion, the Court made findings of fact with respect to some of the allegations of segregation in the S.F.U.S.D. schools. Those findings are set forth in an Appendix to the Court's Order of June 26, 1981, and are incorporated in this decree by reference.

6. At the direction and with the assistance of the Court, the parties have sought to reach a fair and equitable settlement of their differences for the benefit of the children of San Francisco. In the early summer of 1982, the Court and the parties established a Settlement Team, comprised of representatives of the parties and independent co-chairs, named by the Court, to consider the issues in dispute between the parties and to recommend a framework for addressing them. The work of the Settlement Team and the negotiations between the parties in the fall of 1982 have resulted in the agreement set forth herein. As the Settlement Team observed, the S.F.U.S.D. has made significant progress both in desegregation and in educational improvement since the 1971 order of this Court in *Johnson v. San Francisco Unified School District*, 339 F. Supp. 1315 (N.D.Cal.1971), *vacated*, 500 F.2d 349 (9th Cir.1974). The agreement reflected in this Consent Decree is intended to build on these efforts, to address the remaining problems flowing from racial/ethnic concentration, and to assure continued implementation of Educational Redesign as improved by this Consent Decree.

7. The parties, as indicated by the signature of their counsel below, have determined to settle this action, with the Court's approval,

through entry of this Consent Decree, which the parties believe will benefit the children of San Francisco, conserve the resources and time of the parties and the Court, permit educational authorities to devote their attention to sound educational planning and programming, maximize the amount of state and federal financial assistance available to assist S.F.U.S.D. to meet its constitutional and statutory obligations, and serve the best interests of the parties themselves.

8. The parties stipulate and agree that, if proof were presented in formal proceedings, the Court would be justified in making factual findings and legal conclusions sufficient to require the systemwide remedies that are set forth in this Consent Decree.

9. The parties agree that this Consent Decree is final and binding as to the issues resolved herein.

10. In the event objections or challenges are raised to the lawfulness or appropriateness of this Consent Decree, or any provision hereof, or proceedings pursuant hereto, the parties shall defend the lawfulness and appropriateness of the matter challenged. If any such objection or challenge is made in a state court action, the parties shall remove such action to the United States District Court for the Northern District of California.

WHEREFORE, the parties having freely given their consent, the terms of the Decree being within the scope of the Complaint, and the terms of the Decree being fair, reasonable and adequate, it is hereby ORDERED, ADJUDGED, and DECREED:

I. Class Certification

11. That the class of all children of school age who are, or may in the future become, eligible to attend the public schools of the S.F.U.S.D. is an appropriate class to maintain this action, and that the class is adequately represented by named plaintiffs.

II. Student Desegregation

A. General Policies for Implementing Citywide Desegregation

12. A major goal of the provisions of this Consent Decree shall be to eliminate racial/ethnic segregation or identifiability in any S.F.U.S.D.

school, program, or classroom and to achieve the broadest practicable distribution throughout the system of students from the racial and ethnic groups which comprise the student enrollment of the S.F.U.S.D. For purposes of defining the racial/ethnic composition of the system and of each school, nine racial/ethnic groups are identified: Spanish-surname, Other White, Black, Chinese, Japanese, Korean, Filipino, American Indian, and Other Non-White.

13. To achieve the above-stated goal, the following guidelines shall apply:
    a. No school shall have fewer than four racial/ethnic groups represented in its student body.

    b. No racial/ethnic group shall constitute more than 45% of the student enrollment at any regular school, nor more than 40% at the following alternative schools:

    Wallenberg High School, Lawton Middle School, International Studies, Second Community, San Francisco Community, Clarendon, New Traditions, Douglas Traditional, Argonne Elementary, Rooftop, Lilienthal, Lakeshore, Buena Vista, John Swett.

    In the event the percentage of any racial/ethnic group at any of the above-mentioned alternative schools exceeds 40% after September 1983, the S.F.U.S.D. shall apply the provisions of subparagraph (c) to the entering class at such school.

    c. Beginning with the 1983–84 school year, the S.F.U.S.D. shall monitor the entering classes of all regular schools in which a single racial/ethnic group comprises more than 45% of the student enrollment, to assure that students in that racial/ethnic group will not comprise more than 40% of the entering class at any such school.

    d. Beginning with the 1983–84 school year, the trigger point for the granting of Optional Enrollment Requests (OER transfers) shall be lowered from 43% to 40% at both sending and receiving schools.

    e. The S.F.U.S.D., while retaining discretion to initiate, modify or terminate such special programs as magnet or alternative schools or curricula, shall, in exercising its discretion, continue to avoid choosing sites for such special programs which would disproportionately burden any racial/ethnic groups.

    f. The S.F.U.S.D. shall continue to avoid facility utilization policies or

practices, including school openings, closings, conversions, reno-
vations, grade structure changes, boundary changes, or feeder pattern changes, that disproportionately burden any racial/ethnic
group. The S.F.U.S.D. shall also continue to avoid transportation
policies that disproportionately burden any racial/ethnic group.

   g. Except upon agreement of the parties or order of the Court, the
S.F.U.S.D. shall not be precluded from continuing to use optional
attendance or discontiguous assignment zones where they contribute to desegregation.

B. Special Provisions for Certain Designated Schools

14. With respect to each school and racial/ethnic group listed below,
as of September 1983, the maximum percentage of the listed racial/
ethnic group shall be reduced to the percentage specified below:

Alamo Park (Black)	44.9
Bret Harte (Black)	43.0
Bryant (Spanish Surname)	42.5
Downtown (Spanish Surname)	40.0
Edison (Spanish Surname)	42.7
Garfield (Chinese)	41.2
George Moscone (Spanish Surname)	37.0
Hawthorne (Spanish Surname)	40.0
Horace Mann (Spanish Surname)	42.8
Jean Parker (Chinese)	42.7
John Muir (Black)	43.5
John O'Connell (Spanish Surname)	44.5
Junipero Serra (Spanish Surname)	40.8
Leonard Flynn (Spanish Surname)	43.2
Marina (Chinese)	43.6
Spring Valley (Chinese)	41.7
Sutro (Chinese)	39.4
William Cobb (Black)	43.4
William de Avila (Black)	41.0

15. The S.F.U.S.D. shall prepare and submit to the Court no later than
April 1984 and annually thereafter during the term of this Decree

reports on the extent to which special desegregation provisions are needed for other particular schools, or modifications are needed in any of the special provisions contained in this section. The parties shall endeavor in good faith to reach agreement on any such modifications proposed by the S.F.U.S.D., and may seek appropriate action from the Court.

16. On or before June 30, 1983, the parties will submit a joint report to the Court setting forth the extent to which additional educational resources or programs will facilitate implementation of the goals of this Consent Decree at any particular school(s).

C. Special Plan for Bayview-Hunters Point Schools

17. In order to desegregate the three elementary schools and the middle school in the Bayview-Hunters Point area, the S.F.U.S.D. shall adopt, with the approval of the Court, a plan which will, beginning in September 1983, with completion by the end of the 1985–86 school year:

    a. consistent with paragraph 20 of this Decree, convert the Dr. Charles R. Drew School to an academic middle school with increased counseling to help prepare its graduates for the Lowell High School program;

    b. consistent with paragraphs 21–24 of this Decree and Appendix A, reconstitute the Sir Francis Drake School, to which students will be assigned, as a regular K–5 school with an enriched program emphasizing computer science;

    c. consistent with paragraphs 25–27 of this Decree and Appendix B, establish the Dr. George Washington Carver School, to which students will be assigned, as a laboratory school with strong academic emphasis and with a local university as a partner to assist in developing the program; and

    d. consistent with paragraph 28 of this Decree, convert the Pelton Middle School into an academic high school with a curriculum and program modeled after Raoul Wallenberg High School.

    Students who reside in the Bayview-Hunters Point area shall have the option to attend other district schools with transportation provided by the S.F.U.S.D.

18. The S.F.U.S.D. shall declare all staff and administrative positions in the Bayview-Hunters Point Schools open, and shall reconstitute the staff and administration of those schools on the basis of a desegregation plan developed by S.F.U.S.D. and submitted to the Court. The plan shall specify changes in attendance boundaries and methods for selecting staff and administrators appropriate to the new educational programs. The plan shall provide for the assignment of administrators who are strong instructional leaders, with sufficient administrative support.

19. The plan to desegregate schools in the Bayview-Hunters Point area shall focus on improving both the educational quality of the schools and the public perception of the area.

a. Dr. Charles R. Drew School

20. Dr. Charles R. Drew School shall be converted into an academic middle school with an academic program with high quality standards. It shall be renamed Dr. Charles R. Drew Academic Middle School. The newcomer middle school program shall be located at this site if feasible. The Drew staff shall be reconstituted to implement the new program and the S.F.U.S.D. shall provide special assistance in curriculum development, involving one of the area universities if necessary. A joint staff committee shall be established between the Drew School and Lowell High School for course development and implementation of courses that would lead to high secondary-level academic performance. Increased and appropriate counseling staff shall be provided to help prepare Drew students for the Lowell High School program. Transportation shall be provided for students coming from outside the attendance areas.

b. Sir Francis Drake School

21. Sir Francis Drake Elementary School shall be converted from a basic K–5 elementary school to a computer-assisted instruction and computer science and awareness elementary school. This program shall be developed and implemented in cooperation with a local university. The principal assigned to Sir Francis Drake shall if possible have a joint appointment at the university.

22. Students assigned to Sir Francis Drake shall be afforded the opportunity to explore the many uses of computers and computer language with specific emphasis on developing a total awareness of computers and their place in our society. Sir Francis Drake shall have an assigned student attendance area that will enhance its racial/ethnic balance and take advantage of the changing demographics of the community.

23. In order to provide the quality of computer instruction that will be necessary to promote this program, existing staff positions shall be declared open, job descriptions developed, and a new staff selected from those applicants that are qualified. In the event there are not sufficient qualified teachers within the S.F.U.S.D. that meet these requirements for staff, new hires will be solicited to fill any vacancies.

24. The staff shall participate in staff development programs, both in the District and at the local university, that will ensure the continued building of a foundation that is computer-oriented. Each teacher in the program shall be required to give instruction using the computer terminals provided as well as assisting students to program computers and further develop their understanding.

c. Dr. George Washington Carver School

25. Beginning September, 1983, Dr. George Washington Carver Elementary School shall be converted into an academic school, with an assigned attendance area.

26. The program at Dr. George Washington Carver shall build upon an agreement with a university. A specific agreement shall be negotiated between the university selected and the S.F.U.S.D. for the strengthening of the academic program at Carver and for the principal to have a joint appointment with the university, if possible.

27. The S.F.U.S.D., in consultation with the State Defendants and Plaintiffs, shall develop a comprehensive plan for the new academic school and for its relationship with the university as part of the Bayview-Hunters Point plan submitted to the Court pursuant to paragraph 17, above. The educational plan for Dr. George Washington Carver shall extend to all elements of the school's program, organi-

zation, staffing, community and parent relationship, curricular and extra-curricular activities, and relationship with other parts of the public school system.

d. San Francisco Academic High School

28. Pelton Middle School shall be converted into an alternative Traditional Academic High School and shall be renamed San Francisco Academic High School. San Francisco Academic High School shall have a curriculum and program modeled after Raoul Wallenberg High School.

e. Cost of Implementation

29. In order to provide the quality programs that are necessary to promote the desired integration of Dr. Charles R. Drew, Sir Francis Drake, Dr. George Washington Carver and San Francisco Academic High School, the S.F.U.S.D. shall review staffing patterns, class size, program, and buildings. Initial estimates suggest that a comprehensive program of the type herein described for Bayview-Hunters Point may cost between $1 million and $1.5 million in the first year.

f. Special Provisions for Staffing Drew, Drake, Carver, and San Francisco Academic High School

30. The S.F.U.S.D. is authorized by this Consent Decree to select personnel for these four schools, whether from among existing certificated staff or from new hiring of certified and non-certified staff. This flexibility in staffing is essential to successful desegregation of these schools, in light of their substantial reorganization and difficult new missions.

g. Public Information

31. A coordinated public information effort aimed at dealing with public stereotypes about the Bayview-Hunters Point area shall be undertaken by the S.F.U.S.D. in consultation with State Defendants. This effort shall, *inter alia*, consist of the following:
    (a) Publishing a program description of the Dr. George Washington Carver, Dr. Charles R. Drew, Sir Francis Drake and San Francisco

Academic High School, which shall be mailed to the parents of all school-aged children in the city;

(b) Engaging a reputable public relations firm that will collaborate with the principals of the above-named schools to develop and implement a comprehensive public information campaign, the purpose of which shall be to highlight the changing demographics of the area; to promote new private housing development in the area; and to attract new parents and students to the schools by emphasizing the positive changes underway both in terms of quality programming and staffing; and

(c) Working closely with parents and families of the children of San Francisco in actively and positively promoting the educational programs in Hunters Point.

D. State Government Warning on Transfers to Suburban School Districts

32. Within 90 days of approval of this Consent Decree, the State Department of Education shall formally notify suburban school districts that acceptance of students who reside in the S.F.U.S.D., and whose transfer adversely affects desegregation in the school they would otherwise be attending, will disqualify the suburban school district from state aid for such students and may make it liable to school desegregation proceedings. The State Department of Education shall require suburban school districts to give special attention to ending such existing transfers.

E. Military Transportation to Private Schools

33. Transportation by the Defense Department of children who reside on military bases to private schools will undermine the ability of the S.F.U.S.D. effectively to carry out the provisions and purpose of the Consent Decree. In light of this fact, the parties shall submit a joint request to the appropriate military authorities for the termination of Defense Department transportation of children from military bases to private schools, and may seek appropriate assistance from the Court.

III. Desegregation of Faculty, Administrators, and Other Staff

34. The S.F.U.S.D. shall continue to implement a staffing policy such as that contained in Policy No. 4111.1, the goal of which is "to achieve a staff at each school site and District location that will reflect the student population of the District."

35. The S.F.U.S.D. shall assure that faculty and other staff will be equitably assigned throughout the District, within the meaning of applicable legal standards.

IV. Staff Development

36. The S.F.U.S.D., after consultation with the State Defendants, shall develop and submit to the Court and parties no later than April 1, 1983, a comprehensive staff development plan and budget necessary to implement the provisions of this Decree. The plan and budget shall include up to six days per year of staff development, some of which may be outside the regular school calendar, and shall cost no more than $800,000 per year. The training shall address areas identified as essential for staff in school districts undergoing desegregation, such as the following: student discipline procedures and goals; academic achievement and performance goals; teaching in a diverse racial/ethnic environment; parental involvement; and the desegregation goals and provisions of this Consent Decree.

V. Extra-Curricular Activities

37. The parties agree that it is important to ensure that the extra-curricular activities of the S.F.U.S.D. are available to all students on a basis which is consistent with the obligation to avoid segregation and provide equal educational opportunity. Accordingly, the S.F.U.S.D., after consultation with the State Defendants, shall submit to the parties and the Court by May 1, 1983, a program for monitoring extra-curricular activities to find out the extent to which students from the various groups do or do not participate in various activities and to develop methods for informing them fully about their opportunities to participate.

VI. School Discipline

38. The parties agree that it is important in a multi-cultural, multi-racial, multi-ethnic school population undergoing desegregation that discipline be, and be perceived to be, fair and consistent for students from all groups. Accordingly, within 90 days of the Court's approval of this Consent Decree, any party may submit a report to the Court setting forth its views on an appropriate Student Code of Conduct.

VII. Academic Excellence

39. The parties agree that the overall goal of this Consent Decree will require continued and accelerated efforts to achieve academic excellence throughout the S.F.U.S.D. The S.F.U.S.D. shall evaluate student academic progress for the purpose of determining the curricula and programs most responsible for any improved test scores and learning in the District and the extent to which these curricula and programs are available to students of all racial/ethnic groups. The S.F.U.S.D. shall adopt any additional curricula and programs necessary to promote equal educational opportunity.

40. The annual report required in paragraph 44 of this Consent Decree shall include a section on S.F.U.S.D.'s progress toward the goal of academic excellence, setting forth test scores and other evaluative data for each building and for the District as a whole.

41. The S.F.U.S.D. shall continue to assure the availability of academic courses on a basis that is not racially or ethnically discriminatory.

VIII. Parent and Student Participation

42. The parties acknowledge the value in the schools of parent, student, staff, and community representation which reflects the racial/ethnic diversity of a school district which is undergoing desegregation. The S.F.U.S.D. shall continue its effort to encourage and improve participation of parents, students, staff, and community. Any party may submit to the Court by May 1, 1983, its recommendations for any additional steps necessary to assure adequate representation of parents, students, staff, and the community in the implementation of the desegregation goals contained in this Consent Decree.

IX. Housing and Desegregation

43. Because of the critical impact of government housing policies on school segregation, the parties shall engage in the following program, individually and jointly, to try to secure policies and actions by federal, state and local housing agencies that promote rather than impede school desegregation and integration.

    a. Within one month of the entry of this Consent Decree the parties shall submit joint letters to the relevant local, state, and federal agencies requesting information on the location and tenancy of existing subsidized housing in the San Francisco housing market area and asking that the agencies devise policies that will support rather than undermine school desegregation and integration. The letters will request that the concerned agencies meet with the parties to review the impact of existing policies and join in a planning process to devise policies and procedures to avoid segregation in subsidized housing, help integrate existing segregated neighborhoods, and help stabilize existing integrated communities.

    b. The parties shall select an expert who shall be retained for the purpose of reviewing the information obtained from the relevant agencies and prepare an analysis of the extent to which local, state or federal housing policy will undermine or interfere with the implementation of the provisions of this Consent Decree, as well as specific recommendations for changes in the policies and practices of the relevant agencies. Copies of the expert's analysis and recommendations shall be provided to the parties for their comments and alternative recommendations, if any. The parties shall seek to agree on a joint analysis and recommendations.

    c. The joint analysis and recommendations of the parties shall be submitted to the Mayor of San Francisco, the San Francisco Public Housing Authority, the San Francisco Redevelopment Agency, and concerned state and federal agencies. The responses of the agencies will be evaluated by the parties to determine their adequacy and the need for further action. The joint analysis and recommendations, the responses of the relevant agencies and the parties' plans in light of those responses shall be included in the reports to the Court required by subparagraph d below.

d. No later than one year after the entry of this Consent Decree and annually thereafter, the designated expert shall submit to the Court and the parties a report on progress in promoting and achieving policies and actions by housing agencies that promote school desegregation and integration. In addition, each party shall notify the Court and the other parties of housing developments or changes in housing policy that would intensify the problem of school segregation in any part of the District.

e. In evaluating the response of the housing agencies and preparing recommendations, the parties shall consider the following issues, among others: the impact of locating additional housing in areas of the city already racially segregated; the need for the development of tenant selection policies for subsidized family housing projects that will promote integration; the need to stabilize areas that are residentially integrated; the development of policies to maintain residential and school integration in areas undergoing "gentrification"; special counseling efforts to show families with Section 8 certificates housing outside racially isolated areas; automatic termination of involuntary transportation programs when neighborhoods become residentially integrated; and development and improvement of fair housing monitoring and training programs.

X. Reporting and Monitoring

44. The S.F.U.S.D. shall report to the Court no later than August 1, 1983, and annually thereafter for the duration of this Decree on the performance of the S.F.U.S.D.'s responsibilities under this Consent Decree. The Annual Report shall include sections relating to each portion of this Consent Decree, and shall include the identification of any school the S.F.U.S.D. intends to take out of service or otherwise convert from present usage for the coming year. The District shall contract with the State Department of Education to make an independent review of implementation of this Consent Decree at the close of each school year and to submit a report to the Court no later than August 1 for the preceding school year. The parties, by their counsel, shall meet quarterly for the first year, and periodically thereafter, to

review implementation of the Consent Decree and to determine whether any additional monitoring techniques should be proposed to the Court.

XI. The State Role in Financing the Plan

45. The parties agree and the Court finds that the costs of compliance with, and monitoring of, this Consent Decree constitute costs mandated by a final court order for which the S.F.U.S.D. is entitled to reimbursement under Sections 42243.6 and/or 42249 of the California Education Code.

46. Defendant California State Department of Education shall assist the S.F.U.S.D. in documenting its claims for reimbursement under Sections 42243.6 and/or 42249 with respect to the costs of compliance with this Consent Decree, and support such claims before the State Legislature, the State Controller and the State Board of Control.

47. In the event that the S.F.U.S.D. claims for reimbursement are challenged, the S.F.U.S.D. and State Defendant shall report to the Court identifying the difficulties in obtaining reimbursement. Any of the parties may propose to the Court action designed to protect the integrity and timely implementation of the provisions of this Consent Decree.

XII. Retention of Jurisdiction

48. The Court retains jurisdiction of this action for the purpose of receiving the Reports required to be submitted under provisions of this Decree and to enter such additional orders as may be appropriate. At any time after six years from the date of the entry of this Consent Decree, Defendants may move the Court, upon 30 days' notice to Plaintiffs, for dissolution of this Decree. In considering whether to dissolve the Decree, the Court will take into account whether Defendants have substantially complied with the Decree and whether the basic objectives of the Decree have been achieved.

49. The availability of funds will determine the scope and timing of implementation of the provisions of this Decree.

50. Any party to this Decree may at any time propose modification of the Decree to the Court and the other parties.

XIII. Notice and Objections

51. Within ten days of the entry of this Consent Decree, the S.F.U.S.D. shall give notice of this Decree to the class represented by Plaintiffs. The form and content of the notice shall be as set forth in Appendix C to this Decree.

52. The Notice shall be published three times weekly for two consecutive weeks in both the *San Francisco Chronicle* and the *San Francisco Examiner*. It shall be published in a prominent position as a display advertisement, in a type size no smaller than that normally used for news stories in each publication, with a heading in larger, boldface type.

53. The S.F.U.S.D., after consultation with the parties, shall issue a press release on or before the date on which publication of the Notice commences. The press release shall announce the Consent Decree, state that copies thereof will be available at the Court and at the headquarters offices of S.F.U.S.D., and explain the opportunity for interested persons to object in writing and appear at the hearing before this Court on February 14, 1983. The S.F.U.S.D. shall maintain copies of the Notice and of the Consent Decree at its headquarters offices to furnish to persons requesting information concerning the Decree, and shall make such copies available at any press conference concerning the Decree in which District representatives participate.

54. The Notice shall afford members of the class and other affected persons or organizations an opportunity to file written objections to this Decree with the Clerk of the Court within thirty days following the date of the initial publication of the Notice. The Clerk will promptly transmit copies of these objections to counsel of record.

55. The Court will hear oral argument on any timely-filed objections to this Decree at 9:30 a.m. on February 14, 1983.

APPENDIX C
Maps

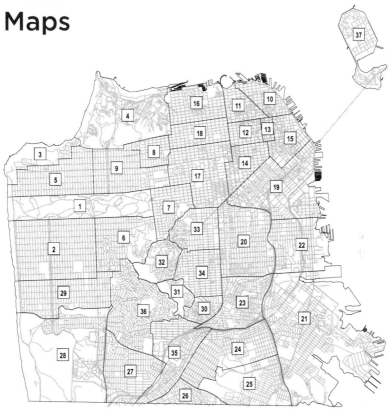

Map 1. San Francisco Neighborhoods. Data Source: City and County of San Francisco Planning Department. (Esri ArcGIS Desktop, 10.6.1)

LEGEND

1. Golden Gate Park
2. Outer Sunset
3. Seacliff
4. Presidio
5. Outer Richmond
6. Inner Sunset
7. Haight Ashbury
8. Presidio Heights
9. Inner Richmond
10. North Beach
11. Russian Hill
12. Nob Hill
13. Chinatown
14. Downtown
15. Financial District
16. Marina
17. Western Addition
18. Pacific Heights
19. South of Market
20. Mission
21. Bayview-Hunters Point
22. Potrero Hill
23. Bernal Heights
24. Excelsior
25. Visitacion Valley
26. Crocker Amazon
27. Oceanview
28. Lakeshore
29. Parkside
30. Glen Park
31. Diamond Heights
32. Twin Peaks
33. Castro/Upper Market
34. Noe Valley
35. Outer Mission
36. West of Twin Peaks
37. Treasure Island

Map 2. San Francisco Unified School District Elementary Schools. Data Source: San Francisco Unified School District. (Esri ArcGIS Desktop, 10.6.1) *Note*: Partial list. Some schools have since closed or been renamed.

LEGEND

1. Alamo
2. Alice Fong Yu Alternative
3. Alvarado
4. Argonne
5. Bret Harte
6. Bryant
7. Buena Vista Alternative
8. Cabrillo
9. César Chávez
10. Claire Lilienthal
11. Cleveland
12. Daniel Webster
13. Dr. Charles R. Drew
14. Dr. William Cobb
15. E. R. Taylor
16. Edison
17. El Dorado

18. Francis Scott Key
19. Garfield
20. George Washington Carver
21. Glen Park
22. Golden Gate
23. Gordon J. Lau (C. Stockton)
24. Grattan
25. Jean Parker
26. John Muir
27. Junipero Serra
28. Lafayette
29. Lakeshore
30. Leonard R. Flynn
31. Malcolm X
32. Marshall
33. McKinley

34. Miraloma
35. Monroe
36. New Traditions
37. Ortega
38. Paul Revere
39. Sanchez
40. Spring Valley
41. Starr King
42. Sunnyside
43. Sunset
44. Sutro
45. Treasure Island
46. Twenty-First Century
47. Ulloa
48. Visitacion Valley
49. West Portal
50. William De Avila
51. Yick Woo

Map 3. San Francisco Unified School District Middle Schools. Data Source: San Francisco Unified School District. (Esri ArcGIS Desktop, 10.6.1) *Note*: Partial list. Some schools have since closed or been renamed.

LEGEND

1. Aptos
2. Luther Burbank
3. Central (never opened)
4. Gloria R. Davis
5. James Denman
6. Everett
7. Francisco
8. Benjamin Franklin

9. A. P. Giannini
10. Herbert Hoover
11. Dr. Martin Luther King Jr. (formerly Portola)
12. James Lick
13. Horace Mann
14. Marina

15. Enola D. Maxwell
16. Pelton (now Thurgood Marshall High)
17. Presidio
18. Roosevelt
19. Visitacion Valley

Map 4. San Francisco Unified School District High Schools. Data Source: San Francisco Unified School District. (Esri ArcGIS Desktop, 10.6.1) *Note*: Partial list. Some schools have since closed or been renamed.

LEGEND

1. Balboa
2. Phillip & Sala Burton Academic (formerly Woodrow Wilson)
3. Downtown
4. Galileo Academy of Science & Technology

5. Abraham Lincoln
6. Lowell
7. Thurgood Marshall Academic (formerly Pelton Middle)
8. Mission

9. John O'Connell Alternative
10. School of the Arts (formerly McAteer)
11. Raoul Wallenberg
12. George Washington

Notes

Introduction

1 Weiner, "Educational Decisions in an Organized Anarchy." The superintendent originally proposed a complex for the predominantly Black southeast corner of the city. But in the end, complexes were created in the predominantly White Sunset ("Park South") and Richmond Districts. As drawn up, Park South comprised eight elementary schools serving just over 3,500 students. Richmond comprised twelve elementary schools serving 5,300 students.

2 *A Report on the Planning and Implementation of the Richmond Educational Complex, 1970–1971,* Office of Innovative Planning, San Francisco Unified School District, San Francisco History Center (hereafter SFHC).

3 Ron Moskowitz, "S.F. Step for New 'Cluster' School Plan," *San Francisco Chronicle,* February 25, 1969.

4 Marjorie Lemlow would go on to run for a seat on the San Francisco Board of Supervisors. Her statement of qualifications for the November 2, 1971, election reads, "I have helped to unify public opinion against forced busing and usurping of parental control. The life of our city depends on the stability of its families and retention of its middle class families within its boundaries." Election Guide, November 2, 1971, General Municipal Election, San Francisco Registrar of Voters, San Francisco Ballot Propositions Database, San Francisco Public Library.

5 Charles Howe, "The 'Goons' Who Struck at the School Meeting," *San Francisco Chronicle,* February 27, 1969; "Incident on Hayes Street," editorial, *San Francisco Chronicle,* February 27, 1969; and "Bloody Row over Busing at School Board Meeting," *San Francisco Chronicle,* February 26, 1969.

6 Jerry Burns, "Alioto Deplores the Violence," *San Francisco Chronicle,* February 27, 1969.

7 The school board conditionally accepted the plan in June 1969 with a requirement that additional revisions be submitted by December. Board approval was contingent on the submission of supplementary information regarding funding, transportation, school–community involvement, facilities, feeder patterns, instructional arrangements, staffing, and evaluation. *A Report on the Planning and Implementation of the Richmond Educational Complex, 1970–1971*, Office of Innovative Planning, SFUSD, SFHC.

8 *Johnson v. San Francisco Unified School District*, 339 F. Supp. 1315 (1971), *vacated and remanded*, 500 F.2d 349 (1974). Plaintiffs representing a group of Black children in public elementary schools filed a civil rights complaint seeking relief against public school officials who they charged with "maintaining and operating a dual school system by means of policies and practices of racial discrimination and segregation." The chronology of the case provided in Judge Weigel's order states that plaintiffs' suit was filed on June 24, 1969. However, the *San Francisco Chronicle* reported that the suit was filed on June 24, 1970 ("S.F. Schools Sued on Desegregation," *San Francisco Chronicle*, June 25, 1970). For a legal history of school segregation in San Francisco through 1978, see Civil Rights Action for Declaratory and Injunctive Relief, Class Action, *SFNAACP v. SFUSD* (Docket File [hereafter DF] 1, filed 6/30/78).

9 Dudley Stone later became William De Avila school (item #50, Map 2). "Jenkins Is 'Sorry' NAACP Filed Suit," *San Francisco Chronicle*, June 25, 1970.

10 Appendix A provides a description of my data and methodology. Several maps are included to help illuminate San Francisco's neighborhood and school dynamics during its period of court supervision (appendix C). Map 1 depicts the city's neighborhoods. In Maps 2, 3, and 4, neighborhood boundaries are overlaid with the elementary, middle, and high schools identified in the book, past and present.

11 *Brown v. Board of Education of Topeka*, 347 U.S. 483 (1954). David Kirp identifies the *Johnson v. SFUSD* court decision as "the first court-ordered desegregation of a large non-Southern city." Kirp, *Just Schools*, 82.

12 *Milliken v. Bradley*, 418 U.S. 717 (1974).

13 *Parents Involved in Community Schools v. Seattle School District No. 1*, 551 U.S. 701 (2007).

14 Clotfelter, *After* Brown; and Orfield et al., *Deepening Segregation in American Public Schools*.

15 For instance, Baker, *Paradoxes of Desegregation*; Anderson, *Little Rock*; Titus, *Brown's Battleground*; Littlejohn and Ford, *Elusive Equality*; K'Meyer, *From Brown to Meredith*; and Erickson, *Making the Unequal Metropolis*.

16 Tolnay, "African American 'Great Migration' and Beyond."

17 Bureau of Intergroup Relations, *Racial and Ethnic Survey of California Public Schools*, 35–46.

18 Contemporary volumes in this vein include Howell Baum's *Brown in Baltimore*, Dionne Danns's *Desegregating Chicago's Public Schools*, and Matthew Delmont's *Why Busing Failed*.

19 Omi and Winant, *Racial Formation in the United States*.

20 Omi and Winant, 55.

21 Omi and Winant, 56.

22 Kim, *Bitter Fruit*. See also Maeda, *Chains of Babylon*.

23 For instance, Campbell, *Institutional Change and Globalization*; Steensland, *Failed Welfare Revolution*; and Béland and Waddan, *Politics of Policy Change*.

24 Scholars have applied an institutional logics framework in numerous fields and on numerous topics. Collectively, this work helps explain how the condition of multiple institutional logics leads to change. Within a field—whether health care, book publishing, or public education—stakeholders maintain, carry, and modify competing sets of material practices and symbolic constructions in political contests for dominance. See, for example, Thornton and Ocasio, "Institutional Logics and the Historical Contingency of Power in Organizations"; Rao, Monin, and Durand, "Institutional Change in Toque Ville"; and Haveman and Rao, "Structuring a Theory of Moral Sentiments."

25 Friedland and Alford, "Bringing Society Back In." See also, Thornton, *Markets from Culture*; Thornton and Ocasio, "Institutional Logics"; and Thornton, Ocasio, and Lounsbury, *Institutional Logics Perspective*.

26 DiMaggio and Powell, "Iron Cage Revisited"; Meyer and Rowan, "Institutionalized Organizations"; Scott and Meyer, "Organization of Societal Sectors"; and Scott, *Institutions and Organizations*. An institution, in its broadest definition, is a rule. It is a social structure that has attained resilience. While organizational institutionalists understand institutions to include formal rules that regulate behavior (e.g., public policy), their focus is typically on informal, taken-for-granted cultural-cognitive and normative frameworks.

27 Scott, *Institutions and Organizations*; and Powell and DiMaggio, introduction.

28 Friedland and Alford, "Bringing Society Back In." See also, Thornton, *Markets from Culture*.

29 Friedland and Alford, "Bringing Society Back In," 248; DiMaggio, "Culture and Cognition"; Greenwood and Suddaby, "Institutional Entrepreneurship in Mature Fields"; and Thornton and Ocasio, "Institutional Logics."

30 Friedland and Alford, "Bringing Society Back In," 248.

31 Friedland and Alford, 256. An "organizational field" refers to those "organizations that, in the aggregate, constitute a recognized area of institutional

life." DiMaggio and Powell, "Iron Cage Revisited," 148. See also, Scott, "Conceptualizing Organizational Fields."

32 California Statutes of 1851, ch. 126, art. III, sec. 1, in "Statutory Segregation of Public School Children by Race in California: 1851–1948" (undated memo), carton 131, folder: "California Statutes, Codes, etc.," Material Prepared by Legal Counsel for Use in Pending Suit Brought against the San Francisco Unified School District, BANC MSS 84/175c, Bancroft Library, University of California, Berkeley (hereafter BANC MSS 84/175c). The memo notes that prior to 1872, California codes regarding education were part of the general state statutes. In 1872, they were moved to the Political Code. In 1929, California established a separate School Code, which, in 1943, became the California Education Code. While 1851 marks the formal start of California's public education system, the "inauguration of free schools on the Pacific Coast" began in 1849. John C. Pelton, "Annual Report of the Superintendent of Public Schools for the Year Ending October 15th, 1867," box 79, San Francisco Unified School District Records, SFHC. For a detailed history of school segregation in California, see Wollenberg, *All Deliberate Speed.*

33 St. Cyprian AME was located on Jackson Street and Virginia Place (between Stockton and Powell Streets). Pelton, "Annual Report, 1867," box 79, SFHC. St. Cyprian became Bethel AME. See Montesano, "San Francisco Black Churches in the Early 1860's." Other cities would follow, and by 1873 there were a reported twenty-one public schools in California for what were then referred to as "colored" students. Wollenberg, *All Deliberate Speed*, 10–11. See also Taylor, *In Search of the Racial Frontier.*

34 Wollenberg, *All Deliberate Speed.*

35 The church operated the school for Chinese students as early as 1853. Wollenberg, *All Deliberate Speed*, 32. See Chang, "Study of the Movement to Segregate Chinese Pupils"; and Pelton, "Annual Report, 1867," box 79, SFHC. See also Notice of Motion for Partial Summary Judgment, *SFNAACP v. SFUSD* (DF190, 6/6/80).

36 "Of Schools," sections 56–58, Pelton, "Annual Report, 1867," box 79, SFHC. Section 53 restricted general admission into public schools to White children. "California Statutes, Codes, etc.," carton 131, BANC MSS 84/175c. On the Chinese School, see Wollenberg, *All Deliberate Speed*, 34.

37 *Ward v. Flood*, 48 Cal. 36 (1874) at 39, 52–57.

38 On the San Francisco school board decision: Wollenberg, *All Deliberate Speed*, 27; and "The Abolishment of Separate Schools for Colored Children," *Pacific Appeal*, August 7, 1875. On the legislative change: "Statutory Segregation" (undated memo), carton 131, folder: "California Statutes, Codes, etc.,"

BANC MSS 84/175c. Section 1662 of the Political Code of 1872 was amended in 1883 with the following: "Every school, unless otherwise provided by law, must be open for the admission of all children between six and twenty-one years of age residing in the district; and the board of trustees or city board of education, have power to admit adults and children not residing in the district, whenever good reason exists therefor. Trustees shall have the power to exclude children of filthy or vicious habits or children suffering from contagious or infectious diseases."

39 Wollenberg, *All Deliberate Speed,* 34–38.

40 The district justified its actions by pointing to a provision in the school law that allowed the exclusion of "the vicious, the filthy and those having contagious and infectious diseases." The courts determined that these conditions could only apply on an individual basis rather than on group stereotypes. *Tape v. Hurley,* 66 Cal. Rptr. 473 (1885).

41 School Law of California (1885), §1662, in "Statutory Segregation" (undated memo), carton 131, folder: "California Statutes, Codes, etc.," BANC MSS 84/175c; and Wollenberg, *All Deliberate Speed,* 41–43. *Wong Him v. Callahan,* 119 Fed. 381 (1902) established that California's segregative policy was in accordance with federal law.

42 A legal question over whether Japanese students could legally be segregated emerged, as the language of the school law provided for the segregation of only "Chinese and Mongolians." Wollenberg, *All Deliberate Speed,* 54.

43 The history of exclusion in San Francisco was quickly forgotten. In 1926, representatives from the North Beach Improvement Association and the Central Council of Civic Clubs presented to the school board a petition signed by 351 parents of Francisco Junior High School. The parents opposed the enrollment of Chinese students at the school. The delegation was informed by the school board that if the district "had established a Chinese School it was not with the thought in mind that the school be a segregated school, but rather with the idea of enabling the children of that section to attend a near-by school." Minutes of the Board of Education, May 18, 1926, in Preble Stolz, Professor of Law, University of California, Berkeley, to Irving G. Breyer, Legal Advisor, SFUSD, February 27, 1963, box 133, folder: "Art Brunwasser Materials," BANC MSS 84/175c.

44 Political Code of 1921, 438, in "Statutory Segregation" (undated memo), carton 131, folder: "California Statutes, Codes, etc.," BANC MSS 84/175c.

45 California Education Code, §8003, 8004 (since repealed), in "Statutory Segregation" (undated memo), carton 131, folder: "California Statutes, Codes, etc.," BANC MSS 84/175c.

46 Hendrick, *Education of Non-Whites in California*.

47 *Mendez v. Westminster School District of Orange County*, 64 F. Supp. 544 (1946). Organizational support for the lawsuit was through LULAC, Santa Ana Chapter No. 147. Arriola, "Knocking on the Schoolhouse Door."

48 For example, the official policy of the El Modena school board required "persons of Mexican descent who were unfamiliar with the English language be required to attend one of the schools set apart." Transcript of Proceedings, *Mendez v. Westminster*, in Arriola, "Knocking on the Schoolhouse Door."

49 *Mendez*, 64 F. Supp. at 549. Mexican and White students were considered to be of the same race. Thus, the court found the school districts to have discriminated on the basis of national origin. *Plessy v. Ferguson*, 163 U.S. 537 (1896). Homer Plessy was considered to be "colored" under Louisiana law and was required to sit in the "colored" car of a train. He argued unsuccessfully that separate cars violated the Thirteenth and Fourteenth Amendments. The ruling allowed for a "separate but equal" distinction that extended to restaurants, public transportation, restroom facilities, and schools.

50 The district court's ruling was affirmed on an appeal that largely argued the federal courts lacked jurisdiction over the state-run public education system. *Westminster v. Mendez*, 161 F.2d 774 (1947).

51 California Education Code, §8003, 8004 (since repealed), in "Statutory Segregation" (undated memo), carton 131, folder: "California Statutes, Codes, etc.," BANC MSS 84/175c. See also *Westminster*, 161 F.2d at 780.

52 For a detailed history of NAACP's struggle to overturn legal school segregation, see Tushnet, *NAACP's Legal Strategy against Segregated Education*; and Kluger, *Simple Justice*.

53 For instance, *Sweatt v. Painter*, 339 U.S. 629 (1950) dealt with the University of Texas Law School's denial of admission of an African American applicant. The Supreme Court determined that a separate legal education could not be equal, but justices reserved judgment on public education.

54 *Plessy*, 163 U.S. 537 (1896).

55 *Missouri ex rel. Gaines v. Canada*, 305 U.S. 337 (1938); *Sipuel v. Oklahoma*, 332 U.S. 631 (1948); and *McLaurin v. Oklahoma State Regents*, 339 U.S. 637 (1950).

56 *Brown*, 347 U.S. at 493.

57 *Brown v. Board of Education (Brown II)*, 349 U.S. 294 (1955).

58 *Brown II*, 349 U.S. at 301. See also Bell, *Silent Covenants*.

59 Orfield et al., *Deepening Segregation*. However, widespread desegregation was relatively short-lived, and districts have gradually resegregated in recent years. Clotfelter, *After Brown*; and Orfield and Lee, *Historic Reversals*.

60 "We Must Study Our School System," editorial, *Sun-Reporter,* June 13, 1959.

61 "We Must Study Our School System," editorial, *Sun-Reporter,* June 13, 1959; "S.O.S. Confab a Success," *Sun-Reporter,* July 11, 1959; and "S.O.S. Confab Set for Aug. 3," *Sun-Reporter,* July 18, 1959. On Spears's testimony, see Kirp, *Just Schools,* 85.

62 Robert L. Carter to Northern Branches, Area and State Conferences (memorandum), October 6, 1961, carton 57, folder 78, National Association for the Advancement of Colored People, Region I, Records, BANC MSS 78/180c, Bancroft Library, University of California, Berkeley (hereafter BANC MSS 78/180c).

63 Testimony of Wilfred T. Ussery, Chair of the San Francisco Chapter of CORE, transcript of the Regular meeting of the Board of Education, September 18, 1962, SFHC. Ussery continues: "That this Board did not affirmatively cause the segregation which exists here in San Francisco does not make such education any the less inferior."

64 "NAACP's 10-Year Campaign," *San Francisco Chronicle,* July 10, 1971.

65 "Schools in West Hit: NAACP Reports Finding Segregation in Survey," *New York Times,* April 21, 1962.

66 Superintendent of Schools Harold Spears asked, "Is it segregation to require children to attend the school in their own neighborhood?" Wallace Turner, "Negroes on Coast Ask School Shift," *New York Times,* August 5, 1962.

67 Central was to occupy the old site of Lowell High School, which, following the 1956 issuance of a bond, had moved to the Lakeshore neighborhood. Decades later, Lowell's admissions policy would become a major issue of contention in San Francisco's school desegregation efforts.

68 Wallace Turner, "Negroes on Coast Ask School Shift," *New York Times,* August 5, 1962. Terry Francois would go on to become San Francisco's first African American supervisor.

69 "The Integration Pattern in S.F.," editorial, *San Francisco Chronicle,* July 23, 1962. An alternate perspective was put forth by the *San Francisco Bulletin*: "It would be folly to gerrymander the district out of all semblance of administrative sanity." Quoted in Kaplan, "San Francisco," 71.

70 Claimants sought an 80–20 White to non-White ratio for the school. The suit was brought on behalf of five White and four Black children from Grattan (including McMurtry's daughter). Kaplan, "San Francisco"; Weiner, "Educational Decisions in an Organized Anarchy"; Weiner, "Participation, Deadlines, and Choice"; McMurtry quoted in "A Challenge in Court on Central High," *San Francisco Chronicle,* August 15, 1962; Correspondence from Citizens Committee for Neighborhood Schools in Harold Spears, Superintendent

(internal memo), August 1963, box 31, SFHC; and Zirpoli quoted in "A Racial Dispute Averted on Coast," *New York Times,* August 26, 1962.

71   *Brock v. Board of Education,* no. 71034, N.D. California (1962). The lawsuit was filed on October 2, 1962, on behalf of 159 Black and White students.

72   California Administrative Code, Title 5, Education, §2010 (approved October 23, 1962).

73   Report of the Ad Hoc Committee of the Board of Education to Study Ethnic Factors in the San Francisco Public Schools, April 2, 1963, box 93, SFHC. In September, the board appointed an ad hoc Committee to Study Ethnic Factors in San Francisco Schools to help quell the debate. Board of Education Resolution #29–18A1, September 18, 1962, SFHC.

74   Breyer to Ad Hoc Committee Meeting, San Francisco Public Schools (Memo), November 15, 1962, in Plaintiffs Fourth Request for Production of Documents, *SFNAACP v. SFUSD* (DF100, c8/79).

75   Report of the Ad Hoc Committee of the Board of Education to Study Ethnic Factors in the San Francisco Public Schools, April 2, 1963, box 93, SFHC.

76   The lawsuit was dismissed following the hiring of a Black human relations officer and the assignment of hundreds of minority students to predominantly White schools. Fraga, Erlichson, and Lee, "Consensus Building and School Reform." An alternate perspective is provided in Weiner, "Educational Decisions in an Organized Anarchy," 47: The SFNAACP dropped its suit "because of the legal difficulties they foresaw in obtaining a favorable judicial ruling."

77   See Weiner, "Educational Decisions in an Organized Anarchy"; Kaplan, "San Francisco"; and Arthur Brunwasser, letter to the editor, *Commentary,* July 1972.

78   Kaplan, "San Francisco." The superintendent sought the data release amid employment discrimination investigations by the California Fair Employment Practices Commission and the U.S. Office of Education.

79   The racial categories used by the district were: *Negro, Oriental,* and *White.*

80   James Benet, "Race Patterns in S.F. Schools Are Revealed," *San Francisco Chronicle,* August 5, 1965.

81   "Racial Disparity in S.F. Schools," editorial, *San Francisco Chronicle,* August 6, 1965.

82   A Report on the Planning and Implementation of the Richmond Educational Complex, 1970–1971, Office of Innovative Planning, SFUSD, box 95, SFHC.

83   Statement of Grandvel A. Jackson, February 7, 1983, *SFNAACP v. SFUSD* (DF293, 2/7/83).

84   Fine, *When Leadership Fails;* Weiner, "Educational Decisions in an Organized Anarchy"; and Weiner, "Participation, Deadlines, and Choice."

85 Weiner, "Educational Decisions in an Organized Anarchy." After years of resistance from the school district, Mayor John Shelley was persuaded by advocates to appoint Laurel Glass, Alan Nichols, and Zuretti Goosby. Mayor Joseph Alioto (a busing opponent who was hired by the school board as a special counsel to defend the district against the SFNAACP's *Brock* lawsuit) appointed David Sanchez and Howard Nemerovski. All of these appointees supported some degree of racial balance. Weiner, "Participation, Deadlines, and Choice."

86 A Report on the Planning and Implementation of the Richmond Educational Complex, 1970–1971, Office of Innovative Planning, SFUSD, SFHC.

87 *Brown,* 347 U.S. at 495. Opinion of the Court delivered by Chief Justice Warren.

1. How Educational Opportunity for San Francisco's African American Students Evolved

1 Veronica Pollard, "Major Plan to Redesign S.F. Schools," *San Francisco Chronicle,* December 30, 1977; Michael Taylor, "S.F. School 'Redesign' OKd," *San Francisco Chronicle,* February 16, 1978; and "Educational Redesign: A Proposal," January 1978, box 1, Robert F. Alioto miscellaneous papers, Hoover Institution Archives, Stanford University (hereafter RFA/HIA).

2 "Educational Redesign: A Proposal," 21, January 1978, box 1, RFA/HIA.

3 See also Report to Federal District Court Regarding Elementary School Desegregation, June 24, 1977, 58, *Johnson v. SFUSD* C-70 1331 SAW, Record Group (hereafter RG) 21, U.S. National Archives and Records Administration (hereafter NARA). The court's ruling is also provided in *Johnson,* 339 F. Supp 1315; Pivnick quoted in Walter Blum, "In the Winter of Redesign," *San Francisco Chronicle & Examiner,* April 30, 1978; Veronica Pollard, "What People Say about S.F. School Plan," *San Francisco Chronicle,* January 18, 1978; Annie Nakao, "Schools Chief's Exit Blocked by Angry Mob," *San Francisco Chronicle,* January 8, 1978; Jack Cheevers, "The Resurrection of San Francisco's Schools," *San Francisco Business,* August 1982; and Affidavit of Robert F. Alioto, *Johnson v. SFUSD,* April 17, 1978, carton 101, folder: "San Francisco Settlement Proposal," BANC MSS 84/175c.

4 *Johnson,* 339 F. Supp. 1315, *vacated and remanded,* 500 F.2d 349.

5 Memorandum of Decision, Judgment, and Decree, July 9, 1971, *Johnson v. SFUSD* C-70 1331 SAW, RG21, NARA.

6 Harry Johanesen, "Chinese Protest School Bus Plans," *San Francisco Chronicle,* June 6, 1971. SFNAACP attorney Arthur Brunwasser recalled: "It was all pure demagoguery. . . . I was really angry at Alioto. He brought the city . . . into a virtual race riot by encouraging people to think they don't have to

obey a federal court order. And I had authorization to cite him for contempt of court for filing and encouraging a violation of a federal court order." Interview, Arthur Brunwasser, January 27, 2010.

7 "NAACP Official Accuses Alioto," *San Francisco Chronicle*, June 8, 1971.

8 As a result of the district's efforts with Operation Integrate, the SFNAACP's secondary education desegregation lawsuit against the SFUSD was voluntarily dismissed in 1976. The case is *O'Neill v. SFUSD*, CA 72–808 RFP (1972).

9 The racial categories under Horseshoe were: *Spanish Surname, Other White, Black/Negro,* and *Asian/Oriental.* "Step One: A Student Assignment Design for September 1974," c1974, SFHC; and "Educational Redesign: A Proposal," January 1978, box 1, RFA/HIA. Under Operation Integrate and Horseshoe, the district took into account nine subgroups in the assignment of students to schools: *Black, Chinese, Spanish Surname, Other White, Filipino, Japanese, Korean, American Indian,* and *Other Non-White.* These categories were determined in 1964, when schools superintendent Harold Spears, facing pressure from various community groups, began annual surveys of the various ethnic groups in the city. Arthur Brunwasser, letter to the editor, *Commentary,* July 1972. Categories have been relatively stable although labels have changed over time (for example, from *Spanish-Surname* to *Spanish-Speaking* to *Latino*).

10 San Francisco Public Schools Commission, "The Educational Components of an Integrated School System," November 17, 1976, SFHC. The San Francisco Public Schools Commission was appointed by State Superintendent of Schools Wilson Riles in January 1975 and was also known as the Riles Commission and the Roth Commission, for the chair, William Matson Roth. The general objectives of the commission were to "identify problems in the School District and to assist in implementing agreed-upon solutions" particularly in the areas of finance and management (5). The commission comprised civic leaders from business, labor, religion, and education, and was supported through grants from local foundations. See also Letter from William M. Roth, Chair, San Francisco Public Schools Commission, December 1, 1976 (DF132, 1/4/80).

11 School closures were projected to yield $4.9 million in savings, reduced busing, $1.6 million. "Educational Redesign: A Proposal," January 1978, box 1, RFA/HIA; Veronica Pollard, "Alioto's Final Plan for Cutting School Budget," *San Francisco Chronicle*, July 29, 1978; Michael Taylor, "S.F. School 'Redesign' OKd," *San Francisco Chronicle*, February 16, 1978; Affidavit of Robert F. Alioto, *Johnson v. SFUSD*, April 17, 1978, carton 101, folder: "San Francisco Settlement Proposal," BANC MSS 84/175c; and Educational Redesign, San Francisco Board of Education Resolution #81–31Sp1.

12 Walter Blum, "In the Winter of Redesign," *San Francisco Chronicle & Examiner*, April 30, 1978; "Educational Redesign: A Proposal," 17, January 1978, box 1, RFA/HIA; Annie Nakao, "Schools Chief's Exit Blocked by Angry Mob," *San Francisco Chronicle*, January 8, 1978; and Alioto quoted in Blum, "In the Winter of Redesign."

13 *Keyes v. School District No. 1, Denver, Colorado*, 413 U.S. 189 (1973). In addition, *Keyes* is significant for extending protection to Latinos ("Hispanos" was the term used by the Colorado Department of Education) since they "suffer identical discrimination" to African Americans ("Negroes"). Brennan quoted in 413 U.S. 189 (1973) at 208 (emphasis added). In his opinion, Justice Brennan refers specifically to *Swann v. Charlotte-Mecklenburg Board of Education*, 402 U.S. 1 (1971), a case in which the court noted a difference between de facto and de jure school segregation. Justice Powell, while concurring in part with *Keyes*, dissented on the question of intent, stating: "The net result of the Court's language, however, is the application of an effect test to the actions of southern school districts and an intent test to those in other sections, at least until an initial de jure finding for those districts can be made. Rather than straining to perpetuate any such dual standard, we should hold forthrightly that significant segregated school conditions in any section of the country are a prima facie violation of constitutional rights." *Keyes*, 413 U.S. at 232. The Ninth Circuit quoted in *Soria v. Oxnard School District Board of Trustees*, 488 F.2d 579 (1973) at 585.

14 Memorandum of Decision, Judgment, and Decree, July 9, 1971, 3, *Johnson v. SFUSD* C-70 1331 SAW, RG21, NARA.

15 Weigel references several cases, including: *United States v. School District 151*, 404 F.2d 1125 (1968); *United States v. Montgomery County Board of Education*, 395 U.S. 225, 231 (1969); and *Coppedge v. Franklin County Board of Education*, 394 F.2d 410 (1968).

16 Intervenors include *Johnson v. SFUSD* (C-71 1877; C-71 2163; C-72 2980); Robert G. Nelson et al., *Intervenor-Appellants* (C-71 1878; C-71 2189); and Guey Heung Lee et al., *Plaintiffs in Intervention-Appellants* (C-71 2105).

17 *Johnson v. SFUSD*, 500 F.2d 349 (1974). The Ninth Circuit also vacated and remanded a decision by Weigel to prevent the intervention of a group of parents of elementary schoolchildren of Chinese ancestry who opposed the reassignment under Horseshoe with instructions to permit their intervention.

18 Interview, Arthur Brunwasser, January 27, 2010.

19 Most SBE members had been appointed by Governor Edmund G. "Pat" Brown Sr. For a discussion on the SBE's activities during this period, see Hendrick, *Education of Non-Whites in California*; California Administrative Code, Title 5, Education, §2010 (October 23, 1962); California Administrative

Code, Title 5, Education, §2011 (February 1963), and §135.3(e) (April 1963); and *Jackson v. Pasadena School District*, 59 Cal.2d 876 (1963).

20 Hendrick, *Education of Non-Whites in California*, 112. Bureau of Intergroup Relations, *Racial and Ethnic Survey of California Public Schools*, 2; and California Administrative Code, Title 5, Education, §2011(c). The regulation, put forth by the State Board of Education in 1962 and amended in 1969, has since been eliminated.

21 Regulations were repealed on March 12, 1970. The Council of the Great City Schools, "Educational Equality/Quality in San Francisco Public Schools" (c1971), 61, box 95, folder 3, SFHC.

22 In 1970, the legislature added §1009.5 to the Education Code: "No governing board of a school district shall require any student or pupil to be transported for any purpose or for any reason without the written permission of the parent or guardian." The California Supreme Court ruled that if construed to bar assignment of pupils to nonneighborhood schools the section would be unconstitutional. *San Francisco Unified School District v. Johnson*, 3 Cal.3d 937 (1971) at 954. The Assignment of Students to Schools Initiative (Proposition 21) proposed to amend the Education Code by adding §1009.6: "No public school student shall, because of his race, creed, or color, be assigned to or be required to attend a particular school." In addition, it repealed a recently passed law (the Bagley Act, AB 724) that added §5002 and §5003 to the Education Code, which (1) established factors for consideration in preventing or eliminating racial or ethnic imbalances in public schools; (2) required school districts to report numbers and percentages of racial or ethnic groups in each school; and (3) required districts to develop plans to remedy imbalances. San Francisco voters narrowly defeated Proposition 21, with 136,180 opposed and 135,948 in favor. San Francisco Registrar of Voters, "General Election Recapitulation of Voters," November 22, 1972. Statewide, the measure passed in a landslide: 4,962,420 (63.1 percent) to 2,907,776 (36.9 percent). Miller, *A Study of California Ballot Measures*.

23 *Santa Barbara School District v. Superior Court*, 13 Cal.3d 315 (1975); *Crawford v. Board of Education of Los Angeles*, 17 Cal.3d 280 (1976); and *NAACP v. San Bernardino City Unified School District*, 17 Cal.3d 311 (1976). The ruling was a clarification of the Court's decision in *Jackson*, 59 Cal.2d 876, which held: "The right to an equal opportunity for education and the harmful consequences of segregation require that school boards take steps, insofar as reasonably feasible, to alleviate racial imbalance in schools regardless of its cause" (881). See also "Plans to Alleviate Racial and Ethnic Segregation of Minority Students," California Administrative Code, Title 5, Sections 90–10;

SFUSD interpretation in H. LeRoy Cannon, SFUSD Legal Advisor, to Lee S. Dolson, President, Members of the Board, Bill Maher, Commissioner Elect, Peter Mezey, Commissioner Elect, Ben Tom, Commissioner Elect, Robert F. Alioto, Superintendent, "Desegregation. Duty of Governing Board to Desegregate Schools Whether Segregation is *De Jure or De Facto*" (internal memo), November 23, 1976, carton 105, folder: "Materials still to be looked at Re: Request to local defs," BANC MSS 84/175c; and California Supreme Court statement in *Crawford*, 17 Cal.3d 280 at 287n1. The California Supreme Court ruling did not immediately jeopardize the Horseshoe plan. Since it was heard in a federal district court, barring a Ninth Circuit or Supreme Court ruling or an act of Congress, the *Johnson* order would remain in effect.

24 California Administrative Code, Title 5, Education, Chapter 7, §90–101, Plans to Alleviate Racial and Ethnic Segregation of Minority Students (adopted 9/8/77, since repealed). See also, California Administrative Register 77, No. 38–7-9–17–77.

25 The earlier report is James S. Coleman and others, "Equality of Educational Opportunity" [also known as the "Coleman Report"] (U.S. Department of Health, Education, and Welfare, 1966). The report describes the benefits of an integrated education for Black students. A supporter of integrated schools, Coleman delivered an address to the American Educational Research Association on April 2, 1975, in advance of a report by the Urban Institute on White flight from cities. While the study, which came to be known as "Coleman's White flight report," did not directly address busing or any other coercive means to desegregate schools, Coleman used it to argue that the federal courts, which while well-intentioned, were contributing to the unintended consequence of exacerbating segregation. "Thus a major policy implication of this analysis is that in an area such as school desegregation, which has important consequences for individuals and in which individuals retain control of some actions that can in the end defeat the policy, the courts are probably the worst instrument of social policy" (12). Coleman, "Recent Trends in School Segregation." Coleman remarked that strategies are "basically producing resegregation, unfortunate strategies that are the outgrowth of court cases." In response, NAACP legal counsel Nathaniel Jones contended that Coleman's seemingly revised position was indicative of declining interest in civil rights by White liberals and that the academic sector was "just not reliable" as a civil rights ally. Coleman and Jones quoted in Paul Delaney, "Long-Time Desegregation Proponent Attacks Busing as Harmful," *New York Times*, June 7, 1975; and quote from Coleman, "Recent Trends in School Segregation," 12. Coleman's provocative remarks and the

attention they generated became a springboard for scholarly debates on the issue. For example, in August 1975, the Brookings Institute hosted a "Symposium on School Desegregation and White Flight" in which several papers (edited by Gary Orfield) emerged critiquing Coleman's position. While the question of causality would remain unsettled among academics, the phenomenon underlying Coleman's comments—the rapid racial shift in urban public schools—had been brought to the fore. Following the Supreme Court's ruling in *Swann,* across the nation, large urban school districts were experiencing significant enrollment declines among White students. For a discussion on the impact of Coleman's second report in academia, see Ravitch, "Social Science and Social Policy." Ravitch notes that in 1968, sixteen of twenty-nine large urban districts had student enrollments that were majority White. By 1976, only eight still had White majorities. Among these twenty-nine districts, San Francisco's loss of White students (percent) was among the highest. Over this period, Atlanta lost 78.3 percent of its White students, Detroit lost 61.6 percent, and San Francisco lost 61.5 percent. (Ravitch's enrollment numbers for SFUSD differ slightly from the enrollment figures provided by SFUSD.) Ravitch, 146–47.

26 Memorandum of Decision, Judgment, and Decree, 7–8, July 9, 1971, *Johnson v. SFUSD* C-70 1331 SAW, RG21, NARA.

27 Research, Planning & Accountability Data Center, "Student Enrollment, 1967–68 to 2008–09," San Francisco Unified School District. The *San Francisco Chronicle* pinned the half-empty schools on "real competition from private schools in San Francisco and the attraction of what is perceived by young parents to be better educational facilities in the suburbs." "Redesigning Our Schools," editorial, *San Francisco Chronicle,* January 3, 1978. While the citywide absentee rate on the first day of the Horseshoe plan was 44 percent, schools in Chinatown experienced absentee rates as high as 76 percent. Only 10 of the 750 Chinatown students showed up to be bused out of the neighborhood that first day. Ron Muskowitz, "Many Absent from School," *San Francisco Chronicle,* September 14, 1971.

28 Fay Fong, coordinator of the Chinatown efforts, vowed that parents would not "accept anything less than an end to busing" before the public school boycott would end. Freedom schools gradually declined in popularity and most Chinese families returned to the school system within a few years. Julie Smith, "Chinese Schools Set to Open," *San Francisco Chronicle,* September 14, 1971. The committee opposed the busing of Chinatown students to schools outside the neighborhood. In addition, there was an "unspoken feeling" of opposition to the busing of non-Chinese students to the neighborhood. Harry Johanesen, "Chinese Protest School Bus Plans," *San Francisco*

Chronicle, June 6, 1971. On the topic of Freedom Schools, see Lum, "Chinese Freedom Schools of San Francisco."

29 Andrew Moss, Senior Statistician, "Evaluation Report #5. SFUSD Integration Department. A 5-Year projection of the Ethnic Composition of SUFSD," April 1, 1976, carton 105, BANC MSS 84/175c. To serve the new matriculates, the district established high school newcomer centers for adults and bilingual education classes for youth speaking Spanish, Tagalog, Chinese, and Vietnamese. Civil Grand Jury Report, 1979–80, RFA/HIA.

30 Affidavit of Robert F. Alioto, April 17, 1978, *Johnson v. SFUSD*, No. C-70 1331 SAW, carton 101, folder: "San Francisco Settlement Proposal," BANC MSS 84/175c. As one example, Alioto: "In the late 1960's new immigrants from Southeast Asia, the Philippines and South and Central America began migrating to San Francisco. At the same time there was a decline in the San Francisco birthrate. This has resulted in a student enrollment in which there is no longer a predominant racial/ethnic group. These facts must be considered when looking at the racial/ethnic balance of our schools." "Educational Redesign: A Proposal," 21, January 1978, box 1, RFA/HIA. These trends continued into the 1980s. By 1985 Chinese students became the largest subgroup in the district, and by 1989, there were more Latino students than Black students.

31 Affidavit of Robert F. Alioto, April 17, 1978, *Johnson v. SFUSD*, No. C-70 1331 SAW, carton 101, folder: "San Francisco Settlement Proposal," BANC MSS 84/175c.

32 Regarding the consent decree: Arthur Brunwasser, Memo to File—*Johnson v. SFUSD*, February 11, 1975, carton 133, folder: "Correspondence of Attys: Brunwasser Files," BANC MSS 84/175c; and Brunwasser to George Krueger, LeRoy Cannon, William Hannawalt, November 4, 1975, carton 133, folder: "Correspondence of Attys: Brunwasser Files," BANC MSS 84/175c. On rescinding settlement agreements: Joseph E. Hall, SFNAACP, to Arthur Brunwasser, March 15, 1976, carton 133, folder: "Correspondence of Attys: Brunwasser Files," BANC MSS 84/175c. Joseph Hall was SFNAACP president from 1975 to 1978.

33 Arthur Brunwasser to Joseph E. Hall, January 9, 1978, box 133, folder: "Correspondence of Atty Brunwasser Files," BANC MSS 84/175c.

34 Thomas I. Atkins was a prominent attorney who was lead counsel of record in school desegregation cases in Detroit, Cleveland, Columbus, Indianapolis, and several other cities. Complaint, Civil Rights Action for Declaratory and Injunctive Relief, *SFNAACP v. SFUSD* (DF1, 6/30/78); and interview, Arthur Brunwasser, January 27, 2010.

35 Thomas Atkins to Joe Hall, February 27, 1978, "Correspondence of Atty.

Brunwasser Files," box 133, folder: "Correspondence of Atty Brunwasser Files," BANC MSS 84/175c.

36 Civil Rights Action for Declaratory and Injunctive Relief, *SFNAACP v. SFUSD* (DF1, 6/30/78). The team of attorneys included Thomas I. Atkins, Nancy B. Reardon, Eva Patterson, Annette Green, Oliver Jones, and Peter Cohn, as well as Nathaniel R. Jones, general counsel for the NAACP Special Contribution Fund, and James Hunt, Susan Ogdie, and Lee Thompson from McCutchen Doyle.

37 Michael Harris, "NAACP Sues to Halt Cutbacks in S.F. Schools," *San Francisco Chronicle*, July 1, 1978.

38 Junius Camp, Supervisor, Community Relations Department to Parents of Guardians of SFUSD Students, "Requests for Correct Racial/Ethnic Identification" (Undated Memo), in Answer to Complaint for Declaratory and Injunctive Relief, *SFNAACP v. SFUSD* (DF12, 8/16/78). Parents were asked to declare on behalf of their children the appropriate category as "considered by themselves, by the school, or by the community." *Other White* was the subgroup for "all Caucasians not counted under Spanish Surname." At various points in time, the district would employ a *Spanish-Speaking* or *Spanish-Surname/Spanish-Speaking* category. The *Asian/Oriental* subgroup brought together Chinese, Japanese, and Korean students. The *Other Non-White* subgroup was mostly composed of other Asian and Pacific Islander populations. The racial and ethnic identification scheme the SFUSD had been using was based on the categories utilized by the State Board of Education for its racial and ethnic surveys of California public schools. Bureau of Intergroup Relations, *Racial and Ethnic Survey of California Public Schools.* See also California Administrative Code, Title 5, §2011, c1978 (since repealed).

39 Memorandum of Decision, Judgment, and Decree, 15, July 9, 1971, *Johnson v. SFUSD* C-70 1331 SAW, RG21, NARA; Memorandum and Order Requiring the Parties to Bus Blacks for School Desegregation, 4, *Johnson v. SFUSD* C-70 1331 SAW, RG21, NARA; and Horseshoe Plan, Submitted by the SFUSD, Version of July 1, 1971, *Johnson v. SFUSD* C-70 1331 SAW, RG21, NARA. On SBE guidelines, see California Administrative Code, Title 5, Education, §2011(c).

40 Andrew Moss, Senior Statistician, SFUSD, "Evaluation Report #5. SFUSD Integration Department. A 5-Year Projection of the Ethnic Composition of SFUSD," April 1, 1976, carton 105, BANC MSS 84/175c; and A Plan for Desegregation and Integration SFUSD, June 9, 1971, carton 105, BANC MSS 84/175c. With the implementation of Operation Integrate, the ±15 percent guidelines were extended to all nine recognized subgroups. Interview, Arthur

Brunwasser, January 27, 2010; and Memorandum of Decision, Judgment, and Decree, 5, July 9, 1971, *Johnson v. SFUSD* C-70 1331 SAW, RG21, NARA. The district submitted Horseshoe; the SFNAACP's plan was dubbed "Freedom." Weigel approved both plans and allowed the district to select the one it would implement. Unsurprisingly, the district opted to implement its own plan.

41 Andrew Moss, Senior Statistician, SFUSD, "Evaluation Report #5. SFUSD Integration Department. A 5-Year Projection of the Ethnic Composition of SUFSD," April 1, 1976, carton 105, BANC MSS 84/175c.

42 "Report: An Educational Redesign for the SFUSD: A Proposal for Consideration," 6, January 6, 1976, carton 101, BANC MSS 84/175c; and "Educational Redesign: A Proposal," 21, January 1978, box 1, RFA/HIA.

43 Affidavit of Robert F. Alioto, 30, April 17, 1978, *Johnson v. SFUSD*, carton 101, folder: "San Francisco Settlement Proposal," BANC MSS 84/175c; Veronica Pollard, "Alioto's Plan Analyzed," *San Francisco Chronicle*, January 19, 1978; SFNAACP statement in Civil Rights Action for Declaratory and Injunctive Relief, 20, *SFNAACP v. SFUSD* (DF1, 6/30/78); For Order Shortening Time and for Temporary Restraining Order, 3–4, *SFNAACP v. SFUSD* (DF9, 8/14/78); Hall quoted in Fairness Hearing, February 14, 1983, *SFNAACP v. SFUSD* (DF289, 2/7/83); Plaintiffs' Report to the Court: A Supplemental Reply to Defendants' Response to Plaintiffs' Motion for Partial Summary Judgment, 10–12, *SFNAACP v. SFUSD* (DF216, 1/23/81); and *Penick v. Columbus Board of Education*, 583 F.2d 787 (1978), affirmed, 443 U.S. 449 (1979).

44 For the 1977–1978 school year, 71 percent of the school district's revenue derived from local sources while 29 percent came from federal and state sources. The share reversed the following year. For the 1978–1979 term, only 31 percent of revenue came from local sources while 69 percent came from federal and state sources. Civil Grand Jury Report, 1978–1979, Robert F. Alioto miscellaneous papers, box 1, Hoover Institution Archives.

45 Proposition 13 amended the state constitution by bringing property values to their 1975 value, limiting property taxes to 1 percent of property value, and restricting reassessments to 2 percent annually. The initiative passed by a 2 to 1 margin on June 6, 1978. Bersin, Kirst, and Liu, *Getting beyond the Facts*; and Michael Harris, "How Prop. 13 Would Affect City Services," *San Francisco Chronicle*, May 22, 1978.

46 Annie Nakao, "School Budget Fight Just Heating Up," *San Francisco Chronicle*, July 30, 1978. The budget of $167.4 million was $23 million less than the prior year's budget. Early projections estimated a budget reduction of as much as 18 percent. Veronica Pollard, "Pleas against S.F. School Cuts," *San*

Francisco Chronicle, August 2, 1978; and "School Budget Fight Just Heating Up," *San Francisco Chronicle,* July 30, 1978. Hooks was quoted during a press conference held after the *SFNAACP* court filing, hours before Prop 13 was to take effect.

47 Stanley Weigel, the judge who presided over the *Johnson* lawsuit, was originally assigned to the case. Weigel recused himself two months after the lawsuit was filed because his son-in-law anticipated a professional relationship with the NAACP Legal Defense and Education Fund in San Francisco. Order of Disqualification, *SFNAACP v. SFUSD* (DF16, 9/6/78). The case was reassigned to Albert Wollenberg who in turn disqualified himself from presiding for having an interest that might have been affected by the outcome. Order of Disqualification, *SFNAACP v. SFUSD* (DF20, 9/13/78). William H. Orrick presided over the case from September 15, 1978, until his retirement in January 2002. Orrick died on August 15, 2003. Motion Requesting the Certification as a Class Action, *SFNAACP v. SFUSD* (DF46, 1/2/79); and Notice of Motion for Partial Summary Judgment, *SFNAACP v. SFUSD* (DF190, 6/6/80).

48 Opinion and Order (Consent Decree), *SFNAACP v. SFUSD,* 576 F. Supp. 34 (1983).

49 *SFNAACP,* 576 F. Supp. 34; Notice of Motion for Dismissal or Abstention, *SFNAACP v. SFUSD* (DF72, 4/13/79); *SFNAACP,* 576 F. Supp. 34; and Plaintiffs' Response to Renewed Motion, *SFNAACP v. SFUSD* (DF225, 8/26/81).

50 Notice of Motion for Partial Summary Judgment, *SFNAACP v. SFUSD* (DF190, 6/6/80); Plaintiffs' Pretrial Statement, *SFNAACP v. SFUSD* (DF236, 3/18/82); and *SFNAACP,* 576 F. Supp. 34.

51 Gary Orfield to the Court, Progress toward a Settlement Agreement, August 10, 1982, in Declaration of Deputy Attorney General John Davison, *SFNAACP v. SFUSD* (DF601, 9/21/90); Notice of Motion for Partial Summary Judgment, *SFNAACP v. SFUSD* (DF190, 6/6/80); and *SFNAACP,* 576 F. Supp. 34, ¶12.

52 Statement of LuLann McGriff, *SFNAACP v. SFUSD* (DF285, 2/7/83).

2. Neighborhood Tensions and Crosstown Busing

1 Supplementary Findings of Fact and Conclusions of Law, 19, *Johnson v. SFUSD* C-70 1331 SAW, RG21, NARA.

2 Proposition H, "Declaration of Policy: In Relation to Busing or Reassigning Elementary School Children," Voter Pamphlet, City and County of San Francisco Propositions, June 2, 1970; and San Francisco Ballot Propositions Database, San Francisco Public Library, retrieved from https://sfpl.org/index.php ?pg=2000027201.

3 Marshall Schwartz, "Mayor Tears into Integration Plan," *San Francisco Chronicle*, June 5, 1971.

4 The survey responses reported in this paragraph are from "What San Francisco Thinks about Busing," *San Francisco Examiner*, August 29, 1971. The poll was carried out for the *Examiner* by Multi-Media Research Company.

5 Proposition P, "Declaration of Policy: Shall the Board of Education Be Elective?," Voter Pamphlet, City and County of San Francisco Propositions, November 4, 1969; and San Francisco Ballot Propositions Database, San Francisco Public Library, retrieved from https://sfpl.org/index.php?pg =2000027201. Another policy declaration (Proposition Q) appearing on the November 1969 ballot asked if the board of education shall be elected by district. The measure failed.

6 There were signs that board opposition to school desegregation was softening. "When we got this order from Judge Weigel, we got it without a trial," recalled Arthur Brunwasser. "And the lawyers in the City Attorney's office . . . weren't putting that much time and effort in it. It appeared to me the school district *wanted* the schools to be desegregated." Interview, Arthur Brunwasser, January 27, 2010.

7 Mike Miller, "The Tenure of Tom Shaheen: An Analysis" (unpublished memo), January 15, 1972, from the personal files of Libby Denebeim.

8 Proposition S, "Elect School Board, at Large," November 2, 1971.

9 Carol Pogash, "Schools—Morena in, Shaheen Out," *San Francisco Progress*, August 30, 1972; and Nanette Asimov, "Thomas Shaheen—1970s S.F. Schools Chief Backed Desegregation," *San Francisco Chronicle*, October 5, 2007.

10 Wirt, *Power in the City*, 293.

11 SFUSD—History of the Board of Education Philosophy and Politics (n.d.), from the personal files of Libby Denebeim. The members of the board of education were Lucille Abrahamson, Zuretta Goosby, John Kidder, plus four members Denebeim identifies as elected on an antibusing platform: Lee Dolson, Eugene Hopp, Father Tom Reed, and Sam Martinez.

12 Memorandum of Decision, Judgment, and Decree, 6–7, July 9, 1971, *Johnson v. SFUSD* C-70 1331 SAW, RG21, NARA.

13 Board of Education policy, adopted August 4, 1936, in Memo from Harold Spears, Superintendent, August 1964, box 93, SFHC.

14 Report of the Ad Hoc Committee of the Board of Education to Study Ethnic Factors in the San Francisco Public Schools, SFUSD, April 2, 1963, box 93, SFHC.

15 Breyer to Ad Hoc Committee Meeting, San Francisco Public Schools (memo), November 15, 1962, in Plaintiffs Fourth Request for Production of Documents, *SFNAACP v. SFUSD* (DF100, c8/79).

16 Citizens Advisory Committee (CAC) Community Information Sub-Committee, "San Francisco School Desegregation. Some Facts and Figures," June 1, 1971, SFHC. The CAC was composed of sixty-five parents, community leaders, and students along with the district. The committee deliberated over several potential plans, including Horseshoe, the plan ultimately adopted. The SFNAACP crafted its own plan, named Freedom. See Weiner, "Educational Decisions in an Organized Anarchy."

17 Citizens Advisory Committee (CAC) Community Information Sub-Committee, "San Francisco School Desegregation. Some Facts and Figures," June 1, 1971, SFHC.

18 "S.F. Integration Plans Are Filed," *San Francisco Chronicle*, June 11, 1971.

19 For Order Shortening Time and for Temporary Restraining Order, 3–4, *SFNAACP v. SFUSD* (DF9, 8/14/78).

20 "Educational Redesign: A Proposal," 21, January 1978, box 1, RFA/HIA.

21 Under Horseshoe, the grade configuration was K–3, 4–6, 7–9, 10–12. "We must discontinue the practice of constantly shifting students from school to school, improve the continuity of instruction, and bring increased stability to the schooling of the learner," noted Alioto. "New grade level configurations . . . must be considered to meet this objective" (3). The gradespans were revised so that elementary schools enrolled kindergarten to fifth-grade students, middle schools enrolled sixth- to eighth-grade students, and high schools enrolled ninth- to twelfth-grade students. "Report: An Educational Redesign for the SFUSD: A Proposal for Consideration, 1-6-76," January 6, 1976, carton 101, BANC MSS 84/175c.

22 Michael Taylor, "S.F. School 'Redesign' OKd," *San Francisco Chronicle*, February 16, 1978; and "Educational Redesign: A Proposal," 22, January 1978, box 1, RFA/HIA.

23 Veronica Pollard, "Major Plan to Redesign S.F. Schools," *San Francisco Chronicle*, December 30, 1977.

24 Veronica Pollard, "Alioto's Plan Analyzed," *San Francisco Chronicle*, January 19, 1978.

25 Under Educational Redesign, schools were consolidated and closed so that while ninety-one elementary schools were in operation during the 1977–1978 school year, only sixty-two were projected to be in operation the following year.

26 During this period, the available district documents typically reported only K–5 transportation data. The district provided transportation for all elementary school students who lived more than one mile from their assigned school as well as students enrolled in certain elementary school programs.

Transportation was provided to middle-school students only if it required multiple transfers or a lengthy travel time on Muni, the city's public transportation system. "Educational Redesign: A Proposal," January 1978, box 1, RFA/HIA.

27 Veronica Pollard, "Major Plan to Redesign S.F. Schools," *San Francisco Chronicle,* December 30, 1977.

28 "Educational Redesign: A Proposal," January 1978, box 1, RFA/HIA. The district projected eight secondary schools would be naturally integrated.

29 Peter Esainko, Statistician, SFUSD Integration Department, "Evaluation Report #7. Ethnic Variations in Busing," March 15, 1976, carton 105, BANC MSS 84/175c.

30 Letter to Mayor George Moscone from Ad Hoc Committee of the Bayview-Hunters Point Community Coordinating Council, (received) January 29, 1976, carton 105, folder: "Materials duplicate of 2 & 3rd Requests," BANC MSS 84/175c.

31 Veronica Pollard, "Alioto's Plan Analyzed," *San Francisco Chronicle,* January 19, 1978.

32 "Educational Redesign: A Proposal," January 1978, box 1, RFA/HIA; and Veronica Pollard, "Alioto's Plan Analyzed," *San Francisco Chronicle,* January 19, 1978.

33 Veronica Pollard, "What People Say about S.F. School Plan," *San Francisco Chronicle,* January 18, 1978; and Veronica Pollard, "Alioto's Plan Analyzed," *San Francisco Chronicle,* January 19, 1978.

34 Veronica Pollard, "What People Say about S.F. School Plan," *San Francisco Chronicle,* January 18, 1978.

35 Veronica Pollard, "What People Say about S.F. School Plan," *San Francisco Chronicle,* January 18, 1978. An added dimension to all of this was the Field Act, which obligated the district to upgrade its schools (several of which were underenrolled) in order to comply with California earthquake standards. "We're being faulted for closing schools," Alioto griped to a *Chronicle* reporter. "I wish [the School Board] closed these schools seven years ago. Some of them should never have been rebuilt, but the Board chose to rebuild them under the Field Act. Now we're living with the sins of the past. . . . We're pumping money into buildings when it should go for kids." Walter Blum, "In the Winter of Redesign," *San Francisco Chronicle & Examiner,* April 30, 1978.

36 "Educational Redesign: A Proposal," January 1978, box 1, RFA/HIA.

37 "Educational Redesign: A Proposal," January 1978, box 1, RFA/HIA.

38 Feilders, *Profile.*

39 Veronica Pollard, "Alioto's Plan Analyzed," *San Francisco Chronicle*, January 19, 1978; and "Educational Redesign: A Proposal," January 1978, box 1, RFA/HIA. Some military families were stationed in the Presidio.

40 Approximately half of the 750 students to be bused from Treasure Island were White. Veronica Pollard, "Alioto's Plan Analyzed," *San Francisco Chronicle*, January 19, 1978.

41 At the time, Treasure Island Annex was an elementary school. The district planned to convert it into a middle school. Veronica Pollard, "Alioto's Plan Analyzed," *San Francisco Chronicle*, January 19, 1978; and "Educational Redesign: A Proposal," January 1978, box 1, RFA/HIA.

42 "Educational Redesign: A Proposal," January 1978, box 1, RFA/HIA.

43 Walter Blum, "In the Winter of Redesign," *San Francisco Chronicle & Examiner*, April 30, 1978.

44 "Another Salvo at School Plan," *San Francisco Chronicle*, January 22, 1978; and Marlin D. Seiders, Petition to Appear, *SFNAACP v. SFUSD* (DF270, 2/4/83).

45 Veronica Pollard, "Alioto's Plan Analyzed," *San Francisco Chronicle*, January 19, 1978. It was the *Chronicle* that described Treasure Island parents as "uncomfortable." Julia Comer was a longtime San Francisco resident and a public school parent. She was chair of a districtwide committee organized to implement a multicultural education program and was a lifetime member of the PTA. Declaration, *SFNAACP v. SFUSD* (DF328, 8/12/83).

46 Veronica Pollard, "Alioto's Plan Analyzed," *San Francisco Chronicle*, January 19, 1978. Even under Horseshoe, with its requirement of busing for all students for part of their elementary education, the burden of busing was disproportionately borne by Black students. While most students walked one span and were bused the other, some students had to double bus; others were able to double walk. Black students were more likely to be the ones who had to double bus. Peter Esainko, Statistician, SFUSD Integration Department, "Evaluation Report #7. Ethnic Variations in Busing," March 15, 1976, carton 105, BANC MSS 84/175c.

47 Veronica Pollard, "Alioto's Plan Analyzed," *San Francisco Chronicle*, January 19, 1978.

48 Veronica Pollard, "What People Say about S.F. School Plan," *San Francisco Chronicle*, January 18, 1978.

49 Veronica Pollard, "Alioto's Plan Analyzed," *San Francisco Chronicle*, January 19, 1978.

50 Civil Rights Action for Declaratory and Injunctive Relief, Class Action, 20, *SFNAACP v. SFUSD* (DF1, 6/30/78).

51 Between 1978 and 1982, the district sought and received grants in excess of $400,000 in order to improve the instructional programs at Carver, Drew, and Drake schools and to secure and fund services to these schools from San Francisco State University. Gloria R. Davis, Administrator, Bayview-Hunters Point Educational Complex, to Aubrey McCutcheon, Attorney, in Local Defendants' Memorandum in Response to Order Dated May 7, 1982, *SFNAACP v. SFUSD* (DF242, 5/14/82).

52 Schainker quoted in Charles Hardy, "San Francisco Desegregation Deal Falling Apart," *San Francisco Examiner,* August 21, 1983.

53 *SFNAACP,* 576 F. Supp. 34, ¶17–18. An additional element of the special plan was extending choice to South Bayshore students. Although most schools had assigned attendance areas (the district's regular schools had assigned attendance areas while its alternative schools were open to all students residing in San Francisco), students living in South Bayshore had the option of attending district schools in other neighborhoods with transportation provided by the school district. Also, the consent decree contained a provision requiring the district to promote the South Bayshore neighborhood and the new academic offerings through the services of a "reputable public relations firm." It was the hope of the SFNAACP and the school district that in the absence of mandated busing, the expanded academic offerings would draw students to the South Bayshore schools and thus help racially integrate them.

54 Petition of Dr. Charles R. Drew Community, *SFNAACP v. SFUSD* (DF190, 2/4/83).

55 Pelton Academic Middle School Parent to the Court (Letter), *SFNAACP v. SFUSD* (DF266, 2/3/83).

56 *SFNAACP,* 576 F. Supp. at 49.

57 "Change in Desegregation Plan Sought," *San Francisco Chronicle,* August 10, 1983.

58 *Webb v. Alioto,* No. 83-3977 (1983) and No. 83-2327 (1983).

59 Declaration, *SFNAACP v. SFUSD* (DF328, 8/12/83).

60 Thomas Atkins, General Counsel, NAACP, to David P. Clisham, Carroll, Burdick & McDonough, July 21, 1983, in Memorandum of Points and Authorities in Support of Motion for Intervention, *SFNAACP v. SFUSD* (DF327, 8/12/83); and Order, *SFNAACP v. SFUSD* (DF439, 9/25/86).

61 Charles Hardy, "San Francisco Desegregation Deal Falling Apart," *San Francisco Examiner,* August 21, 1983.

62 Statement of Barbara Holman, *SFNAACP v. SFUSD* (DF273, 2/4/83).

63 *SFNAACP,* 576 F. Supp. 34, ¶45.

64 Memorandum of Points and Authorities in Support of an Adjudication of Civil Contempt, *SFNAACP v. SFUSD* (DF306, 8/10/83).

65 Charles Hardy, "San Francisco Desegregation Deal Falling Apart," *San Francisco Examiner*, August 21, 1983.

66 Dexter Waugh, "Bayview Boycott of One-Way Busing," *San Francisco Examiner*, September 7, 1983. Some students were to be bused as far away as Ulloa and 46th Street in the Sunset District, literally on the other side of town.

67 Amelia Ashley-Ward, "The Fight to Re-Open Drew," *Sun-Reporter*, September 14, 1983.

68 Burford and Webb quoted in Dexter Waugh, "Bayview Boycott of One-Way Busing," *San Francisco Examiner*, September 7, 1983.

69 Amelia Ashley-Ward, "The Fight to Re-Open Drew," *Sun-Reporter*, September 14, 1983.

70 Stipulation Pursuant to Consent Decree Paragraph 50 and Order Modifying Consent Decree, *SFNAACP v. SFUSD* (DF353, 11/29/83).

71 Fairness Hearing, Morning Session, Reporter's Transcript, February 14, 1983, *SFNAACP v. SFUSD* (DF352, 11/16/83).

72 Comments and Objections Submitted by the Mexican American Legal Defense and Educational Fund as Amicus Curiae, *SFNAACP v. SFUSD* (DF272, 2/4/83).

73 Comments and Objections Submitted by the Mexican American Legal Defense and Educational Fund as Amicus Curiae, *SFNAACP v. SFUSD* (DF272, 2/4/83).

74 Comments and Objections Submitted by the Mexican American Legal Defense and Educational Fund as Amicus Curiae, *SFNAACP v. SFUSD* (DF272, 2/4/83).

75 *SFNAACP*, 576 F. Supp. 34, ¶13(b), ¶14.

76 *SFNAACP*, 576 F. Supp. at 50; and Irene Dea Collier, Chairperson, SFUSD Bilingual Community Council, to the Court (Letter), *SFNAACP v. SFUSD* (DF269, 2/4/83).

77 Irene Dea Collier, Chairperson, SFUSD Bilingual Community Council, to the Court (Letter), *SFNAACP v. SFUSD* (DF269, 2/4/83).

78 Joaquin G. Avila and others (MALDEF) to the Court, *SFNAACP v. SFUSD* (DF272, 2/4/83).

79 Joaquin G. Avila and others (MALDEF) to the Court, *SFNAACP v. SFUSD* (DF272, 2/4/83).

80 Class definition, *SFNAACP*, 576 F. Supp. 34, ¶11; and Statement from Morris Baller, Counsel, MALDEF, Morning Session, Reporter's Transcript, February 14, 1983, *SFNAACP v. SFUSD* (DF352, 11/16/83).

81 Joaquin G. Avila and others (MALDEF) to the Court, *SFNAACP v. SFUSD* (DF272, 2/4/83).

82 Written Statement of Position of Myra G. Kopf, *SFNAACP v. SFUSD* (DF268, 2/4/83).

83 *SFNAACP,* 576 F. Supp. at 49.

84 Memorandum of the MALDEF, as Amicus Curiae, in Support of Plaintiffs' Motion for Civil Contempt, *SFNAACP v. SFUSD* (DF339, 9/8/83).

85 Irma D. Herrera, Director, Educational Programs, MALDEF, (letter) June 14, 1983, Records of Mexican American Legal Defense and Educational Fund (MALDEF), M673, box 142, folder 1, Stanford University Special Collections; and "NAACP v. SFUSD community meeting" (handwritten notes), May 12, 1983, June 21, 1983, June 29, 1983, Records of MALDEF, M673, box 141, folder 11, Stanford University Special Collections.

86 Stipulation Pursuant to Consent Decree Paragraph 50 and Order Modifying Consent Decree, *SFNAACP v. SFUSD* (DF353, 11/29/83).

3. Choosing Schools, Preserving Segregation

1 Applications for Temporary Attendance Permit to Attend a School other than the Assigned, SFUSD Integration Department Form c1975, c1977; and Answer to Complaint for Declaratory and Injunctive Relief, *SFNAACP v. SFUSD* (DF12, 8/16/78). By 1977, the Integration Department handled TAP requests.

2 *Lau v. Nichols,* 414 U.S. 563 (1974); Sanchez Resolution (San Francisco Board of Education #46-11A7, June 1974); and Fairness Hearing Statement of Joseph Hall, *SFNAACP v. SFUSD* (DF289, 2/7/83).

3 "Educational Redesign: A Proposal," January 1978, box 1, RFA/HIA. Argonne/ Golden Gate Elementary had a year-round program, New Traditions School had multiage and multigrade student groupings, and Downtown featured an experience-based work-study program.

4 Deposition of Albert Cheng, February 22, 1980, *SFNAACP v. SFUSD* (DF180, 5/27/80).

5 Declaration of Margery J. Levy in Opposition to the SFUSD Proposed Sibling Policy, in Plaintiffs' Response to SFUSD'S Position, *SFNAACP v. SFUSD* (DF356, 5/29/84). Levy was former director of the Desegregation and Integration Office (1974–1977) and current chair of the district's Affirmative Action Review Committee.

6 National Lawyers Guild to Harold Spears, Superintendent, August 4, 1961, in Harold Spears, "The Proper Recognition of a Pupil's Racial Background in the San Francisco Unified School District," June 19, 1962, SFHC.

7 *O'Neill v. SFUSD*, CA 72-808 RFP (1972).

8 Margery Levy, Director, Office of Integration, to Steven Morena, Superintendent, "Report of Pre-Trial Conference—Secondary School Desegregation Suit," February 6, 1975, carton 102, folder: "Ofc. Integ/Deseg: notes of meeting with Judge Peckham on Second Deseg," BANC MSS 84/175c.

9 Declaration of Donald I. Barfield, *SFNAACP v. SFUSD* (DF1231, 4/11/01). TAP transfers were requested from across the racial/ethnic subgroups. From 1973 to 1975, Chinese students had the largest TAP granted to student enrollment ratio among the district recognized subgroups. Bob Walker, Planning Specialist, Integration Office, to Margery J. Levy, Director, Integration Department, in Affidavit of Robert F. Alioto, November 11, 1975, *Johnson v. SFUSD*, carton 102, folder: "Ofc. Integ/Deseg. Concerns of Chinatown No. Beach area," BANC MSS 84/175c.

10 Civil Rights Action for Declaratory and Injunctive Relief, 19–20, *SFNAACP v. SFUSD* (DF1, 6/30/78).

11 "Educational Redesign: A Proposal," January 1978, box 1, RFA/HIA.

12 See, for example, Local Defendants' 1984–1985 Annual Report, *SFNAACP v. SFUSD* (DF395, 8/1/85).

13 For the 1978–1979 term, Sir Francis Drake was projected to be 91.3 percent Black; Carver, 90.5 percent Black; Drew, 80.6 percent Black. For Order Shortening Time and for Temporary Restraining Order, Segregative Impact of Local Defendants' Plans, *SFNAACP v. SFUSD* (DF9, 8/14/78).

14 The district promised a minimum of $225,000 for the improvement of these schools' educational programs and to engage the services of the staff of a major university. *SFNAACP v. SFUSD* (DF12, 8/16/78).

15 Isadore Pivnick, Asst. Supt. School Operations Division, Letter to Parents, May 15, 1978, in Answer to Complaint for Declaratory and Injunctive Relief, *SFNAACP v. SFUSD* (DF12, 8/16/78).

16 For Order Shortening Time and for Temporary Restraining Order, Segregative Impact of Local Defendants' Plans, *SFNAACP v. SFUSD* (DF9, 8/14/78).

17 *Green v. County School Board of New Kent County (Virginia)*, 391 U.S. 430 (1968). With *Green*, the court established six factors to be considered when determining whether a district was unitary: composition of the student body, faculty, staff, transportation, extracurricular activities, and facilities.

18 United States Commission on Civil Rights, *Southern School Desegregation*, 88.

19 United States Commission on Civil Rights, *Federal Enforcement of School Desegregation*, 16.

20 *Brown II*, 349 U.S. at 301.

21 *Alexander v. Holmes County Bd. of Ed.*, 396 U.S. 19 (1969).

22 United States Commission on Civil Rights, *Federal Enforcement of School Desegregation,* 14.

23 For Order Shortening Time and for Temporary Restraining Order, Segregative Impact of Local Defendants' Plans, *SFNAACP v. SFUSD* (DF9, 8/14/78).

24 The SFNAACP's request for a Temporary Restraining Order was denied on August 16, 1978, and a subsequent appeal to the Ninth Circuit failed.

25 *SFNAACP,* 576 F. Supp. 34.

26 Gary Orfield, "Progress toward a Settlement Agreement" (memo), August 10, 1982, in Declaration of Deputy Attorney General John Davison in Support of the State Defendants' Opposition to Plaintiffs' Motion to Modify the Consent Decree, *SFNAACP v. SFUSD* (DF601, 9/21/90).

27 *SFNAACP,* 576 F. Supp. 34, ¶13(d).

28 Consent Decree Fairness Hearing Statement, *SFNAACP v. SFUSD* (DF268, 2/4/83). Kopf was elected to the Board of Education in 1978. She would go on to serve on the board until 1990.

29 Reporters Transcript (morning session), February 14, 1983, *SFNAACP v. SFUSD* (DF352, 11/16/83).

30 Statement of Grandvel A. Jackson Re: Fairness of Consent Decree, 1–2, *SFNAACP v. SFUSD* (DF293, 2/7/83).

31 Fairness Hearing, Morning Session, Reporter's Transcript, 25, February 14, 1983, *SFNAACP v. SFUSD* (DF352, 11/16/83).

32 Statement of Barbara Holman, *SFNAACP v. SFUSD* (DF273, 2/4/83).

33 Statement of Margery Levy, *SFNAACP v. SFUSD* (DF284, 2/4/83).

34 Reporter's Transcript, 6, December 30, 1982, *SFNAACP v. SFUSD* (DF861, 7/22/97).

35 Opinion and Order (Consent Decree), *SFNAACP,* 576 F. Supp. 34.

36 State of the City Address, Office of the Mayor, 10/9/1984, box 1, folder 119, RFA/HIA.

37 Carver was 61.6 percent Black for the 1984–1985 school year; New Traditions was 41.5 percent White and King was 41.1 percent Black. Local Defendants' 1984–85 Annual Report, *SFNAACP v. SFUSD* (DF395, 8/1/85).

38 California Education Code, §42243.6 and §42249.

39 Court Reporter's Transcript, June 7, 1984, *SFNAACP v. SFUSD* (DF504, 3/12/88).

4. From Race Conscious to Race Neutral

1 To recap, on June 30, 1978, the San Francisco chapter of the NAACP filed a lawsuit charging the local school district with engaging in discriminatory practices and maintaining a segregated school system (*SFNAACP v. SFUSD*

C-78–1445 WHO). The court eventually certified the SFNAACP as class representative of not just all Black public schoolchildren—as the lawsuit originally asserted—but of "all the school children, heretofore, now or hereafter eligible to attend the public elementary and secondary schools of the SFUSD." Following several years of minor legal machinations, in 1983 the parties avoided the prospect of an expensive, racially divisive, and politically contentious trial by entering into a consent decree settlement over the appropriate means by which San Francisco would desegregate its schools. The goal of the consent decree was "to eliminate racial/ethnic segregation or identifiability in any SFUSD school, program, or classroom and to achieve the broadest practicable distribution throughout the system of students from the racial and ethnic groups which comprise the student enrollment of the SFUSD." The nine recognized racial and ethnic subgroups were: African American, Chinese, Latino, Korean, Japanese, Filipino, American Indian, "Other Non-White," and "Other White."

2 The 1983 settlement placed the 45 percent subgroup cap on all public schools except for fourteen alternative schools that had a cap of 40 percent (Wallenberg High School, Lawton Middle School, International Studies, Second Community, San Francisco Community, Clarendon, New Traditions, Douglas Traditional, Argonne Elementary, Rooftop, Lilienthal, Lakeshore, Buena Vista, and John Swett). At the time, students were assigned to schools based primarily on neighborhood boundaries. The district carved small satellite feeder zones of several blocks each with a demographic profile that would help maintain an otherwise racially concentrated school's racial balance. Some schools needed only one feeder zone. Other schools required multiple feeder zones. If any school exceeded the enrollment caps imposed by the consent decree, the district was to restrict the entering classes so as to gradually bring it into compliance.

3 Because more than 40 percent of the student population at Lincoln, Washington, and Galileo High Schools was Chinese, some of these students would need to be reassigned to other (less popular) schools under Cornejo's proposal.

4 Lowell High School is the top feeder school to the University of California system in the state and is the recipient of numerous accolades and praise. In 1986, the *New York Times* named Lowell one of the top forty-five schools in the nation.

5 Diane Curtis, "Top Rated Lowell a Pressure Cooker," *San Francisco Chronicle*, June 11, 1986.

6 "Yee Decries S.F. School Plan," *AsianWeek*, August 19, 1988.

7 "Lowell Quota Would Be Unfair," editorial, *San Francisco Chronicle*, August 11, 1988. The *San Francisco Examiner* was more circumspect, arguing that "as long as the district maintains one academically superior high school, Lowell, entrance cannot be colorblind," but acknowledging that the burden of the new proposal would be unevenly borne across the nine subgroups. "S.F. Schools Rethink the Ethnic Mix," editorial, *San Francisco Examiner*, August 11, 1988.

8 CADC 30th Anniversary Program, "CADC History," March 1988, Berkeley Ethnic Studies Library; and correspondence, Louis Hop Lee, October 27, 2009.

9 Correspondence, Louis Hop Lee, October 27, 2009.

10 Roland Quan to Ramon Cortines regarding Proposed "Refinements" to Desegregation Plan, August 18, 1988, box 4, folder 4, Records of the Chinese American Democratic Club, California Ethnic and Multicultural Archives, University of California, Santa Barbara (hereafter CEMA 49).

11 Correspondence, Louis Hop Lee, October 27, 2009. As Doug Chan recalls, the very first CADC member to recognize the looming crisis with the consent decree was Clifford Lee, a deputy state attorney general. "Cliff was the first guy to perceive the problem, talk up the fact that the consent decree struck at the core interests of the Chinese American community, and that the consent decree was worthy of challenge. Senior CADC members such as Harold [Yee], the late Roland Quan, and Louis [Hop Lee] blessed the idea, and the younger folks ran with the idea." Correspondence, Doug Chan, August 13, 2009.

12 Leslie Yee to Roland Quan, September 3, 1988, box 3, folder 8, CEMA 49.

13 "School Integration Consent Decree," CADC, [no date, but probably late 1988/ early 1989], box 10, folder 3, CEMA 49.

14 Leonard Greene, "Busing Plan in Peril as Chinese Students Tilt Balance in S.F.," *San Francisco Chronicle*, October 2, 1989. Henry Der is a longtime education advocate. He is a former member of the SFUSD Affirmative Action Review Committee (1975–1976), SFUSD Educational Redesign Committee (1978–1979), and Citizens Advisory Committee on the Selection of the SFUSD Superintendent (1986–1987).

15 "Fairness or Discontent: Lowell High Freshman," *Voice*, Fall 1993.

16 For example, a student who had fifty-seven points could have had fifty-nine if she received an A in eighth-grade English rather than a B.

17 Interview, Steve Phillips, July 23, 2009.

18 Local Defendants 1984–85 Annual Report, *SFNAACP v. SFUSD* (DF395, 8/1/85). All regular schools had at least four subgroups, only one regular

school had a subgroup that comprised more than 45 percent of its student body (George Washington Carver had a Black enrollment of 61.6 percent). Only two alternative schools had a subgroup that comprised more than 40 percent of their student bodies (New Traditions had a White enrollment of 41.5 percent and Dr. Martin Luther King Jr. had a Black enrollment of 41.1 percent).

19 *SFNAACP,* 576 F. Supp. 34, ⁋39.

20 Basic Information about School Reconstitution, Waldemar Rojas to All CSIP Participants (memo), May 8, 1995, in Report by Local Defendants, *SFNAACP v. SFUSD* (DF839, 8/15/95).

21 "S.F. Schools' Success Story," editorial, *San Francisco Examiner,* August 18, 1989.

22 Local Defendants' 1997–98 Annual Report, *SFNAACP v. SFUSD* (DF873, 7/31/98). Desegregation funding provided for in California Education Code, §42243.6 and §42249.

23 Gary Orfield (Consent Decree Monitor) to the Court, October 14, 1991, in Unpublished Order, *SFNAACP v. SFUSD* (DF662, 11/8/91).

24 Gary Orfield (Consent Decree Monitor) to the Court, October 14, 1991, in Unpublished Order, *SFNAACP v. SFUSD* (DF662, 11/8/91).

25 Gary Orfield (Consent Decree Monitor) to the Court, October 14, 1991, in Unpublished Order, *SFNAACP v. SFUSD* (DF662, 11/8/91).

26 The Committee of Experts was chaired by Gary Orfield and included Barbara L. Cohen, Gordon Foster, Robert L. Green, Paul Lawrence, David S. Tatel, and Fred Tempes. Desegregation and Educational Change in San Francisco—Findings and Recommendations on Consent Decree Implementation, *SFNAACP v. SFUSD* (DF673, 6/26/92); Nanette Asimov, "S.F. Schools Criticized on Teaching of Minorities," *San Francisco Chronicle,* June 27, 1992; and Brief of Objections, *SFNAACP v. SFUSD* (DF750, 4/22/93).

27 Notice by Intervenor-Plaintiffs to Intervene, *SFNAACP v. SFUSD* (DF703, 1/26/93).

28 Peter Schmidt, "Language Minorities Seek Place," *Education Week,* February 17, 1993.

29 Declaration of Claire J. Merced, *SFNAACP v. SFUSD* (DF714, 1/26/93); and Motion by Plaintiffs-Intervenors META, *SFNAACP v. SFUSD* (DF704, 1/26/93). META began in 1983 as a project to address immigrant education issues of Harvard University Center for Law and Education. It eventually spun off and established offices in Somerville, Massachusetts, and San Francisco, California, and claimed to have been actively involved in most major language rights cases of the period. This was also an opportunity for orga-

nized labor to attempt to intervene. The United Educators of San Francisco (UESF) filed a motion to intervene in 1993. Most of the concern centered on the impact school reconstitution would have on its members. UESF's motion to intervene was ultimately denied. UESF Motion to Intervene, *SFNAACP v. SFUSD* (DF726, 3/10/93).

30 Memorandum of points and authorities in support of motion for leave to intervene, *SFNAACP v. SFUSD* (DF705, 1/26/93). META represented the petitioners; Irma Herrera was a staff attorney at MALDEF and in charge of MALDEF's motion to intervene in 1982–1983.

31 Declaration by Henry Der Regarding Motion to Intervene, *SFNAACP v. SFUSD* (DF718, 1/26/93).

32 Desegregation and Educational Change in San Francisco, 20, *SFNAACP v. SFUSD* (DF673, 6/26/92).

33 Memorandum of Points and Authorities in Support of Motion for Leave to Intervene, *SFNAACP v. SFUSD* (DF705, 1/26/93).

34 Declarations by Anthony Ramirez, Assistant Superintendent in the Department of Integration, Ligaya Avenida, Program Director in the Bilingual Education Department, E. Anthony Anderson, High School Operations Department Supervisor, and Susan Wong, Supervisor of the Pupil Services Department, Countering the Claims Made by META Declarants, in Response by Local Defendants, *SFNAACP v. SFUSD* (DF730, 3/25/93). The Board of Education voted to oppose META's motion to intervene on March 22, 1993.

35 Declaration by Angie Fa, *SFNAACP v. SFUSD* (DF761, 5/7/93).

36 Letter to Tony Ramirez From Leland Yee RE: Comments on Integration Consent Decree Action Plan, March 19, 1993, in Declaration by Leland Yee, *SFNAACP v. SFUSD* (DF758, 5/7/93).

37 School board members Tom Ammiano, Carlota Del Portillo, Angie Fa, Steve Phillips, and Leland Yee voted to support META's motion to intervene; members Dan Kelly and Jill Wynns voted against. In Order Extending Time to File Appropriate Pleadings, *SFNAACP v. SFUSD* (DF752, 4/22/93).

38 Declaration by Tom Ammiano on Behalf of Defendant SFUSD Regarding META Motion to Intervene, *SFNAACP v. SFUSD* (DF760, 5/7/93).

39 Declaration by Steve Phillips, *SFNAACP v. SFUSD* (DF759, 5/7/93).

40 Declaration by Steve Phillips, *SFNAACP v. SFUSD* (DF759, 5/7/93).

41 Declaration of Irma D. Herrera, *SFNAACP v. SFUSD* (DF707, 1/26/93).

42 Declaration by Sui-Ming Wan, *SFNAACP v. SFUSD* (DF715, 1/26/93).

43 Response by Multicultural Education Re: Opposition Memorandum, *SFNAACP v. SFUSD* (DF745, 4/1/93).

44 Memorandum Decision and Order (Denying Motion to Intervene, Granting Amicus Curiae Status), *SFNAACP v. SFUSD* (DF774, 7/22/93).

45 Memorandum Decision and Order (Denying Motion to Intervene, Granting Amicus Curiae Status), *SFNAACP v. SFUSD* (DF774, 7/22/93).

46 The Latino Group consisted of Mujeres Unidas y Activas, Alianza, Padres Unidos, Susana Salinas, Noemi Ortiz, and her two daughters, Nadia and Adriana. The Asian Group consisted of Chinese for Affirmative Action, Sui-Ming Wan, and her two daughters, Jacky and Wynne. *SFNAACP v. SFUSD* (DF774, 7/22/93).

47 Desegregation and Educational Change in San Francisco, 20–21, *SFNAACP v. SFUSD* (DF673, 6/26/92).

48 The neighborhoods most affected were Chinatown, North Beach, Parkside, Richmond, Sunset, and Western Addition Districts. Leonard Greene, "Busing Plan in Peril as Chinese Students Tilt Balance in San Francisco," *San Francisco Chronicle,* October 2, 1989.

49 Leonard Greene, "Busing Plan in Peril as Chinese Students Tilt Balance in San Francisco," *San Francisco Chronicle,* October 2, 1989.

50 Leonard Greene, "Busing Plan in Peril as Chinese Students Tilt Balance in San Francisco," *San Francisco Chronicle,* October 2, 1989.

51 Leonard Greene, "Busing Plan in Peril as Chinese Students Tilt Balance in San Francisco," *San Francisco Chronicle,* October 2, 1989. Lulann McGriff had worked on school desegregation issues for the SFNAACP since the mid-1970s. She served as chapter president from 1987 to 1994. Nanette Asimov, "Guardian at the School Gate," *San Francisco Chronicle,* November 3, 1996.

52 Deborah Escobedo and Irma Herrera, META to Attorneys in SFNAACP, November 16, 1992, in Declaration of Deborah Escobedo in Support of Motion for Intervention, *SFNAACP v. SFUSD* (DF706, 1/26/93).

53 Declaration by Henry Der, *SFNAACP v. SFUSD* (DF718, 1/26/93).

54 Andrew Leonard, "Class Action," *San Francisco Bay Guardian,* April 7, 1993.

55 Correspondence, Louis Hop Lee, October 27, 2009.

56 Interview, Amy Chang, February 10, 2010.

57 Interview, Steve Phillips, July 23, 2009.

58 "Resolution on SFUSD Consent Decree," *Fiery Dragon News,* March 1993; and Brief of Objections, Chinese American Democratic Club, *SFNAACP v. SFUSD* (DF750, 4/22/93). See also "CADC and the Consent Decree," *Fiery Dragon News,* May 1993. From the perspective of CADC, at least part of the resistance by the board and superintendent to addressing the enrollment cap issue was the considerable amount of state funding that flowed through

the consent decree. Interview, Amy Chang, February 10, 2010. There were some exceptions, though. Mayor Dianne Feinstein and Supervisor Quentin Kopp expressed their support. Correspondence, Louis Hop Lee, October 27, 2009.

59 *Fiery Dragon News,* April 1993. Several CADC members were actively involved throughout the course of the consent decree campaign, including recently elected board member Henry Louie, Lee Cheng, a law student and alumnus of Lowell, and Amy Chang, the chair of the task force and CADC's public spokesperson on the consent decree; "Lowell H.S.—Admissions Change or Spare Change," *Fiery Dragon News,* June 1993. Some of the rhetoric was more incendiary. The CADC described the impact of the consent decree as scapegoating innocent children of Chinese descent as "San Francisco's own form of 'ethnic cleansing.'" *Fiery Dragon News,* June 1993.

60 Nanette Asimov, "Students Battle for Admission to Top S.F. School," *San Francisco Chronicle,* April 19, 1993.

61 Andrew Leonard, "Class Action," *San Francisco Bay Guardian,* April 7, 1993.

62 CADC Press Packet, July 1994, from the personal records of Douglas Chan.

63 Interview, Victor Seeto, September 2, 2009. Relations were strained but not destroyed. Henry Louie recalls that "while the tension existed [over the consent decree] . . . there were still a lot of opportunities for the two organizations to work together on issues of common interest." Interview, Henry Louie, September 2, 2009.

64 Brief of Objections, Chinese American Democratic Club, *SFNAACP v. SFUSD* (DF750, 4/22/93).

65 Interview, Steve Phillips, July 23, 2009. Peter Cohn had been a member of the NAACP's National Board of Directors and Western regional attorney for NAACP activities in California and eight other Western states. He became the SFNAACP's primary contact on consent decree implementation and monitoring activities from its establishment. Response by META Regarding Opposition Memorandum, *SFNAACP v. SFUSD* (DF745, 4/1/93).

66 Nanette Asimov, "Lowell High Fails Desegregation Test," *San Francisco Chronicle,* September 9, 1993.

67 The task force was chaired by Paul Warren, dean of the University of San Francisco School of Education. "It's tough," said Warren to a *Chronicle* reporter. "Unless public schools find a way to address the issues at the forefront of this discussion—equity and excellence—they're in deep trouble." Nanette Asimov, "Lowell High Fails Desegregation Test," *San Francisco Chronicle,* September 9, 1993; "Lowell High School Admissions Panel Update," *Fiery Dragon News,* CADC, November 1993; "Fairness or Discontent:

Lowell High Freshman," *Voice*, Fall 1993; and Nanette Asimov, "Clone Lowell High, Education Panel Says," *San Francisco Chronicle*, December 22, 1993.

68 "Lowell High School Admissions Panel Update," *Fiery Dragon News*, November 1993.

69 Nanette Asimov, "Clone Lowell High, Education Panel Says," *San Francisco Chronicle*, December 22, 1993.

70 Lee Cheng of the CADC consent decree task force felt that "the judiciary and the judicial route was a much more effective and efficient way to go." Interview, Lee Cheng, August 22, 2009.

71 Amy Chang to Doug Chan (handwritten note), July 17, 1994, in CADC Press Packet, July 1994, from the personal records of Douglas Chan.

72 Leslie Yee to Roland Quan, September 3, 1988, box 3, folder 8, CEMA 49.

73 Correspondence, Louis Hop Lee, October 27, 2009.

74 Interview, Lee Cheng, August 22, 2009. Declaration by Amy Chang, *Ho v. SFUSD* (DF432, 6/3/99). The legal luncheon was held on December 7, 1993, at the Grand Palace Restaurant. Interview, Amy Chang, February 10, 2010. Details on the search for potential lawyers and the legal luncheon culled from: interview, Henry Louie, September 2, 2009; interview, David Levine, July 30, 2009; and interview, Anthony Lee, September 30, 2009.

75 Interview, Daniel Girard, August 24, 2009. Henry Louie recalls that approximately ten firms sent representatives to the legal luncheon. Interview, Henry Louie, September 2, 2009.

76 Interview, Daniel Girard, August 24, 2009.

77 As the CADC campaign was ramping up, in early 1994, the court approved an amendment to the consent decree that included, among other items, extending the 40 percent enrollment cap to every alternative school in the district (previously, only a designated subset of alternative schools were held to the cap) and deleting the section placing more restrictive caps on certain subgroups at certain designated schools (¶14). Amended 1983 Consent Decree, *SFNAACP v. SFUSD* (DF804, 3/9/94).

78 "The Admission of Chinese Students to San Francisco High Schools," *Fiery Dragon News*, April 1994.

79 Interview, Lee Cheng, August 22, 2009.

80 Interview, Henry Louie, September 2, 2009.

81 Interview, Henry Louie, September 2, 2009; interview, Ron Chun, August 26, 2009; and Hannah Nordhaus, "Desegregation Suit Spawns New Bar Foundation," *Recorder*, January 17, 1995. AALF held a fund-raising dinner attracting Asian American professionals from the Bay Area. The money raised went toward various miscellaneous expenses including filing charges, and printing and reproduction costs.

82 Interview, Henry Louie, September 2, 2009.

83 In addition to the SFUSD, the action was filed against the district superintendent Bill Rojas, the school board, the State Board of Education, California Department of Education, and the state superintendent of education. On January 12, 1995, the court added the SFNAACP as a defendant. Minutes, *Ho v. SFUSD* (DF27, 1/12/95).

84 CADC Press Packet, July 1994, from the personal records of Douglas Chan.

85 中黑:族裔限額 *Sing Tao Daily,* May 27, 1994. [Original: 三藩市華裔家長反對設族裔上限的混合教育政策，本來是有節有理. 學校應打開大門招生，不分種族，按客觀公平的原則取錄.]

86 Nanette Asimov, "S.F. Schools Sued on Enrollment," *San Francisco Chronicle,* July 12, 1994.

87 Nanette Asimov, "S.F. Schools Sued on Enrollment," *San Francisco Chronicle,* July 12, 1994.

88 Amy Chang describes the legal campaign as "a David versus Goliath story." Correspondence, February 12, 2010.

89 Defendants moved to dismiss on the basis res judicata and collateral estoppel. Memorandum Opinion and Order Denying Motion to Dismiss (DF44, 9/28/95). As I describe below, the judge's order came soon after the Supreme Court delivered its opinion in *Missouri v. Jenkins,* an important school desegregation case. See also, Peter Schmidt, "Chinese-American Parents in S.F. Win Round in Court," *Education Week,* October 11, 1995; Venise Wagner, "Court Challenge Advances on S.F. School Racial Caps," *San Francisco Examiner,* September 29, 1995; and Rex Bossert, "Case against Schools 'Cap' to Go Forward," *Daily Journal,* September 29, 1995.

90 Memorandum Decision and Order, March 8, 1996, *Ho v. SFUSD* (DF66, 3/12/96).

91 Notice of Motion for Partial Summary Judgment, *SFNAACP v. SFUSD* (DF190, 6/6/80).

92 Interview, Stuart Biegel, May 22, 2009.

93 San Francisco Board of Education Policy for Lowell Admissions (#62–13SP1).

94 Nanette Asimov, "Lowell Freshmen Reflect New Entry Rules," *San Francisco Chronicle,* August 28, 1996.

95 Motion for Summary Judgment, *Ho v. SFUSD* (DF68, 7/23/96); and 98 California Daily Opinion Service 4275 (hereafter CDOS). Changes in desegregation and affirmative action jurisprudence that underlie Ho's claim for summary judgment are detailed below.

96 Opinion Denying Motion for Summary Judgment, *Ho v. SFUSD* (DF116, 5/5/97).

97 Rojas continued: "However, race or ethnicity is considered as a factor in

determining whether the student population of a SFUSD school is within the guidelines set forth in Paragraph 13 of the Consent Decree and sometimes a student is not permitted to enroll if the school is overcrowded or outside the guideline." 98 CDOS 4277.

98 Orrick found that "plaintiffs failed to show an absence of a factual dispute relating to the necessity of relief, efficacy of alternative remedies, flexibility and duration of relief, waiver provisions, relationship of numerical goals to the relevant population, and impact on relief on third parties." 98 CDOS 4275.

99 "Judge Blocks Bid to Ax Quotas in S.F. Schools," *Education Week,* May 21, 1997. As a young lawyer, Alex Pitcher provided assistance to Thurgood Marshall in cases that set the stage for *Brown.* Gregory Lewis, "Cancer Claims Civil Rights Warrior at 73," *San Francisco Examiner,* January 7, 2000.

100 *Milliken v. Bradley,* 418 U.S. 717 (1974). *Milliken* placed restrictions on the busing allowed under *Swann* by ruling that in the absence of constitutional violations, suburban districts were not required to be part of central city integration plans.

101 *Milliken v. Bradley,* 418 U.S. 717 (1974) at 745: "Without an interdistrict violation and interdistrict effect, there is no constitutional wrong calling for an interdistrict remedy."

102 *Milliken v. Bradley,* 418 U.S. 717 (1974) at 740.

103 *Board of Education of the Oklahoma City Public Schools v. Dowell,* 498 U.S. 237 (1991); and *Freeman v. Pitts,* 503 U.S. 467 (1992).

104 The three-part *"Dowell/Freeman"* test was used in 2005 to determine whether to extend the consent decree to June 2007 or to allow it to expire. *Freeman,* 503 U.S. at 491. Third part quoted in *Dowell,* 498 U.S. at 250.

105 *Missouri v. Jenkins,* 515 U.S. 70 (1995).

106 The dissenting justices were Souter, Stevens, Ginsburg, and Breyer.

107 By 1995, the district had been reimbursed over $300 million in desegregation expenses by the State of California. Annual Report of the Local Defendants, *SFNAACP v. SFUSD* (DF776, 7/30/93); and Notice by Defendants, *SFNAACP v. SFUSD* (DF 874, 7/31/98).

108 "The Supreme Court Lurches Backwards," editorial, *San Francisco Chronicle,* July 7, 1995.

109 *Bakke v. Regents of University of California,* 18 Cal.3d 34 (1976) at 62.

110 *Regents of the University of California v. Bakke,* 438 U.S. 265 (1978) at 320.

111 *Bakke v. Regents of University of California,* 18 Cal.3d 34 (1976) at 62.

112 Warren Weaver Jr., "Justice Dept. Brief 1 of 58 in Bakke Case," *New York Times,* September 20, 1977.

113 Warren Weaver Jr., "Justice Dept. Brief 1 of 58 in Bakke Case," *New York Times,* September 20, 1977.

114 *Regents of the University of California v. Bakke,* 438 U.S. 265 (1978).

115 *Bakke,* 438 U.S. at 320. In affirming that the special admissions program was unlawful, Justice Powell was joined by Chief Justice Burger and Justices Stewart, Rehnquist, and Stevens. In allowing that a properly devised admissions program might involve the consideration of race, Powell was joined by Justices Brennan, White, Marshal, and Blackmun.

116 "Who Won?," editorial, *New York Times,* June 29, 1978.

117 *City of Richmond v. J.A. Croson Co.,* 488 U.S. 469 (1989); and *Adarand Constructors, Inc. v. Pena,* 515 U.S. 200 (1995) at 494.

118 *Adarand,* 515 U.S. at 229.

119 *Adarand,* 515 U.S. at 235.

120 *Adarand,* 515 U.S. at 237; and *Croson,* 488 U.S. at 507.

121 Liu, "Beyond Black and White."

122 Executive Order to End Preferential Treatment and to Promote Individual Opportunity Based on Merit (#W-124–95, June 1, 1995).

123 Yumi Wilson and Kenneth Garcia, "Wilson Signs Away Affirmative Action," *San Francisco Chronicle,* June 2, 1995.

124 Prohibition against Discrimination or Preferential Treatment by State and Other Public Entities, Initiative Constitutional Amendment (Proposition 209), Text of Proposed Law, California Secretary of State.

125 The U.C. Regents approved the ban on preferential treatment in admissions (Special Policy 1) and contracting and employment (Special Policy 2) in July 1995. The policies were repealed in 2001. However, restrictions instituted through Proposition 209 remain in place.

126 Carol Ness and Annie Nakao, "Voters Back Ban on Affirmative Action by 55–45 Percent," *San Francisco Chronicle,* November 6, 1996.

127 Remarks on Affirmative Action at the National Archives and Records Administration, *Public Papers of the Presidents of the United States—William J. Clinton, 1995. Book II, July 1 to December 31, 1995* (Government Printing Office, 1995), 1106–13. See also, "Clinton Plans a Review of Affirmative Action Programs," *New York Times,* February 24, 1995.

128 The case is *Hopwood v. Texas,* 78 F.3d 932. The decision was abrogated by the Supreme Court in 2003. *Grutter v. Bollinger,* 539 U.S. 306.

129 "California and Affirmative Action," *Hearing before the Committee on the Judiciary, United States Senate,* April 30, 1996.

130 "California and Affirmative Action," *Hearing before the Committee on the Judiciary, United States Senate,* April 30, 1996, 47.

131 Executive Order 13050 of June 13, 1997, *President's Advisory Board on Race,* Federal Register, Vol. 62 No. 116.

132 "State-Sanctioned Discrimination in America," *Hearing before the Committee on the Judiciary, United States Senate,* June 16, 1997. The hearing is archived at http://www.c-spanvideo.org/program/86872–1.

133 "State-Sanctioned Discrimination in America," *Hearing before the Committee on the Judiciary, United States Senate,* June 16, 1997, 38.

134 Charlene F. Wong to Jennie A. Horn, Supervisor, Educational Placement Center, March 25, 1994, Attachment to Revised Expert Witness Statement of Henry Der, *Ho v. SFUSD* (DF331, 2/3/99). Patrick Wong was eventually allowed to enroll into Lincoln High School, his fourth choice.

135 "State-Sanctioned Discrimination in America," *Hearing before the Committee on the Judiciary, United States Senate,* June 16, 1997, 39.

136 See, for example, statements by Senators Hatch (November 4, 1997) and Sessions (November 9, 1997) on the floor of the U.S. Senate in opposition to the nomination of Bill Lann Lee to assistant attorney general for civil rights and remarks by Elaine Chao on the President's Initiative on Race (April 29, 1998, and July 9, 1998).

137 Interview, Daniel Girard, August 24, 2009. Loen's testimony was discussed on the June 16, 1997, PBS broadcast of *NewsHour with Jim Lehrer.*

138 Full Board, Public Session Minutes, California State Board of Education, September 12, 1997, in Declaration by Janet Sommer, *SFNAACP v. SFUSD* (DF869, 10/21/97).

139 Quoted in Alethea Yip, "New Support in School Desegregation Case," *AsianWeek,* September 5, 1997.

140 Full Board, Public Session Minutes, California State Board of Education, September 12, 1997, in Declaration by Janet Sommer, *SFNAACP v. SFUSD* (DF869, 10/21/97). The State Board of Education was represented by John Yoo, a professor of law at University of California, Berkeley. Eventually, Patrick Manshardt of the Individual Rights Foundation served as counsel.

141 The assertion was made through the spokesperson for the state superintendent, Doug Stone. Quoted in Alethea Yip, "New Support in School Desegregation Case," *AsianWeek,* September 5, 1997. See also, John Yoo and Eric George, "When Desegregation Turns into Discrimination," *Wall Street Journal,* May 26, 1998.

142 Nanette Asimov, "Wilson Sides with S.F. Chinese Americans on Schools Lawsuit to End Court-Supervised Desegregation," *San Francisco Chronicle,* August 21, 1997.

143 Alethea Yip, "New Support in School Desegregation Case," *AsianWeek*, September 5, 1997.

144 For instance, CADC supported efforts by the Association of Chinese Teachers (TACT) to increase their representation. Correspondence, Louis Hop Lee, October 27, 2009. See also, Ramon Cortines, Superintendent of Schools, SFUSD, to Roland Quan, President, CADC, June 28, 1988, box 3, folder 8, CEMA 49.

145 Alethea Yip, "New Support in School Desegregation Case," *AsianWeek*, September 5, 1997.

146 Correspondence, Louis Hop Lee, October 27, 2009.

147 CADC Press Packet, July 1994, from the personal records of Douglas Chan.

148 Interview, Henry Louie, September 2, 2009.

149 Interview, Doug Chan, August 26, 2009.

150 Interview, Henry Der, September 2, 2009.

151 The intricacies of the legal proceedings during this period of the consent decree are clearly detailed in cocounsel for plaintiff David Levine's "Chinese American Challenge." The paper and my interview with Professor Levine were invaluable to me in writing the following sections.

152 *Ho by Ho v. San Francisco Unified School Dist.*, 147 F.3d 854 (1998). No findings of fact had been supplied by the district court. The panel majority noted that the normal way of adjudication is "first the facts, then the decision of the district court, then the appeal. In a case where facts are critical, we cannot change this order of business." Plaintiffs had also sought a writ of mandamus directing the court not to proceed with the trial (scheduled for September 1998), which was also denied. *Ho by Ho*, 147 F.3d at 861.

153 *Ho by Ho*, 147 F.3d 8 at 865. This section is aided by interviews with Stuart Biegel, May 22, 2009; David Levine, July 30, 2009; and Daniel Girard, August 24, 2009. I thank Stuart Biegel for pointing out that the appeal could have simply been dismissed for lack of jurisdiction, with no further involvement from the Ninth Circuit.

154 *Ho by Ho*, 147 F.3d at 863.

155 *Ho by Ho*, 147 F.3d at 865.

156 Interviews, David Levine, July 30, 2009; Stuart Biegel, May 22, 2009; and Daniel Girard, August 24, 2009. See also Levine, "Chinese American Challenge." The dissenting judge agreed with much of the majority opinion. However, he argued that the conclusory statements by the district meant that "neither the trial judge nor we had before us any genuinely contested facts sufficient either to create a genuine issue, or to deprive an appellate court of jurisdiction." *Ho by Ho*, 147 F.3d at 866.

157 *Ho by Ho,* 147 F.3d at 865.

158 Nanette Asimov, "S.F. Schools Plan Drastic Budget Cut," *San Francisco Chronicle,* June 22, 1998. At the time, SFUSD enrolled approximately sixty-four thousand students.

159 At the time the consent decree was approved, California's Education Code contained a provision allowing for the full reimbursement by the state for all court-ordered desegregation costs incurred by school districts. Subsequently, in 1985, the Education Code was amended to require a reimbursement of 80 percent of expenditures in excess of the amount expended for the 1984–1985 year, adjusted for districtwide enrollment growth and cost of living (Statutes of 1985, Chapter 180, §42247). Beginning with the 1994–1995 term, SFUSD (along with other districts) fell into a dispute with the state when it failed to reimburse districts for allowable expenses over the course of a number of years. For example, for the 1994–1995 term, the state controller approved $30,306,296 but SFUSD only received $28,163,550. Similarly, for the 1995–1996 term, the controller approved $38,736,742 but SFUSD only received $28,164,000. In 1998, the legislature appropriated funds to cover the shortfall but this line item was vetoed by Governor Wilson. The issue came to a head in 1999 when Superintendent Rojas publicly called for monies past due to be provided. "It's appropriate for me to complain this year, because I didn't get the money this year or the year before that or the year before that," complained Rojas. "We have not received [desegregation] funds for '94, '95 or '96." Eric Brazil and Robert Salladay, "Cash for S.F. Schools Comes with Lecture," *San Francisco Chronicle,* March 19, 1999. For the 1996–1997 school term, SFUSD claimed $35,952,302 in desegregation expenses; for 1997–1998, SFUSD claimed $36,950,429 in desegregation expenses; for 1998–1999, SFUSD claimed $37,624,000 in desegregation expenses. See Defendants' 1992–1993 Annual Report, *SFNAACP v. SFUSD* (DF776, 7/30/93); Defendants' 1997–1998 Annual Report (Volume II), *SFNAACP v. SFUSD* (DF874, 7/31/98); Defendants' 1998–1999 Annual Report, *SFNAACP v. SFUSD* (DF1035, 8/4/99); Consent Decree Monitor's Annual Report, Paragraph 44 Independent Review, 1996–1997 (DF865, 9/29/97); and Consent Decree Monitor's Annual Report, Paragraph 44 Independent Review, 1998–1999 (DF1033, 7/29/99).

160 In March, Orrick scheduled a trial for September 22, 1998. Order for Civil Pretrial Conference, *Ho v. SFUSD* (DF146, 3/2/98). During an August status conference, Orrick vacated the September trial date and scheduled a trial for February 8, 1999. Minutes, *Ho v. SFUSD* (DF208, 8/28/98). See Levine, "Chinese American Challenge," for a detailed chronicle of activities that took

place following the appeals court remand. The parties filed several motions regarding "discovery, expert witnesses, and the scope of trial" (75).

161 *Ho,* 59 F. Supp. 2d at 1025.

162 Joseph Remcho and Robin Johansen, senior partners at Remcho, Johansen & Purcell, were retained.

163 Levine, "Chinese American Challenge," 96.

164 Levine, 96–97.

165 The special master appointed by Judge Orrick was Thomas Klitgaard.

166 Proposed Modifications to the Consent Decree, *SFNAACP v. SFUSD* (Memorandum, DF876, 10/15/98).

167 "Regular schools: student populations shall reflect the District's student geographical and socio-economic distributions. SFUSD will divide the city into geographic zones, reserve at least 25% of seats at regular schools for neighborhood students, and allow an additional 10% of the seats for siblings. If a regular school becomes oversubscribed, the District will use a lottery system to determine admission. Alternative schools: attendance to these schools will be based on pass/fail qualifying criteria and a lottery and shall reflect plus or minus 10% of the student geographical distribution, again based on reasonable geographic zones. This will assure that alternative schools will be accessible to the entire SFUSD population." Memorandum by State Defendant, *SFNAACP v. SFUSD* (DF876, 10/15/98).

168 Proposed Modifications to the Consent Decree, *SFNAACP v. SFUSD* (Memorandum, DF876, 10/15/98).

169 Levine, "Chinese American Challenge," 97.

170 "The parties have not submitted a single declaration or any other piece of evidence to support their stipulation to modify the Decree." Memorandum Decision and Order, *SFNAACP v. SFUSD* (DF904, 12/2/98).

171 Memorandum Decision and Order, *SFNAACP v. SFUSD* (DF904, 12/2/98).

172 Opinion and Order, *Ho v. SFUSD,* 59 F. Supp. 2d at 1029n2.

173 Opinion and Order, *Ho v. SFUSD,* 59 F. Supp. 2d at 1029n2.

174 Order, *Ho v. SFUSD* (DF271, 11/20/98). For a discussion, see Levine, "Chinese American Challenge," 75.

175 Levine, 76.

176 For a rich description of the final push toward settlement, see Levine, 99–100.

177 "It would have been a very divisive trial," remarked Stuart Biegel, who had heard that one side of the courtroom was nearly all African American and the other side was nearly all Chinese American. Interview, Stuart Biegel, May 22, 2009. Judge Orrick commended the parties for saving weeks of trial

that would have been "emotional." Reporter's Transcript, February 17, 1999, *Ho v. SFUSD* (DF403, 4/16/99). The Court: "The years of litigation that were certain to result from a trial in the Ho action, regardless of the outcome, would have been very expensive. A great deal of that expense would have been borne by the taxpayers. In addition, the trial and subsequent litigation likely would have been extremely divisive in the community. The case had attracted considerable attention from the press in the weeks before trial. On the day trial was to begin, the courtroom was filled with press and concerned citizens. The Court has no doubt that a settlement of this action, if possible, would have been preferable to a lengthy, racially divisive trial." Opinion and Order, *Ho v. SFUSD*, 59 F. Supp. 2d 1021 at 25.

178 Reporter's Transcript, February 17, 1999, *Ho v. SFUSD* (DF403, 4/16/99).

179 *SFNAACP*, 59 F. Supp. 2d 1025–1027.

180 "Except as related to the language needs of the student or otherwise to assure compliance with controlling federal or state law." *SFNAACP*, 59 F. Supp. 2d 1025–1027, ¶C.

181 For the *Ho* plaintiffs, this was an important victory. "The days of racial bean-counting are over," remarked Amy Chang. Joan Walsh, "A New Racial Era for San Francisco Schools," *Salon*, February 18, 1999.

182 "The parties acknowledge that SFUSD officials have the duty and authority to determine lawful criteria for admission to all schools in the SFUSD." Opinion and Order, *SFNAACP v. SFUSD*, 59 F. Supp. 2d at 1025–1027.

183 Julian Guthrie and Eric Brazil, "Judge OKs Settlement to End Consent Decree," *San Francisco Examiner*, April 21, 1999. Among the protesters were U.C. Berkeley students who fought to preserve higher education affirmative action. BAMN Outreach Flier c1999.

184 Julian Guthrie and Eric Brazil, "Judge OKs Settlement to End Consent Decree," *San Francisco Examiner*, April 21, 1999.

185 Request by Rahel Tekeste, *Ho v. SFUSD* (DF387, 4/7/99).

186 Letter to Judge Orrick from Diane Chin on Behalf of Chinese for Affirmative Action, Chinese Progressive Association, Chinatown Youth Center, and Two Community Leaders, Gordon Chin and Reverend Harry Chuck, *Ho v. SFUSD* (DF395, 4/7/99).

187 Diane Chin, "End of Decree Hurts Chinese American Children," opinion, *San Francisco Chronicle*, March 17, 1999.

188 Progress Made, Challenges Remaining in San Francisco School Desegregation, Report of the Consent Decree Advisory Committee to the Federal District Court, San Francisco, California, *Ho v. SFUSD* (DF292, 1/19/99). The

Consent Decree Advisory Committee included Laureen Chew, Robert L. Green, Hoover Liddell, Gary Orfield, J. David Ramirez, and Gwen Stephens.

189 "From the beginning the basic strategy of the decree was to accomplish desegregation and make educational opportunity more equal, while providing more good educational choices for all students. In the 1990s the effort has been to extend its most effective remedies from the Bayview-Hunter's Point community to the entire city and to reach groups not previously sharing fully in the remedy." Progress Made, Challenges Remaining in San Francisco School Desegregation, Report of the Consent Decree Advisory Committee to the Federal District Court, San Francisco, California, *Ho v. SFUSD* (DF292, 1/19/99).

190 Gary Orfield, "Report on the Proposed Settlement," April 15, 1999, in Order, *Ho v. SFUSD* (DF404, 4/16/99).

191 Opinion and Order, *SFNAACP v. SFUSD*, 59 F. Supp. 2d 1021 (1999), ¶ C. The parties acknowledge that SFUSD officials have the duty and authority to determine lawful criteria for admission to all schools in the SFUSD. The parties further acknowledge that in setting those criteria, state and federal laws provide that district officials may consider many factors, including the desire to promote residential, geographic, economic, racial, and ethnic diversity in all SFUSD schools. However, race or ethnicity may not be the primary or predominant consideration in determining such admission criteria. Further, the SFUSD will not assign or admit any student to a particular school, class, or program on the basis of the race or ethnicity of that student, except as related to the language needs of the student or otherwise to assure compliance with controlling federal or state law.

192 David Ely was an expert in demographic analysis and had been a consultant and retained expert in several cases regarding redistricting, reapportionment, and the redrawing of school attendance zones. Amendment to Summary of Witness Testimony for Trial by Defendant Delaine Eastin, State Superintendent of Public Instruction, *Ho v. SFUSD* (DF303, 1/25/99). Ely's analysis was based on 1990 Census data, the court monitor cautioned, and thus an assignment system based on his computer modeling would need to be carefully monitored. Report of the Consent Decree Monitor, July 29, 1999, *SFNAACP v. SFUSD* (DF1033, 7/29/99).

193 In the proposed settlement, the parties agreed to a preliminary injunction that would immediately remove the racial and ethnic classifications. See 59 F. Supp. 2d at 1026, ¶ H. Preferences were given to siblings of current enrollees, children living in certain zip codes, and to children living near a school.

194 Levine, "Chinese American Challenge," 109.

5. Creating Diverse Schools through Choice

1 See, for example, Local Defendants' 1984–85 annual report (DF395, 8/1/85).

2 *SFNAACP,* 576 F. Supp. At 54–55.

3 Although Lowell was an alternative school, its process for admission was separate from the OER application. Students wishing to attend School of the Arts completed an OER form and a special application and went through an audition process.

4 Report of the Consent Decree Monitor, September 29, 1997, *SFNAACP v. SFUSD* (DF865, 9/29/97).

5 Some students could not attend the school designated by their home address because doing so would cause the school to violate its subgroup enrollment cap or because the school had reached its enrollment limit. If a seat subsequently became available at the designated school, preference would be given to a bumped student.

6 For example, during the 1996–1997 school year, the priority went to students with permanent addresses with 94110, 94124, and 94134 zip codes. The enrollment priority for students living in 94110, which spanned the Mission District and Bernal Heights, was changed the following year. Report of the Consent Decree Monitor, July 31, 1998, *SFNAACP v. SFUSD* (DF875, 7/31/98). "Our community [in Bernal Heights] had been pretty blue-collar for a long time, but I think it had definitely already started to undergo some gentrification. . . . I think it was specifically because of Bernal Heights [that] they changed the rule. . . . At least for the 94110 one, you had to also show low-income to get that priority," recalls Deena Zacharin, director of the SFUSD Office of School/Family Partnership and cofounder of Parents for Public Schools—San Francisco. "Somebody kind of got aware of the fact that not the whole 94110 was necessarily low-income." Interview, Deena Zacharin, September 30, 2009; and interview, K. C. Jones, August 11, 2009.

7 For the 1991–1992 term, of the 11,363 OERs processed by the SFUSD, the district granted 6,842. That year, 25,371 of the 63,806 SFUSD students were on an Optional Attendance Permit. Local Defendants' 1991–1992 Annual Report, *SFNAACP v. SFUSD* (DF679, 7/31/92).

8 Declaration by David Aldape, Alianza, *SFNAACP v. SFUSD* (DF711, 1/26/93). See also Declaration by Richard Maggi, Latin American Teachers Association, *SFNAACP v. SFUSD* (DF713, 1/26/93); and Declaration by Susana Salinas, Bilingual Advisory Committee, *SFNAACP v. SFUSD* (DF719, 1/26/93).

9 Report of the Consent Decree Monitor, 11, July 29, 1999, *SFNAACP v. SFUSD* (DF1033, 7/29/99).

10 Interview, Mark Sanchez, June 15, 2009. The issue elicited a wide range of responses, with some informants considering it to be more widespread than others. The claim is based on several interviews, including Matt Kelemen, August 11, 2009; Dan Kelly, September 8, 2009; Hydra Mendoza, October 20, 2009; Jill Wynns, June 16, 2009; Caroline Grannan, June 30, 2009; and Dan Kelly, September 8, 2009. See also Diana Walsh, "Big Scramble to Get Kids into Choice Schools," *San Francisco Examiner,* December 23, 1990; and Nanette Asimov, "Racial Fakery Gets Kids into Better S.F. Schools," *San Francisco Chronicle,* December 9, 1990.

11 Declaration of Donald I. Barfield, *Ho v. SFUSD* (DF538, 4/11/01).

12 Rojas was noted for his strong support of several elements of the consent decree, including reconstitution, and for presiding over a period when student test scores increased. Fraga, Rodriguez, and Erlichson, "Desegregation and School Board Politics." See also Nanette Asimov, "Rojas' Record Can't Be Denied," *San Francisco Chronicle,* June 21, 1999.

13 Declaration of Donald I. Barfield, Attachment C-5, C-7, *SFNAACP v. SFUSD* (DF1228, 4/11/01).

14 Report of the Consent Decree Monitor, July 29, 1999, 54, *SFNAACP v. SFUSD* (DF1033, 7/29/99). Rojas was interviewed by the court monitor on June 14, 1999.

15 Eric Brazil and Robert Salladay, "Lawmakers Scold Rojas over School Cuts," *San Francisco Chronicle,* March 18, 1999. Concerns over financial mismanagement plagued the superintendent throughout his term. Allegations emerged soon after the 1999 bond issuance of $60 million (part of a $90 million school bond approved on June 3, 1997, through Proposition A). Subsequently, a city audit concluded that the SFUSD needed a better system to manage its financial reporting. "The San Francisco Unified School District Cannot Accurately Account for the Revenues and Expenditures of Its $90 Million 1997 Bond Issue," January 24, 2005, Office of the Controller, City Services Auditor, City and County of San Francisco.

16 Julian Guthrie, "Improvement May Be Smoke and Mirrors," *San Francisco Examiner,* April 12, 1999.

17 Julian Guthrie, "School Shocker: Rojas Quitting," *San Francisco Chronicle,* April 23, 1999.

18 Nanette Asimov, "Rojas' Record Can't Be Denied," *San Francisco Chronicle,* June 21, 1999.

19 Deputy Superintendent Linda Davis served as interim superintendent for the 1999–2000 school year, becoming the first woman and the first African American to lead San Francisco's schools. Arlene Ackerman became

the first woman and the first African American to permanently hold the superintendency.

20 Amendment to Summary of Witness Testimony for Trial by Defendant Delaine Eastin, State Superintendent of Public Instruction, *Ho v. SFUSD* (DF303, 1/25/99).

21 Levine, "Chinese American Challenge." Presumably, the *Ho* attorneys anticipated a system similar to Horseshoe but with race-neutral assignments.

22 Proposed New Student Assignment Plan, in Declaration by D. Barfield, *SFNAACP v. SFUSD* (DF1070, 11/23/99). Donald Barfield, Deputy Director for Institutional Development at WestEd, served as a consultant to the SFUSD in the development of the PNSAP.

23 Proposed New Student Assignment Plan, in Declaration by D. Barfield, *SFNAACP v. SFUSD* (DF1070, 11/23/99).

24 Poverty level was to be determined by participation in the Free/Reduced Lunch Program, CalWORKs, or public housing. Academic achievement was to be determined through standardized test scores. Following the 1999 settlement, the district began tracking additional subgroups. For the 2000–2001 application track, the district had the following subgroups: African American, American Indian, Chinese, Filipino, Hispanic/Latino, Japanese, Korean, White, Arabic, Samoan, Southeast Asian, Middle Easterner, and Other Non-White. As agreed upon in the settlement, applicants could also choose a "decline to state" category. Order Denying Plaintiffs' Motion, *SFNAACP v. SFUSD* (DF1117, 1/14/00).

25 Proposed New Student Assignment Plan, 7–8, in Declaration by D. Barfield, *SFNAACP v. SFUSD* (DF1070, 11/23/99).

26 Examples of special programs include special education, gifted and talented education, and language programs.

27 Proposed New Student Assignment Plan, in Declaration by D. Barfield, *SFNAACP v. SFUSD* (DF1070, 11/23/99).

28 Policy for Lowell Admissions (San Francisco Board of Education #62–13SP1).

29 In what would become an ongoing problem, some parents and guardians did not participate in the choice process. Common explanations revolved around insufficient culturally and linguistically competent outreach on the part of the district. Students who did not make any choice requests were "assigned by default." This population of students, as one might imagine, tended to be among the most educationally disadvantaged in the district.

30 Nanette Asimov, "How SF's New School Choice Process Will Work," *San Francisco Chronicle*, November 18, 1999.

31 Proposed New Student Assignment Plan, 6, in Declaration by D. Barfield, *SFNAACP v. SFUSD* (DF1070, 11/23/99).

32 Memorandum of Points and Authorities in Opposition by Plaintiff, *SFNAACP v. SFUSD* (DF1092, 12/10/99); and Levine, "Chinese American Challenge," 112.

33 *SFNAACP,* 59 F. Supp. 2d at 1025.

34 I thank David Levine for this characterization. Interview, David Levine, July 30, 2009.

35 Order, *SFNAACP v. SFUSD* (DF1089, 12/17/99).

36 Reporter's Transcript, December 17, 1999, Hearing, *SFNAACP v. SFUSD* (DF1159, 4/11/00).

37 Nanette Asimov, "S.F. District OKs Race-Neutral School Plan," *San Francisco Chronicle,* January 7, 2000.

38 Michael Harris, SFNAACP attorney. In Nanette Asimov, "S.F. District OKs Race-Neutral School Plan," *San Francisco Chronicle,* January 7, 2000.

39 *SFNAACP,* 576 F. Supp. 53, ¶12.

40 *SFNAACP,* 576 F. Supp. 53, 58, ¶39.

41 See, for example, Report of the Consent Decree Monitor, 1998, *SFNAACP v. SFUSD* (DF875, 7/31/98).

42 The plan "seeks to achieve two intertwined and overriding objectives . . . : first, to eliminate existing segregation (and vestiges of past segregation) in SFUSD's schools, programs, and classrooms, and second, to improve the academic achievement of all students, but particularly those students whose performance has lagged behind others in SFUSD—African American and Latino students, and students who are English language Learners ('ELL') of many different ethnicities." Excellence for All: A Five-Year Comprehensive Plan to Achieve Educational Equity in the San Francisco Unified School District, Revision of January 24, 2002, 1.

43 "SFUSD Reaches Out to the Community," *Sun-Reporter,* March 15, 2001.

44 Interview, David Campos, July 29, 2009; and Report of the Consent Decree Monitor, July 31, 2003, *SFNAACP v. SFUSD* (DF1340, 7/31/03).

45 Annual Report of the Consent Decree Monitor, July 31, 2002, 110n80, *SFNAACP v. SFUSD* (DF1306, 7/31/02).

46 Julian Guthrie, "New S.F. Plan Uses Race to Assign Students," *San Francisco Chronicle,* March 2, 2001.

47 Katie Savchuk, "Plan May Save Desegregation Funds," *Lowell,* April 6, 2001.

48 Order, *SFNAACP v. SFUSD* (DF1235, 4/20/01).

49 Amended Stipulation and [Proposed] Order Re: Modification and Termination of Consent Decree, *SFNAACP v. SFUSD* (DF1244, 7/11/01); and Order, *SFNAACP v. SFUSD* (DF1245, 7/11/01).

50 Memorandum Opinion and Order, *SFNAACP v. SFUSD* (DF1272, 10/24/01).

51 The stipulation continued: "As the SFUSD shall have, by December 31, 2005, taken all practicable actions to achieve unitary status, including eliminating

any vestiges of past de jure racial or ethnic discrimination to the extent practicable and complying with the Consent Decree substantially and in good faith for a reasonable period, the SFUSD and the State shall oppose any attempt to extend, by motion or otherwise, the Consent Decree beyond December 31, 2005."

52 Attachment A, Amended Stipulation and [Proposed] Order Re: Modification and Termination of Consent Decree, *SFNAACP v. SFUSD* (DF1244, 7/11/01); and Order, *SFNAACP v. SFUSD* (DF1245, 7/11/01).

53 Amending ¶13(j) of the Consent Decree, Amended Stipulation and [Proposed] Order Re: Modification and Termination of Consent Decree, 4, *SFNAACP v. SFUSD* (DF1244, 7/11/01); and Order, *SFNAACP v. SFUSD* (DF1245, 7/11/01).

54 Excellence for All: A Five-Year Comprehensive Plan to Achieve Educational Equity in the San Francisco Unified School District, Revision of January 24, 2002.

55 Order by Executive Committee Case Reassigned to William H. Alsup, *Ho v. SFUSD* (DF581, 1/11/02).

56 Excellence for All: A Five-Year Comprehensive Plan to Achieve Educational Equity in the San Francisco Unified School District, Revision of January 24, 2002, 97.

57 Since the Diversity Index Lottery was employed only in schools with more applicants than seats available and only for students changing schools (thus, primarily the entry grades of kindergarten, sixth grade, and ninth grade), its impact on schools' demographic profiles was gradual and uneven.

58 "History of the Student Assignment Method," SFUSD.

59 Enrollment Guide, 2003–2004 Enrollment Period, San Francisco Unified School District.

60 Annual Report of the Consent Decree Monitor, July 31, 2002, *SFNAACP v. SFUSD* (DF1306, 7/31/02).

61 Excellence for All: A Five-Year Comprehensive Plan to Achieve Educational Equity in the San Francisco Unified School District, Revision of January 24, 2002, Attachment M. Band One assignments based on GPA (English, math, social studies, and science grades for seventh and eighth grade) and SAT-9/STAR (reading comprehension and math scores). Maximum score for the first two years would be 73 points, after which the maximum was 89 points.

62 Annual Report of the Consent Decree Monitor, July 31, 2003, *SFNAACP v. SFUSD* (DF1340, 7/31/03).

63 Although early versions of the Diversity Index proposed reserving seats in schools throughout the district in order to evenly distribute students who did not participate in the choice process, there was no such provision in the implemented version. "It wouldn't be practical," mused former Supervisor

Mark Sanchez. "If you hold . . . positions open . . . you're going to have a riot, I mean there will be a riot." Interview, Mark Sanchez, June 15, 2009. Hydra Mendoza, school board commissioner and former executive director of Parents for Public Schools, recalls that in the early 2000s, the number of students that did not apply reached into the thousands, primarily from the low-income neighborhoods of Bayview-Hunters Point and Visitacion Valley. Interview, Hydra Mendoza, October 20, 2009. Hoover Liddell, a longtime cabinet-level district employee stated: "For poor kids, I've never seen complete choice. We have, for example, Gloria R. Davis, which is out in Hunters Point . . . and when they closed the school . . . [parents] could get first choice of any school. . . . Only about seven parents opted to choose a school out of one hundred and forty." Interview, Hoover Liddell, October 24, 2009.

64 Report of the Consent Decree Monitor, July 31, 2003, *SFNAACP v. SFUSD* (DF1340, 7/31/03); and Report of the Consent Decree Monitor, August 1, 2005 (DF1439, 8/1/05). The most segregated schools were also among the most underperforming schools in the district.

65 Report of the Consent Decree Monitor, July 31, 2003, *SFNAACP v. SFUSD* (DF1340, 7/31/03).

66 Sandra Halladey, "Choosing a School in the New San Francisco Order," opinion, *San Francisco Chronicle*, November 23, 1999. "School reform begins with enrollment" is a quotation from this article.

67 Sandra Halladey and Deena Zacharin, letter to the editor, *San Francisco Chronicle*, November 13, 1999.

68 Sandra Halladey, "S.F. Schools Are Better than Reports—Go See," opinion, *San Francisco Chronicle*, March 26, 1999. Deena Zacharin recalls having a less than positive notion of public schools as her daughter was reaching school age. But then, she said, "I went to the school, and I remember, like the first visit, just being blown away and thinking, 'Oh, my God, this would be a great place for my daughter!' It was really diverse, and the kids were really interactive with the teacher, and their little hands were up answering. Nobody was throwing spitballs or whatever that I thought was going to happen, and no one was running up and down the hallway." Interview, Deena Zacharin, September 30, 2009.

69 Though part of a national organization, PPS-San Francisco enjoys relative autonomy. "We're very different, we're incredibly independent. We're independently funded, and we really serve the needs of our communities, so we have differences," stated Ellie Rossiter, Director of PPS-SF. Interview, Ellie Rossiter, July 28, 2009.

70 Interview, Sandra Halladey, August 26, 2009.

71 Diane Curtis, "Parents Rough It to Get Kids into Alternative Schools," *San*

Francisco Chronicle, January 14, 1985; "Lining Up for Class," editorial, *San Francisco Chronicle*, January 15, 1985; interview, Victor Seeto, September, 2, 2009; interview, Deena Zacharin, September 30, 2009; and correspondence, Amy Chang, February 12, 2010.

72 Diana Walsh, "Big Scramble to Get Kids into Choice Schools," *San Francisco Examiner*, December 23, 1990.

73 Interview, Sandra Halladey, August 26, 2009.

74 Interview, Hydra Mendoza, October 20, 2009.

75 Interview, Dana Woldow, August 5, 2005; interview, Caroline Grannan, June 30, 2009; interview, Deena Zacharin, September 30, 2009; and interview, Sandra Halladey, August 26, 2009. See also Nanette Asimov, "Frustration about Schools Is on the Rise," *San Francisco Chronicle*, September 16, 1991.

76 Interview, Sandra Halladey, August 26, 2009.

77 Interview, Deena Zacharin, September 30, 2009.

78 Interview, Hydra Mendoza, October 20, 2009.

79 Interview, Sandra Halladey, August 26, 2009.

80 Interview, Sandra Halladey, August 26, 2009.

81 A common refrain among advocates was: "How can we pit diversity against quality? Why can't we have high achieving schools for all kids?"

82 Der, "Resegregation and Achievement Gap," 315.

83 Interview, Ellie Rossiter, July 28, 2009.

6. The Enduring Appeal of Neighborhood Schools

1 "The Assignment Method set forth . . . was developed and adopted by the SFUSD, and the decision to use that particular Assignment Method was not taken at the request of any party or imposed by the Court." Stipulation and [Proposed] Order Re: Modification and Termination of Consent Decree, *SFNAACP v. SFUSD* (DF1244, 7/11/01).

2 Although the consent decree was terminated in 2005, the Diversity Index remained the district's student assignment system.

3 Memorandum and Order, *Ho v. SFUSD* (DF573, 10/24/01).

4 Susan Shors Letter to the Court, September 4, 2001, in Order, *SFNAACP v. SFUSD* (DF1251, 9/7/01).

5 Interview, Daniel Girard, August 24, 2009. Also in interview, David Levine, July 30, 2009.

6 The Supreme Court, in *Hunt v. Cromartie*, 526 U.S. 547 (1999), determined that challenging a facially race-neutral plan requires showing that race was the predominant motivation in choosing the race-neutral factors. Orrick wrote: "There is no evidence before the Court from which the Court can con-

clude that the District's race neutral diversity index is an unconstitutional proxy for race." Memorandum and Order, *Ho v. SFUSD* (DF573, 10/24/01).

7 David Levine was identified as cocounsel and assisted Girard in matters relating to particular areas of expertise. Anthony Lee and Gordon Fauth rounded out the legal team. To be sure, ties with CADC and AALF remained throughout the years. "We certainly had our input," recalls AALF and CADC board member Henry Louie. "They never did anything without saying: *This is what we think will work for us.* And, you know, invariably, we [would] defer to them." Interview, Henry Louie, September 2, 2009.

8 Interview, Henry Louie, September 2, 2009.

9 See interview, Ron Chun, August 26, 2009; and Henry Louie Letter to the Court, September 1, 2001, in Order, *SFNAACP v. SFUSD* (DF1251, 9/7/01).

10 *Parents Involved in Community Schools v. Seattle School District No. 1,* 551 U.S. 701 (2007); *Grutter v. Bollinger,* 539 U.S. 306 (2003); *Gratz v. Bollinger,* 539 U.S. 244 (2003); and interview, Lee Cheng, August 22, 2009.

11 Victor Seeto Letter to the Court, September 5, 2001, in Order, *SFNAACP v. SFUSD* (DF1251, 9/7/01).

12 Henry Louie Letter to the Court, September 1, 2001, in Order, *SFNAACP v. SFUSD* (DF1251, 9/7/01).

13 Elsewhere, Gray identifies herself as a member of the Black Leadership Forum. Venise Wagner, "Blacks Losing Clout in S.F.," *San Francisco Chronicle,* October 29, 2000.

14 Letter to the Court from Naomi Gray, in Order, *SFNAACP v. SFUSD* (DF1251, 9/7/01).

15 *SFNAACP,* 576 F. Supp. 54–56 (1983), ¶17–31.

16 Statement to the Health, Family and Environment Committee, Board of Supervisors, San Francisco, March 12, 1998, in Order, *SFNAACP v. SFUSD* (DF1251, 9/7/01). Earlier that year, Gray asked: "What has busing accomplished and what has the consent decree accomplished? Busing has been almost one way—our kids heading out (of the Bayview). And look at our kids' test scores. You have to wonder when there's so much money going into something and still such poor outcome." Julian Guthrie, "S.F. School Race-Bias Case Trial Starts Soon," *San Francisco Examiner,* February 14, 1999.

17 Approximately 60 percent of kindergarten, 69 percent of middle school, and 45 percent of high school students who requested a particular neighborhood school had been accommodated. Julian Guthrie, "Enrollment Wraps Up," *San Francisco Chronicle,* May 3, 2002.

18 Julian Guthrie, "Enrollment Wraps Up," *San Francisco Chronicle,* May 3, 2002.

19 The school attendance boundaries were based on pre-Horseshoe lines. On

top of this, in order to facilitate compliance with the enrollment caps, a system of satellite zones was created.

20 Enrollment Guide, 2003–2004, San Francisco Unified School District, 9.

21 "Under the new assignment process, after placement of students with program needs and siblings of existing students, students residing in the school's attendance area (and whose parents list that school as one of five choices) will receive an enrollment priority so long as they contribute to increasing multifaceted diversity at the school (without regard to race or ethnicity). Thereafter, all applicants (from the attendance area and elsewhere) will be considered for each available seat. . . . Students whose attendance area based on home address is a satellite zone (that is, a geographic area that is not contiguous to the school of assignment and is generally located at some distance from the school) require special consideration. These students will be treated as living in the attendance area of their highest choice school that has an attendance area, and will receive equal consideration with those students actually living in that area." Excellence for All: A Five-Year Comprehensive Plan to Achieve Educational Equity in the San Francisco Unified School District, Revision of January 24, 2002, 98.

22 Annual Report of the Consent Decree Monitor, July 31, 2002, *SFNAACP v. SFUSD* (DF1306, 7/31/02).

23 Annual Report of the Consent Decree Monitor, July 31, 2002, *SFNAACP v. SFUSD* (DF1306, 7/31/02).

24 "Yee's 3-Prong Plan to Erase S.F. School Enrollment Woes," *San Francisco Chronicle,* May 21, 2002; "Divide and Demagogue," editorial, *San Francisco Chronicle,* June 4, 2002. Even in the near-impossible event that the Board of Supervisors approved his proposal, it would have needed to pass muster with the school board and the State Board of Education. Ultimately, proponents of such a plan would need to prove that splitting the district would not promote discrimination or segregation.

25 Magary wrote his comments on a local school blog. Nanette Asimov, "Yee's 3-Prong Plan to Erase S.F. School Enrollment Woes," *San Francisco Chronicle,* May 21, 2002.

26 Rachel Gordon, "Divvying Up Schools—S.F. City Hall Agog," *San Francisco Chronicle,* May 31, 2002. In his capacity at Lawyers Committee, Harris served as counsel for the SFNAACP in the *SFNAACP* and *Ho* cases.

27 "Divide and Demagogue," editorial, *San Francisco Chronicle,* June 4, 2002.

28 San Francisco Board of Supervisors, Resolution No. 379–02, Adopted June 3, 2002, Approved June 14, 2002. "Bravo!" wrote Diane Chin, director of CAA. "Leno's leadership in reaching out to a diverse coalition of parents, students, educators and community groups that represented all the communities of

San Francisco to support this vision was important—helping to foster a momentum to provide the support our public schools need right now." Diane Chin, "Keep Schools United," letter to the editor, *San Francisco Chronicle,* June 6, 2002.

29 Yee: "If I had my druthers, we'd look at another individual school district [for the western half of the city], but that's not going to happen." Tiffany Maleshefski, "Admissions Outrage Escalates," *AsianWeek,* April 11, 2003.

30 Enrollment Guide, 2003–2004, San Francisco Unified School District, 9. Sandra Halladey recalls PPS-SF being part of the conversation: "I remember sitting with Hydra [Mendoza] and Tony Anderson, who was the head of the EPC at that time when the Diversity Index was first being talked about, and very supportive of the Diversity Index but also really trying to let the bureaucrats at the district know that they would not get buy-in from parents if the end result was just: You go to the school that you add the most diversity to. . . . And we're like: No, you need to do it by the choice." Interview, Sandra Halladey, August 26, 2009.

31 The district reported the following: 87 percent of kindergarteners, 91 percent of sixth graders, and 81 percent of ninth graders were assigned a school of choice; 67 percent of kindergarteners, 73 percent of sixth graders, and 64 percent of ninth graders were assigned to their top choice. Tiffany Maleshefski, "Diversity Furor," *San Francisco Independent,* March 29, 2003.

32 Tiffany Maleshefski, "Diversity Furor," *San Francisco Independent,* March 29, 2003.

33 Tiffany Maleshefski, "Diversity Furor," *San Francisco Independent,* March 29, 2003. Some high school students who had positive experiences at the less popular schools of Mission and Galileo confided that neighborhood schools may not be the sole issue. "Many Asian parents don't want their kids going to schools that don't have the words Lowell, Lincoln or Washington in them," remarked Dolores Lee, a student at Galileo. "They think that if their kids go to a school with a perceived bad reputation, then their kids will be looked down upon and lose face." Crystal Cao, a student at Mission, agreed. Reputation is also a worry of parents. May Chow, "S.F. Schools Assignment Controversy Continues: Some Students Say Distance Doesn't Matter," *AsianWeek,* April 18, 2003.

34 Ray Delgado, "New Offers on S.F. School Assignments," *San Francisco Chronicle,* April 10, 2003.

35 Zhao's daughter Lona was not offered an assignment to any of her chosen high schools (Lowell, Lincoln, and Washington). Although Zhao lived only several blocks away from Lincoln, his daughter was assigned to Burton on the east side.

36 三藩市联合校区排位风波报道之十：战果扩大，未获全胜, *Chinese Times*, April 10, 2003. [Original: 他呼籲所有小学和初中的家长继续出来, 帮助高中生的家长们抗争 [...] 大家异口同声说: "不接受."]

37 May Chow, "S.F. Schools Assignment Controversy Continues: Some Students Say Distance Doesn't Matter," *AsianWeek*, April 18, 2003. The meeting was called by San Francisco Supervisor Fiona Ma.

38 For the 2003–2004 school year, approximately 34 percent of the ninth graders in the school district identified as Chinese; at Washington, 49 percent of the incoming ninth-grade class identified as Chinese; at Lincoln, approximately 57 percent of the incoming ninth-grade class identified as Chinese. San Francisco Unified School District, Profiles, 2003–2004.

39 Ray Delgado, "Schools Forum Ends in Anger," *San Francisco Chronicle*, May 1, 2003.

40 Washington High School received approximately 2,800 requests for 591 available seats. Lincoln High School received approximately 3,200 requests for its 586 available seats. 三藩市联合校区排位风波报道之十：战果扩大，未获全胜, *Chinese Times*, April 10, 2003; and Ray Delgado, "Schools Forum Ends in Anger," *San Francisco Chronicle*, May 1, 2003.

41 The special hearing was held on April 29, 2003. Ray Delgado, "Schools Forum Ends in Anger," *San Francisco Chronicle*, May 1, 2003.

42 Ray Delgado, "Schools Forum Ends in Anger," *San Francisco Chronicle*, May 1, 2003.

43 Ray Delgado, "Schools Forum Ends in Anger," *San Francisco Chronicle*, May 1, 2003.

44 Caroline Grannan, "SFUSD Shell Game," letter to the editor, *AsianWeek*, May 16, 2003.

45 The parent's name is Zhang Yi. 路漫漫兮其修遠 家長爭取子女區內上學紀實, *Sing Tao Daily*, May 20, 2003. [Original: 家長張藝憤怒地指出: "如果我們的孩子連鄰近的學校都去不了, 學區憑什麼要我們支持放發教育公債?"] The school facilities bond passed in November 2003 with support from two-thirds of San Francisco voters (Proposition A).

46 Ray Delgado, "Parents Storm Ackerman's Office," *San Francisco Chronicle*, May 20, 2003; 路漫漫兮其修遠家長爭取子女區內上學紀實, *Sing Tao Daily*, May 20, 2003; Daniel Quach, "Chronicle Biased for S.F. Superintendent," letter to the editor, *AsianWeek*, May 30, 2003; Joan Walsh, "John Zhao's Crusade," *San Francisco Magazine*, September 1, 2003; and interview, Matt Kelemen, August 11, 2009.

47 Ray Delgado, "Parents Storm Ackerman's Office," *San Francisco Chronicle*, May 20, 2003. Matt Kelemen, a special assistant to the superintendent who

attended the meeting, described it as "probably the scariest day we've ever had at the district." Interview, Matt Kelemen, August 11, 2009.

48 "Parents Behaving Badly," editorial, *San Francisco Chronicle*, May 23, 2003.

49 Ackerman, who is African American and had been bused to an all-White high school, remarked: "Well, it's really too painful for me. I'm sitting here now as a product of that time, as somebody who bore the pain of desegregating schools. We couldn't even have lunch with the other kids in the lunchroom. So, I have this very vivid history and pain around this issue. And these are people who've been the recipients of what the civil rights movement achieved." Joan Walsh, "John Zhao's Crusade," *San Francisco Magazine*, September 1, 2003.

50 Interview, Matt Kelemen, August 11, 2009.

51 Joan Walsh, "John Zhao's Crusade," *San Francisco Magazine*, September 1, 2003.

52 Joan Walsh, "John Zhao's Crusade," *San Francisco Magazine*, September 1, 2003.

53 On the division between the two groups, John Zhao said, "From the beginning, I was never interested in forming a formal organization with a formal name. Once PFNSA was formed, it was a political group and I don't want to be part of a political group because I'm not interested in that." May Chow, "Parent Group Fights for Neighborhood Schools: Kids Boycotting Schools in San Francisco," *AsianWeek*, September 19, 2003.

54 Tiffany Maleshefski, "Parents Keep Kids Out of First Day of School," *AsianWeek*, August 29, 2003.

55 Heather Knight, "Chinese Americans End School Protest," *San Francisco Chronicle*, October 3, 2003.

56 Julie Soo, "Chinese Americans Still Feel Left Out of the School Diversity Dialogue," *AsianWeek*, June 10, 2004.

57 For example, to entice parents to consider high schools beyond Lowell, Lincoln, and Washington, Ackerman promised to establish a Chinese immersion program at Balboa and to increase the number of advanced placement classes at Galileo. Tiffany Maleshefski, "Admissions Outrage Escalates," *AsianWeek*, April 11, 2003. With the focused attention from the district central office and a committed onsite staff, over a period of years Balboa and Galileo developed into well-regarded high schools of choice in their own right. See interviews with Caroline Grannan, June 30, 2009; Sandra Halladey, August 26, 2009; and Frank Chong, October 6, 2009.

58 Julian Guthrie, "Parents and Teachers May Soon Control S.F. School Funds," *San Francisco Chronicle*, March 16, 2002.

59 Weighted Student Formula was incorporated in Excellence for All, 68–69; Julian Guthrie, "Parents and Teachers May Soon Control S.F. School Funds," *San Francisco Chronicle*, March 16, 2002.

60 Julian Guthrie, "Parents and Teachers May Soon Control S.F. School Funds," *San Francisco Chronicle*, March 16, 2002. Parents and teachers in SFUSD are served by the Second District of the California Congress of Parents, Teachers, and Students. In addition to the PTA, Parents for Public Schools also registered their support for weighted student formulas.

61 Under some weighted student formula plans, particularly when site councils are provided wide latitude over personnel line items, "there is an economic interest in getting rid of experienced teachers that completely sidesteps whether or not they're effective or working." However, the union was satisfied that across schools, regardless of neighborhood or quality, there was a relatively even distribution of experienced teachers. "The whole myth that teachers will work at a bad school for a few years and then they'll just want to get out and go to a good school simply didn't [hold]." Interview, Dennis Kelly, August 13, 2009.

62 Students and Teachers Achieving Results Brochure, Attachments to the State Board of Education Annual Report, Attachment 15.1, *SFNAACP v. SFUSD* (DF1342, 8/15/03).

63 STAR Initiative elementary schools: Bret Harte, Carver, Chávez, Cleveland, Drew, El Dorado, Fairmount, Flynn, Glen Park, Golden Gate, Malcolm X, Marshall, McKinley, Milk, Monroe, Muir, Revere, Sanchez, Serra, Starr King, Swett, Treasure Island, and Webster. STAR Initiative middle schools: Burbank, Davis, Denman, Everett, Franklin, King, Lick, Mann, and Maxwell. STAR Initiative high schools: Balboa, Burton, Galileo, Marshall, McAteer, Mission, and O'Connell. Excellence for All: A Five-Year Comprehensive Plan to Achieve Educational Equity in the San Francisco Unified School District, Revision of January 24, 2002, Attachment H.

64 Report of the Consent Decree Monitor, 67, July 31, 2002, *SFNAACP v. SFUSD* (DF1306, 7/31/02).

65 The STAR program provided: (1) *School Personnel.* Instructional reform facilitators, long-term substitutes, parent liaisons, middle school advisors, and volunteer mentors/tutors; (2) *District Support.* Instructional walk-throughs, school site plan review processes, leadership development workshops; and (3) *Resources.* Test-prep packets, extended learning packets, $150 for teaching supplies for each teacher, additional resources to enhance libraries, and resources for parent centers. Students and Teachers Achieving Results Brochure, Attachments to the State Board of Education Annual Report, Attachment 15.1, *SFNAACP v. SFUSD* (DF1342, 8/15/03).

66 "Our data holistically suggest that the STAR Schools Program clearly benefits participating schools." Report of the Consent Decree Monitor, July 31,
2002, 67, *SFNAACP v. SFUSD* (DF1306, 7/31/02). "The District's STAR
schools program is aggressively targeting low performing schools, and we
commend the District for its ongoing efforts in this regard." Report of the
Consent Decree Monitor, July 31, 2003, 85, *SFNAACP v. SFUSD* (DF1340,
7/31/03). See also interview, Dan Kelly, September 8, 2009.

67 Report of the Consent Decree Monitor, July 31, 2003, 85, *SFNAACP v.
SFUSD* (DF1340, 8/5/03).

68 The comparison was based on 2003 Academic Performance Index base
scores for African American students in Los Angeles, Oakland, Sacramento
City, Long Beach, and San Diego. Supplemental Report of the Consent Decree Monitor, Stuart Biegel, March 12, 2004, *SFNAACP v. SFUSD* (DF1356,
3/12/04).

69 Minutes, Evidentiary Hearing, August 3, 2004, *SFNAACP v. SFUSD* (DF1374,
8/3/04); and Order Denying Proposed Extension of Consent Decree, *SFNAACP
v. SFUSD*, 413 F. Supp. 2d 1051 (2005).

70 Order Denying Proposed Extension, *SFNAACP*, 413 F. Supp. 2d at 1061.

71 Heather Knight, "Arlene Ackerman S.F. School Chief to Point to Back-to-
Basics Success," *San Francisco Chronicle*, January 21, 2004; and Heather
Knight, "Dream Schools Strive to Raise Bar for Kids," *San Francisco Chronicle*, August 30, 2004. The Dream Schools initiative was based on schools
founded by Lorraine Monroe in Harlem. "Flat out, flat out: the mission is all
these kids are going to college," Monroe told a group of Bayview-Hunters
Point parents. "We're saying everybody in the Dream Schools is gifted and
talented. We're going to surprise everybody and astonish the kids in terms of
what they're capable of doing." Heather Knight, "Fanfare Follows OK of Plan
for Charter Dream Schools," *San Francisco Chronicle*, March 19, 2004.

72 Heather Knight, "Plan for Smaller Schools," *San Francisco Chronicle*, January 22, 2004. "Who wouldn't want that?," asked school board member
Sandra Lee Fewer, recalling Ackerman's promise to provide private school
education for public school children. "I knew parents, Black parents that
pulled their kids out from other schools and brought them there, and it became racially segregated schools. And, you know, with racially segregated
schools . . . you have hard-to-fill slots for teachers. It is hard to attract the
best and brightest. And those children there, they need . . . exceptional
teaching." Interview, Sandra Lee Fewer, August 4, 2009.

73 The first Dream Schools were Charles Drew Elementary, Twenty-First Century Academy (K–8), and Gloria R. Davis Middle schools. In 2005, the
school board voted to rename Twenty-First Century Academy to Willie L.

Brown Jr. College Preparatory Academy, in honor of the city's first African American mayor. The plan was to create a Dream School corridor from preschool to high school, with Gloria R. Davis Middle School adding one grade a year until it reached twelfth grade. However, this was never done, and the school was closed in 2007 because of low enrollment and a poor achievement record. Heather Knight, "Arlene Ackerman S.F. School Chief to Point to Back-to-Basics Success," *San Francisco Chronicle,* January 21, 2004; Heather Knight, "Dream Schools Strive to Raise Bar for Kids," *San Francisco Chronicle,* August 30, 2004; and Jill Tucker, "Davis Middle School to Close in Bayview," *San Francisco Chronicle,* January 11, 2007.

74 Interview, Hoover Liddell, October 24, 2009.

75 "Superintendent Says Quality Segregated Schools an Option," *San Francisco Examiner,* May 17, 2005.

76 "Dream Schools Plan Angers Union," *San Francisco Chronicle,* February 6, 2004.

77 "Union Won't Resist Dream Plan," *San Francisco Chronicle,* February 12, 2004. Teachers attending the school board meeting expressed no reservations with reapplying for their positions. In April, the district reported receiving four hundred applications for the one hundred open teacher and administrator positions. "Applicants Begin Lining Up for Dream Schools Positions," *San Francisco Chronicle,* April 30, 2004.

78 Stipulation and Order, *Ho v. SFUSD* (DF624, 10/19/04).

79 "Dream Schools Strive to Raise Bar for Kids," *San Francisco Chronicle,* August 30, 2004.

80 "City's Dream Schools Open Doors on a New Era," *San Francisco Chronicle,* August 31, 2004.

81 Reporter's Transcript, Proceedings, October 14, 2005, *SFNAACP v. SFUSD* (DF1496, 1/25/06).

82 Reporter's Transcript, Proceedings, October 14, 2005, *SFNAACP v. SFUSD* (DF1496, 1/25/06).

83 Plans were made for Dream Schools in the Mission District (Sanchez Elementary, Everett Middle, John O'Connell High), Bernal Heights (Paul Revere Elementary), Western Addition (Ben Franklin Middle), and Potrero Hill (Enola Maxwell Middle, Treasure Island K–8). The board subsequently closed Ben Franklin, Treasure Island, and Enola Maxwell. Heather Knight, "Dream Schools Program to Expand," *San Francisco Chronicle,* October 1, 2004.

84 "Fanfare Follows OK of Plan for Charter Dream Schools," *San Francisco Chronicle,* March 19, 2004. Although some students were less enthused with

the initiative. "All the change I have seen from the Dream School is that we wear uniforms and the administration has made a lot more rules that interfere with the students learning," wrote John O'Connell senior Blaise Didier (O'Connell became a Dream School in 2005). Letter to the Court from Blaise Didier, *SFNAACP v. SFUSD* (DF1464, 10/12/05).

85 Interview, Carl Barnes, August 13, 2009.

86 Interview, Sandra Lee Fewer, August 4, 2009. Referring to the disciplinary environment at Dream Schools, Supervisor Fewer continued, "And I am not Black, but I went out to visit the schools, and, I don't know, I have issue with the young, White teachers screaming at Black kids all day."

87 Interview, Dan Kelly, September 8, 2009.

88 "The Dream School was torpedoed by the teacher's union in the beginning," stated former school board commissioner Dan Kelly. "I think the Dream Schools could have been successful if the teachers union hadn't selectively opposed them." Interview, Dan Kelly, September 8, 2009.

89 "Long Days at Dream Schools," *San Francisco Chronicle,* October 5, 2004.

90 Eddie Chin, Heather Hiles, Dan Kelly, and Jill Wynns were considered to be Ackerman backers; Sarah Lipson, Eric Mar, and Mark Sanchez were vocal critics.

91 "Schools' Politics Focus on Ackerman," *San Francisco Chronicle,* October 12, 2004. See also "Blacks Concerned Board Race May Divide Vote and Hurt Superintendent," *San Francisco Sun-Reporter,* July 15, 2004.

92 "Will Pressure Force Ackerman to Retire?," *San Francisco Sun-Reporter,* August 11, 2005. The school board was faced with a $22 million budget gap. Closing schools had to be part of the calculus. "The budget crisis is so severe, and we just have no other options," Commissioner Mar stated. "Budget Squeeze Threatens School, the Island's Treasure," *San Francisco Chronicle,* May 24, 2005.

93 Final Supplemental Report of Consent Decree Monitor Regarding Desegregation and Academic Achievement, December 28, 2005, *SFNAACP v. SFUSD* (DF1494, 12/28/05).

94 "S.F. Schools Are Resegregating, Monitor Charges," *San Francisco Chronicle,* January 4, 2006.

95 Interview, Jill Wynns, June 16, 2009.

96 "Chinese Americans Renew School Placement Push," *San Francisco Chronicle,* March 31, 2005.

97 "New Plan Pitched for Neighborhood Schools," *San Francisco Chronicle,* May 17, 2005.

98 Interview, Norman Yee, May 19, 2009.

99   Lisa Schiff, "School Beat: Redefining Student Assignment," *BeyondChron*, May 19, 2005; and Community Advisory Committee on Student Assignment, "Recommendations for Student Assignment in the San Francisco Unified School District," February 22, 2005. Because of new immigrants from Mexico, Central America, and Asia, neighborhoods (including Bayview-Hunters Point) were ever more diverse.

100 Order Scheduling Hearing Re: Proposed Modifications to Consent Decree, Attachment, *SFNAACP v. SFUSD* (DF1443, 8/26/05).

101 Response to Written Public Comments Filed with Court in Response to Notice of Proposed Modification of Consent, *Ho v. SFUSD* (DF692, 10/12/05).

102 Response to Written Public Comments Filed with Court in Response to Notice of Proposed Modification of Consent, *Ho v. SFUSD* (DF692, 10/12/05). Reverend Amos Brown, writing in his capacity as head of the SFNAACP, made similar comments to the court.

103 Chan lived in the 94134 zip code. Response to Written Public Comments Filed with Court in Response to Notice of Proposed Modification of Consent, *Ho v. SFUSD* (DF692, 10/12/05).

104 This demographic information was determined by noting the zip codes and surnames of respondents. Response to Public Comments Regarding Proposed Settlement, *Ho v. SFUSD* (DF692, 10/12/05).

105 Response to Public Comments Regarding Proposed Settlement, *Ho v. SFUSD* (DF692, 10/12/05).

106 "Superintendent Says Quality Segregated Schools an Option," *San Francisco Examiner*, May 17, 2005.

Conclusion

1   "Judge Criticizes Desegregation Plan," *San Francisco Chronicle*, October 21, 2005. The public hearing on the modifications to the consent decree was held on October 14, 2005. See also *SFNAACP v. SFUSD* (DF1469, 10/14/05).

2   The consent decree had previously received a three-year extension, from December 31, 2002, to December 31, 2005. Order Denying Proposed Extension, *SFNAACP*, 413 F. Supp. 2d at 1063.

3   *SFNAACP*, 59 F. Supp. 2d 1021, 1038.

4   *Ho by Ho v. SFUSD*, 147 F.3d at 865.

5   Reporter's Transcript, Proceedings, October 14, 2005, *SFNAACP v. SFUSD* (DF1496, 1/25/06).

6   Reporter's Transcript, Proceedings, October 14, 2005, *SFNAACP v. SFUSD* (DF1496, 1/25/06).

7   Order Denying Proposed Extension, *SFNAACP*, 413 F. Supp. 2d at 1072.

8   Order Denying Proposed Extension, *SFNAACP*, 413 F. Supp. 2d at 1072.

Alsup refers to the failed attempts by MALDEF, META, CAA, UESF, and others to formally intervene in the case.

9 Reporter's Transcript, Proceedings, October 14, 2005, *SFNAACP v. SFUSD* (DF1496, 1/25/06).

10 Reporter's Transcript, Proceedings, October 14, 2005, *SFNAACP v. SFUSD* (DF1496, 1/25/06).

11 Reverend Derrick Eva was associate pastor of Providence Baptist Church. Reporter's Transcript, Proceedings, October 14, 2005, *SFNAACP v. SFUSD* (DF1496, 1/25/06).

12 Reporter's Transcript, Proceedings, October 14, 2005, *SFNAACP v. SFUSD* (DF1496, 1/25/06).

13 Supplemental Report of the Consent Decree Monitor, April 11, 2005, *Ho v. SFUSD* (DF651, 4/11/05).

14 Reporter's Transcript, Proceedings, October 14, 2005, *SFNAACP v. SFUSD* (DF1496, 1/25/06); and "Judge Criticizes Desegregation Plan," *San Francisco Chronicle*, October 21, 2005.

15 Alsup determined that counsel failed to show how modifying the consent decree would satisfy the *Dowell/Freeman* test or an alternative legal standard for modifying consent decrees in institutional reform cases (the so-called *Rufo* standard). *SFNAACP*, 413 F. Supp. 2d at 1064–1072.

16 *Freeman*, 503 U.S. at 490.

17 Order Denying Proposed Extension, *SFNAACP*, 413 F. Supp. 2d at 1063.

18 Letter to Judge William Alsup from David Johnson, December 28, 2005, *SFNAACP v. SFUSD* (DF1495, 1/17/06).

19 Final Supplemental Report of the Consent Decree Monitor Regarding Desegregation and Academic Achievement, December 28, 2005, 5, *SFNAACP v. SFUSD* (DF1494, 12/28/05).

20 Final Supplemental Report of the Consent Decree Monitor Regarding Desegregation and Academic Achievement, December 28, 2005, 8, *SFNAACP v. SFUSD* (DF1494, 12/28/05).

21 The district was less successful at meeting the consent decree's additional integrative elements: eliminating racial identifiability in every classroom and program.

22 In a dust-up that generated considerable press, a well-known political figure was accused of pulling strings at the Educational Placement Center to attain a better school. The incident was vividly recalled by several informants years after it occurred.

23 For example, Kucsera and Orfield, "New York State's Extreme School Segregation"; Clark and Maas, "Schools, Neighborhoods, and Selection"; Whet Moser, "Chicagoland Schools: For Blacks, the Most Segregated in the

Country," *Chicago Magazine,* September 20, 2012; Ronald Brownstein, "Why Poverty and Segregation Merge at Public Schools," *Atlantic,* November 12, 2015; Elizabeth Harris, "School Segregation Persists in Gentrifying Neighborhoods, Maps Suggest," *New York Times,* December 15, 2015; and Dana Goldstein, "'Threatening the Future': The High Stakes of Deepening School Segregation," *New York Times,* May 10, 2019.

24 In the 1970s, the Department of Justice supervised cases representing 540 school districts. As of 2007, the United States was a party to 266 school desegregation lawsuits. U.S. Commission on Civil Rights, *Becoming Less Separate?*; and U.S. Government Accountability Office, *K–12 Education.* A 2014 survey conducted by the nonprofit investigative newsroom ProPublica identified 328 school districts under a desegregation order. Yue Qiu and Nikole Hannah-Jones, "A National Survey of School Desegregation Orders," *ProPublica,* December 23, 2014.

25 *Brown,* 347 U.S. at 493.

Bibliography

Archive and Manuscript Collection

San Francisco Public Library
    Daniel E. Koshland San Francisco History Center
      San Francisco Unified School District (SFHC)
Stanford University
    Hoover Institution Archives
      Robert F. Alioto Miscellaneous Papers (RFA/HIA)
    Special Collections
      MALDEF (M673)
University of California
    California Ethnic and Multicultural Archives, Davidson Library,
    U.C. Santa Barbara
      Chinese American Democratic Club (CEMA 49)
Bancroft Library, U.C. Berkeley (BANC MSS)
    NAACP, Region I, records (78/180c)
    SFNAACP Material Prepared by Legal Counsel (84/175c)

Government Archives

National Archives and Records Administration, Pacific Region (RG 21, NARA)
    Johnson v. SFUSD
Federal Records Center, San Bruno
    SFNAACP v. SFUSD
    Ho v. SFUSD

Newspapers (Partial List)

AsianWeek
Chinese Times
Daily Journal
New York Times
San Francisco Bay Guardian
San Francisco Chronicle
San Francisco Examiner
San Francisco Sun-Reporter
Sing Tao Daily

Newsletters

Fiery Dragon (CADC)
New Views (SFUSD)
The Insider (SFUSD)
Voice (CAA)

Anderson, Karen. *Little Rock: Race and Resistance at Central High School.* Princeton, N.J.: Princeton University Press, 2010.

Arriola, Christopher. "Knocking on the Schoolhouse Door: *Mendez v. Westminster,* Equal Protection, Public Education, and Mexican Americans in the 1940's." *La Raza Law Journal* 8, no. 166 (1995): 160–207.

Baker, Scott. *Paradoxes of Desegregation: African American Struggles for Educational Equity in Charleston, South Carolina, 1926–1972.* Columbia: University of South Carolina Press, 2006.

Baum, Howell. *Brown in Baltimore: School Desegregation and the Limits of Liberalism.* Ithaca, N.Y.: Cornell University Press, 2010.

Béland, Daniel, and Alex Waddan. *The Politics of Policy Change: Welfare, Medicare, and Social Security Reform in the United States.* Washington, D.C.: Georgetown University Press, 2012.

Bell, Derrick. *Silent Covenants: Brown v. Board of Education and the Unfulfilled Hopes for Racial Reform.* New York: Oxford University Press, 2004.

Bersin, Alan, Michael W. Kirst, and Goodwin Liu. *Getting beyond the Facts: Reforming California School Finance.* Berkeley, Calif.: The Chief Justice Earl Warren Institute on Race, Ethnicity and Diversity, University of California, Berkeley Law School, 2008.

Bureau of Intergroup Relations, Office of Compensatory Education. *Racial and Ethnic Survey of California Public Schools. Part One: Distribution of Pupils, Fall, 1966.* California State Department of Education, 1967.

Campbell, John L. *Institutional Change and Globalization*. Princeton, N.J.: Princeton University Press, 2004.

Chang, Francis Yung. "A Study of the Movement to Segregate Chinese Pupils in the San Francisco Public Schools up to 1885." PhD diss., Stanford University, 1936.

Clark, William, and Regan Maas. "Schools, Neighborhoods and Selection: Outcomes across Metropolitan Los Angeles." *Population Research and Policy Review* 31, no. 3 (2012): 339–60.

Clotfelter, Charles T. *After* Brown: *The Rise and Retreat of School Desegregation*. Princeton, N.J.: Princeton University Press, 2004.

Coleman, James S. "Recent Trends in School Segregation." *Educational Researcher* 4, no. 7 (1975): 3–12.

Danns, Dionne. *Desegregating Chicago's Public Schools: Policy Implementation, Politics, and Protest, 1965–1985*. New York: Palgrave Macmillan, 2014.

Delmont, Matthew. *Why Busing Failed: Race, Media, and the National Resistance to School Desegregation*. Oakland: University of California Press, 2016.

Der, Henry. "Resegregation and Achievement Gap: Challenges in San Francisco School Desegregation." *Berkeley La Raza Law Journal* 15, no. 1 (2004): 308–16.

DiMaggio, Paul. "Culture and Cognition." *Annual Review of Sociology* 23 (1997): 263–87.

DiMaggio, Paul, and Walter W. Powell. "The Iron Cage Revisited: Institutional Isomorphism and Collective Rationality in Organizational Fields." *American Sociological Review* 48 (1983): 147–60.

Erickson, Ansley. *Making the Unequal Metropolis: School Desegregation and Its Limits*. Chicago: University of Chicago Press, 2016.

Feilders, John F. *Profile: The Role of the Chief Superintendent of Schools*. Belmont, Calif.: Fearon Education, 1982.

Fine, Doris R. *When Leadership Fails: Desegregation and Demoralization in the San Francisco Schools*. New Brunswick, N.J.: Transaction Books, 1986.

Fraga, Luis R., Bari A. Erlichson, and Sandy Lee. "Consensus Building and School Reform: The Role of the Courts in San Francisco." In *Changing Urban Education*, edited by Clarence N. Stone, 66–92. Lawrence: University Press of Kansas, 1998.

Fraga, Luis R., Nick Rodriguez, and Bari A. Erlichson. "Desegregation and School Board Politics: The Limits of Court-Imposed Policy Change." In *Besieged: School Boards and the Future of Education Politics*, edited by William G. Howell, 102–28. Washington, D.C.: Brookings Institution Press, 2005.

Friedland, Roger, and Robert R. Alford. "Bringing Society Back In: Symbols, Practices, and Institutional Contradictions." In *The New Institutionalism in*

Organizational Analysis, edited by Walter W. Powell and Paul DiMaggio, 232–66. Chicago: University of Chicago Press, 1991.

Greenwood, Royston, and Roy Suddaby. "Institutional Entrepreneurship in Mature Fields: The Big Five Accounting Firms." *Academy of Management Journal* 49 (2006): 27–48.

Haveman, Heather A., and Hayagreeva Rao. "Structuring a Theory of Moral Sentiments: Institutional and Organizational Coevolution in the Early Thrift Industry." *American Journal of Sociology* 102 (1997): 1606–51.

Hendrick, Irving G. *The Education of Non-Whites in California, 1849–1970.* Los Angeles: R. and E. Research Associates, 1977.

Kaplan, John. "San Francisco" [Condensed from "Race and Education in San Francisco," a report to the United States Commissioner of Education]. *Law & Society Review* 2 (1967): 64–78.

Kim, Claire Jean. *Bitter Fruit: The Politics of Black-Korean Conflict in New York City.* New Haven, Conn.: Yale University Press, 2000.

Kirp, David L. *Just Schools: The Idea of Racial Equality in American Education.* Berkeley: University of California Press, 1982.

Kluger, Richard. *Simple Justice: The History of* Brown v. Board of Education *and Black America's Struggle for Equality.* New York: Vintage, 2004.

K'Meyer, Tracy. *From* Brown *to* Meredith*: The Long Struggle for School Desegregation in Louisville, Kentucky, 1954–2007.* Chapel Hill: University of North Carolina Press, 2013.

Kucsera, John, and Gary Orfield. "New York State's Extreme School Segregation: Inequality, Inaction, and a Damaged Future." Los Angeles: The Civil Rights Project/Proyecto Derechos Civiles, 2014.

Levine, David. "The Chinese American Challenge to Court-Mandated Quotas in San Francisco's Public Schools: Notes from a (Partisan) Participant-Observer." *Harvard BlackLetter Law Journal* 16 (2000): 39–145.

Littlejohn, Jeffrey, and Charles Ford. *Elusive Equality: Desegregation and Resegregation in Norfolk's Public Schools.* Charlottesville: University of Virginia Press, 2012.

Liu, Caitlin M. "Beyond Black and White: Chinese Americans Challenge San Francisco's Desegregation Plan." *Asian Law Journal* 5 (1998): 341–52.

Lum, Phillip A. "The Chinese Freedom Schools of San Francisco: A Case Study of the Social Limits of Political System Support." PhD diss., University of California, Berkeley, 1975.

Maeda, Daryl J. *Chains of Babylon: The Rise of Asian America.* Minneapolis: University of Minnesota Press, 2009.

Meyer, John W., and Brian Rowan. "Institutionalized Organizations: Formal

Structure as Myth and Ceremony." *American Journal of Sociology* 83 (1977): 340–63.

Miller, Tony. *A Study of California Ballot Measures 1884 to 1993.* California Secretary of State, 1994.

Montesano, Phillip M. "San Francisco Black Churches in the Early 1860's: Political Pressure Group." *California Historical Quarterly* 52, no. 2 (1973): 145–52.

Omi, Michael, and Howard Winant. *Racial Formation in the United States: From the 1960s to the 1990s.* New York: Routledge, 1994.

Orfield, Gary, Mark D. Bachmeier, David R. James, and Tamela Eitle. *Deepening Segregation in American Public Schools.* Cambridge, Mass.: Harvard Project on School Desegregation, 1997.

Orfield, Gary, and Chungmei Lee. *Historic Reversals, Accelerating Resegregation, and the Need for New Integration Strategies.* Los Angeles: The Civil Rights Project/Proyecto Derechos Civiles, University of California, Los Angeles, 2007.

Powell, Walter W., and Paul J. DiMaggio. Introduction to *The New Institutionalism in Organizational Analysis,* edited by Walter W. Powell and Paul J. DiMaggio, 1–38. Chicago: University of Chicago Press, 1991.

Rao, Hayagreeva, Philippe Monin, and Rodolfe Durand. "Institutional Change in Toque Ville: Nouvelle Cuisine as an Identity Movement in French Gastronomy." *American Journal of Sociology* 108 (2003): 795–843.

Ravitch, Diane. "Social Science and Social Policy: The 'White Flight' Controversy." *Public Interest* 51 (1978): 135–49.

Scott, W. Richard. "Conceptualizing Organizational Fields: Linking Organizations and Societal Systems." In *Systemrationalität und partialinteresse: Festschrift für Renate Mayntz,* edited by H. U. Derlien, U. Gerhardt, and F. W. Scharpf, 203–21. Baden-Baden, Germany: Nomos Verlagsgesellschaft, 1994.

Scott, W. Richard. *Institutions and Organizations.* Thousand Oaks, Calif.: Sage Publications, 1995.

Scott, W. Richard, and John W. Meyer. "The Organization of Societal Sectors." In *Organizational Environments: Rituals and Rationality,* edited by John W. Meyer and W. Richard Scott, 129–53. Newbury Park, Calif.: Sage, 1983.

Steensland, Brian. *The Failed Welfare Revolution: America's Struggle over Guaranteed Income Policy.* Princeton, N.J.: Princeton University Press, 2008.

Taylor, Quintard. *In Search of the Racial Frontier: African Americans in the West, 1528–1990.* New York: W. W. Norton and Company, 1998.

Thornton, Patricia H. *Markets from Culture: Institutional Logics and Organizational Decisions in Higher Education Publishing.* Stanford, Calif.: Stanford University Press, 2004.

Thornton, Patricia H., and William Ocasio. "Institutional Logics." In *The Sage Handbook of Organizational Institutionalism,* edited by Royston Greenwood, Christine Oliver, Kerstin Sahlin-Andersson, and Roy Suddaby, 99–129. Thousand Oaks, Calif.: Sage Publications, 2008.

Thornton, Patricia H., and William Ocasio. "Institutional Logics and the Historical Contingency of Power in Organizations: Executive Succession in the Higher Education Publishing Industry, 1958–1990." *American Journal of Sociology* 105 (1999): 801–43.

Thornton, Patricia, William Ocasio, and Michael Lounsbury. *The Institutional Logics Perspective: A New Approach to Culture, Structure, and Process.* New York: University of Oxford Press, 2012.

Titus, Jill. Brown's *Battleground: Students, Segregationists, and the Struggle for Justice in Prince Edward County.* Chapel Hill: University of North Carolina Press, 2011.

Tolnay, Stewart E. "The African American 'Great Migration' and Beyond." *Annual Review of Sociology* 29, no. 1 (2003): 209–32.

Tushnet, Mark V. *The NAACP's Legal Strategy against Segregated Education, 1925–1950.* Chapel Hill: University of North Carolina Press, 1987.

United States Commission on Civil Rights. *Becoming Less Separate? School Desegregation, Justice Department Enforcement, and the Pursuit of Unitary Status.* Washington, D.C., 2007.

United States Commission on Civil Rights. *Federal Enforcement of School Desegregation.* Washington, D.C., 1969.

United States Commission on Civil Rights. *Southern School Desegregation, 1966–67.* Washington, D.C., 1967.

United States Government Accountability Office. *K–12 Education: Better Use of Information Could Help Agencies Identify Disparities and Address Racial Discrimination.* Report to Congressional Requesters. Washington, D.C., 2016.

Weiner, Stephen S. "Educational Decisions in an Organized Anarchy." PhD diss., Stanford University, 1972.

Weiner, Stephen S. "Participation, Deadlines, and Choice." In *Ambiguity and Choice in Organizations,* 2nd ed., edited by James G. March and Johan P. Olsen, 225–50. Bergen, Norway: Universitetsforlaget, 1979.

Wirt, Frederick M. *Power in the City: Decision Making in San Francisco.* Berkeley: University of California Press, 1974.

Wollenberg, Charles. *All Deliberate Speed: Segregation and Exclusion in California Schools, 1855–1975.* Berkeley: University of California Press, 1976.

Wollenberg, Charles. "*Mendez v. Westminster*: Race, Nationality, and Segregation in California Schools." *California Historical Quarterly* 53, no. 4 (1974): 317–32.

Index

RAND QUINN is associate professor of education at the University of Pennsylvania.